Empire Building is a book about the meeting and transformation of cultures: those of Victorian Britain and the Ottoman Middle East. The author looks at how the architecture of cities like Istanbul, Jerusalem and Cairo dazzled and beguiled Victorian travellers, and how British writers tried to describe and comprehend those effects. He examines Britain's rising influence in this area and how this was to be manifested in new buildings.

The first half of this book argues that by the mid-nineteenth century a particular kind of architectural orientalism had emerged in Britain. This could be seen in a variety of forms: in the scholarship of architects such as Owen Jones and the writing of John Ruskin, for instance, as well as in the popular context of the Great Exhibition and a number of neo-Islamic buildings. The question of how this related to Britain's actual imperial power in the Middle East is addressed in the second part of the book. Through an examination of European presence in three key cities – Istanbul, Alexandria and Jerusalem – and of the problem of devising and realizing an architectural expression of that presence in a number of eclectic styles, a very different picture of East–West relations is portrayed, one that has many lessons for today.

The book uncovers and re-examines several key issues for Victorians: most notably the place that politics, religion and racial theory played in their conception of the architecture of other cultures; and, conversely, how their ideas of national identity took on different and sometimes unresolved forms in their own architecture. At the heart of this book is the first sustained discussion of the relation between orientalism – both Victorian and modern revisionist ideas of it – and the built environment.

Mark Crinson is Lecturer in the History of Art at the University of Manchester.

EMPIRE BUILDING

Orientalism and Victorian Architecture

•

MARK CRINSON

London and New York

First published 1996
by Routledge
11 New Fetter Lane, London EC4P 4EE

Simultaneously published in the USA and Canada
by Routledge
29 West 35th Street, New York, NY 10001

© 1996 Mark Crinson

Typeset in Garamond and Franklin Gothic by
Solidus (Bristol) Limited
Printed and bound in Great Britain by Redwood Books, Trowbridge, Wiltshire

British Library Cataloguing in Publication Data
A catalogue record for this book is available from the British Library

Library of Congress Cataloguing in Publication Data
Crinson, Mark.
Empire building: orientalism and Victorian architecture/Mark Crinson.
p.   cm.
Includes bibliographical references and index.
1. Architecture–Great Britain–Islamic influences.
2. Architecture, Modern–Great Britain–Islamic influences.
3. Architecture, Victorian–Great Britain.   4. Exoticism in
architecture–Great Britain.   5. Architecture, Islamic–Middle East–
–influence.   I. Title.
NA967.5.V53C75   1996
720′.941′09034–dc20   95–26418

ISBN 0–415–13940–6 (hbk)
0–415–13941–4 (pbk)

For my father, Bill Crinson

CONTENTS

PLATES

•

ACKNOWLEDGEMENTS

•

This book would not have been possible without the financial support of an almost embarrassingly large number of institutions, to all of whom I owe great thanks: the Thouron Foundation, the University of Pennsylvania, the American Research Center in Turkey, the Kress Foundation (Kress Fellowship), the Paul Mellon Centre for Studies in British Art (Paul Mellon Centre Fellowship), the Center for Advanced Studies in the Visual Arts (Chester Dale Fellowship), and the British Academy.

Numerous people have helped me with their expertise. The staffs of the following institutions have all been particularly efficient and welcoming: the Fine Arts Library, University of Pennsylvania; the RIBA British Architectural Library; the British Library; the Prints and Drawings Collection of the Victoria and Albert Museum; Rhodes House Library, Oxford; the Bodleian Library, Oxford; the Royal Commonwealth Society Library; and the Public Record Office. Individual curators who have guided me through their collections and shown interest and support in my work include Neil Bingham of the RIBA Drawings Collection, Jaromir Malek of the Griffith Institute, Gill Grant of the Middle East Centre (Oxford), and Michael Bulman of the Israel Trust of the Anglican Church. Mrs A. de Cosson and Mrs Vivien Betti both graciously made their collections available to me. Peter Burton and Michael Pollard have helped with the photographs. The many people who have answered my enquiries with plentiful information, hospitality and goodwill include Canon Peter Armstrong, John and Molly Cloak, Revd C. Coussmaker, Michael Darby, Revd J. M. V. Drummond, Tony Greenwood, Robert Ilbert, Kresten Jesperson, Paul Joyce, Iain Kelly, Arieh Klein, Howard Levett, Angela Mace, Ali Muslubas, Ayse Nasir, Charles Newton, J. R. Paterson, Harley Preston, Inci Saltikgil, the late Sir John Summerson, and Mercedes Volait.

This work began and was developed at the University of Pennsylvania, a marvellous place of learning and discussion. Renata Holod's graduate course on 'Colonial Architecture in the Islamic World' and David Brownlee's teaching were the starting points for many of my lines of thought. My friends and fellow graduates in Philadelphia offered the best kind of support: especially Joshua Bernstein, Jeffrey Cohen, Rebecca Foote, Peter Kohane, Mike Lewis, Dede Ruggles, and Ajay Sinha. My students and colleagues at the University of Manchester continue to provide a fertile ground for ideas.

I owe thanks to Routledge's anonymous readers, and to those of earlier versions of this work at the Architectural History Foundation, New York. Joe Mordaunt Crook read drafts of all the chapters and offered comments and consistent encouragement. Jules Lubbock, an inspirational collaborator on another book, commented on a draft of the whole work. David Brownlee's unflagging advice and enthusiasm gave direction and drive to my first stumbling efforts. Tristan Palmer at Routledge has been a model editor.

Lastly, the most special thanks to Katy and Eva.

PHOTOGRAPHIC CREDITS

ABBREVIATIONS

•

BIHR: Borthwick Institute of Historical Research (Hickleton
               Papers), York
BM Add.:   British Museum, Additional Manuscripts
BP: Bonomi Papers in the possession of Mrs de Cosson
CEAJ: *Civil Engineer and Architect's Journal*
CMJ: Archives of the Church's Ministry among the Jews (once the
               London Society for the Promotion of Christianity Amongst
               the Jews), Bodleian Library, Oxford
DGE: Diocese of Gibraltar in Europe, Diocesan Office Archives
DNB: *Dictionary of National Biography* (1885–)
FO: Foreign Office Papers, Public Record Office
GI: Griffith Institute, Ashmolean Museum, Oxford
GLRO: Greater London Record Office
ITAC: Israel Trust of the Anglican Church, Jerusalem
JI: *Jewish Intelligence*
PMJ: Palestine Mission Journal, Israel Trust of the Anglican
               Church, Jerusalem
PRO: Public Record Office, Kew
Report OSPGA: *Report of the Oxford Society for Promoting the Study of Gothic
               Architecture*
RIBA: Royal Institute of British Architects, Drawings Collection
RIBA BAL: Royal Institute of British Architects, British Architectural
               Library
RIBAJ: *Royal Institute of British Architects Journal*
SMDB: St Mark's Deed Box, St Mark's Church, Alexandria
SPG: Society for the Propagation of the Gospel
SPGJ: *Society for the Propagation of the Gospel, Journals*
T: Treasury Papers, Public Record Office

USPG: Archives of the United Society for the Propagation of the
                Gospel, Rhodes House Library, Oxford
V&A: Prints and Drawings Collection, Victoria and Albert
                Museum
Works: E. T. Cook and Alexander Wedderburn, *The Works of John
                Ruskin*, London: George Allen, 1903–12
Works: Board of Works Papers, Public Record Office

INTRODUCTION

•

Victorian colonial architecture seems bound to provoke stock responses in its viewers. At two extremes, it either stands for the rapacity and racial self-delusion of empire, or for a world of lost glory and forgotten convictions. A third reaction, perhaps less political than these, simply finds nothing but absurdity in the image, say, of a Lincolnshire church modified and set down on the hot, dusty *maidan* of some tropical city. Is Englishness imposed on these locations? Is it threatened by them? Or is it instead exposed as a silly chimera by such relocation? This book was initiated in the belief that to maintain any of these responses was to foreclose enquiry, to caricature and therefore to misunderstand the complex magnitude both of colonialism and of archi-tecture. At the same time what has sustained it is the conviction that if, without false neutrality, we can demythologize this architecture it will offer compelling insight not just on nineteenth-century British architecture and imperial history, but perhaps also on architecture in today's globalized, supposedly post-colonial era.

This book looks at British architecture in the Near East as one of two neighbouring facets of nineteenth-century British imperial culture. The other facet is the Islamic and Byzantine architecture of the Near East, as seen through the eyes of Victorian architects and writers. By addressing these related topics the book attempts specifically to understand the role played by the built environment in focusing western interest and influence upon an Islamic part of the world.

For Victorians, Islam was often interchangeable with the group of ideas about art, religion, society, history and geography that made up the 'Orient'. On various levels the Victorian obsession with this imaginary Orient is well known; its typical products were the racy travel books and engraved Biblical landscapes or the countless objects from ottomans to soup tureens that used eastern forms or allusions to stimulate exotic fantasy. But this general cultural phenomenon was all the more powerful for having strong roots both in scholarship and in the newly professionalizing fields such as architecture. Most of the major architects and architectural theorists of the Victorian era, from Owen Jones, through James Fergusson and John Ruskin to William Burges, were also profoundly interested in the arts of the eastern Mediterranean, although they might strongly differ as to whether they found a confirmation of certain forms of western belief and practice or an antidote to them. It was in seeking to analyse the character of those arts, and in erecting several remarkable new buildings in a part of the world with which this Orient was associated, that these Victorians tested their eclectic theories to the limits and helped to forge some elements of the new ideology out of which twentieth-century architecture was born, and long before Le Corbusier's *Voyage d'Orient*. In addition these buildings exemplified some of the practices, values and beliefs that accompanied colonial modernization in the area.

Few terms in the study of imperialism are uncontested. 'Orient' has problems which have already been indicated and will be developed later, but other terms are no less loaded and disputable, especially because of the continuing struggles over land and identity in the region. 'Near East', although usually replaced today by the equally problematic 'Middle East', is retained here to denote the Ottoman girdle of the eastern Mediterranean, particularly Turkey, Palestine and Egypt. At the beginning of the nineteenth century the Ottoman Empire, centred on the Sultan and his Porte (imperial government) in Istanbul, stretched much further than this – from the Balkans to Baghdad and from Algeria to Aden. Its history from then until 1923 is one of reform and gradual disintegration as internal and external pressures strained its ramshackle construction. 'Near East' serves not only to indicate an area but also to summon up the attitudes of a historical period.

These attitudes helped to bring about that particular economic and political relationship between Britain and large parts of the Ottoman Empire, similar to that, say, between Europe and South America, which can usefully be summed up by another term, 'informal imperialism'.[1] This was not necessarily a stage along a development towards formal rule, but a certain form of imperialism by which control was established through the ostensibly peaceful means of free trade and economic integration into the orbit of European power.[2] The most obvious results of this relationship were extraterritorial privileges, European investment in major modernization schemes (with new banking facilities), the rise of a western-educated corps of mediators, a ruling class increasingly emulating the forms of European culture, and the flooding of markets with western manufactures. Although cities were dramatically reshaped and expanded, less studied has been the erection of new buildings for the small European communities that helped to manage these developments. No part of the area was under Britain's formal constitutional rule during this period, yet its trade became so dominated by Britain and other European powers that its own society and economy were remoulded and then sustained or forced into a state of underdevelopment by these external forces, sometimes with such stress that, as happened in Egypt in 1882, Britain stepped in to protect its economic interests through formal rule. Thus, unlike British India, which could be understood as an alternative satellite of British power, the Near East was seen, in specific and narrowly defined ways, as peripheral to Britain's centre. At the same time there were shifting metropolitan relationships between, say, London and Alexandria, Alexandria and Cairo, Cairo and Istanbul, and Istanbul and Jerusalem, even in this short period.

British buildings did not simply arrive with the first British diplomats or traders to reside in the major cities of the Ottoman Empire. If they had, then there would have been British buildings in Istanbul, Cairo and Izmir by at least the seventeenth century. It was only with the growth of stronger diplomatic, missionary and commercial ties that the British gained the confidence to form their own communities. With these came the moment covered by this book, that period starting in the mid-nineteenth century when a need emerged for an architecture which would not just house the various communal requirements (because that could be done largely by renting property) but, more importantly, which would give these communities prestige and establish a vital presence for them. And so, in major ports such as Istanbul and Alexandria, embassies, consulates, churches, hospitals, and even post offices and prisons were constructed or proposed. In other towns and cities, particularly Jerusalem, British religious groups established missions often requiring purpose-built structures, especially chapels, hospitals and schools.

The informal status of British presence also means that for historians its architecture raises different issues from those buildings that might appear visually similar in Britain or India. British architecture in the Near East at this time was not plentiful and it was rarely grandiose, certainly not by comparison either with equivalent British buildings in India or, say, with French buildings in Algeria at this time. Nor, as a desultory flick through the pages of any architectural periodical will reveal, does it compare with the level of activity at the end of the century, the Age of Empire. Yet it had a significance that went beyond its size or expense. As an embodiment of British presence architecture was the form in which British ambitions and identities were made physically apparent. Sometimes it might attempt symbolically to negotiate the transition into formal rule. But more broadly, it was an architecture that exemplified and epitomized a range of notions about integration and alliance, religious and national identity, missionary intent and economic potency. It was therefore often an architecture of allegory, though that allegory was neither a simple manifestation of intentions nor a reflection of context. The significance of these buildings was felt in Britain especially, for they were hotly competed for, often reproduced and reviewed, and usually the subject of lofty religious and political debate within journals, institutes and government bodies.

It follows that the acts of building in the Near East and of writing about Near Eastern architecture are crossed and circled by the broader themes of racial theory, tourism, religious and social programmes, commercial and political agendas. These in their turn, like a sea of icebergs, are only the visible forms above a more submerged order of beliefs and massing of knowledge. But rather than seeing architecture as merely subjected to these ideas, I hope to indicate that the experience of material and conceptual constraints within the production of architecture itself helped to form or remould ideology.

One major assumption is that, for architects and architectural commentators of the time, their ideas about the Near East were only partly formed by direct experience. (Indeed, of the major figures discussed here, Ruskin and Viollet-le-Duc never visited the Near East, and Fergusson only visited it many years after he had written extensively about it.) It could be said that, like other westerners, they viewed the Islamic world through the various lenses of orientalism. To put this another way, there were various means to structure and elaborate responses, particularly through racial and religious categories, but these were all limited by a series of linked ideas about the East: for instance, that huge areas of the world and disparate cultures were in fact unified in an ethnically dominated condition locked forever in a stage of history long bypassed by the West. Whether orientalism involved assimilative or hierarchical systems of thought, its role was to enable and justify the logic of growing western domination. The cultural sphere was a partner of the economic sphere, rather than being an effect of it. This, at least, taking his cue from the work of the French philosopher-historian Michel Foucault, was the influential thesis of Edward Said's *Orientalism* (1978).

Most useful to Said were Foucault's ideas about power and knowledge and how they work through discourses (or discursive formations). Power and knowledge are intimately bound up, power having a productive, disciplinary relation to the creation of knowledge and its working on subjects. Power ramifies through all modern societies, helping to establish dynamic conjunctions, or discourses, of texts, operations and institutions producing those forms of knowledge that undergird modernity and define its others: health, madness, sexuality, and, for Said, orientalism. But Said added a non-Foucauldian twist to this, arguing that orientalism was not just some discourse conducted through the invisible apparatus of modernity but was linked to a hegemonic dominance: here, the more visible actions of western imperialism on the East.

Said's book, in which orientalism was dissected and anathematized in the scholarship and literature of the nineteenth century, has caused such a shift in thinking that, where previously orientalism was taken as a purely descriptive term meaning the study of and fascination with the East that arose with the Enlightenment, now it commonly implies this new sense of a knowledge closely and insidiously linked to power and diffused through many different activities. Orientalism was thus a form of cultural paternalism that reduced, abstracted and restructured a myriad variety of histories and societies into a totalizing tightly knit group of essentialist tropes and repetitious patterns, the 'complementary opposite' to the culture of the orientalist.[3] The main problem with this, however, is that it risks doing to any object or text that touches on the Orient what it claims orientalism did to its putative subjects; homogenizing them, making them mere examples of an orientalist discourse, rather than differentiated expressions – perhaps even ambiguous, compromised or ineffective – of the various forms taken by colonialism, some of which may be far from hostile to colonized cultures. Therefore while the idea of a discourse offers exciting ways to rethink the relation between what have often been thought of as discrete areas of cultural activity, one must be wary of its tendency to collapse the fractured qualities and strengths and perhaps significant positions of its objects in one essentializing discourse entirely owned by the colonizer.

Said's more recent work, while still barely concerned with the built environment, does offer some interesting ways of conceptualizing the relationship between colonial architecture, overtly orientalist writing about architecture, and other forms of British culture. In his book *Culture and Imperialism* (1993), Said used Raymond Williams's concept of 'structures of feeling' to argue that imperialism is the defining feature of modern experience, sending its ripples through the culture of the modern West and from there back to the empire. Whilst I am wary of the implicit claim that effects of empire are all-pervasive, this idea has confirmed my understanding of how different parts of, say, John Ruskin's *Stones of Venice* (1851–3) can depend on an imperial horizon even when they do not ostensibly concern it, and furthermore that the experience of imperialism has to be reckoned into the evolution of modernist forms in the arts, including architecture. At least one of Said's assumptions in this book – that culture is more than a mere accompaniment and in fact plays a key role in imperialism – can be tested out in a new way through architecture, especially if the imperial horizon is refined to the more specific context of economic or informal imperialism. Finally, the most stimulating idea in Said's book, if perhaps also the most elusive, is that of 'contrapuntal reading': to see imperial themes as playing off domestic or metropolitan themes, with order and meaning created by and within this very interplay.

While there is much in both of Said's books that is suggestive, especially his example of how to rework unequal imperial relationships back into the dominant culture, his general thesis attributes too absolute a power to colonialism, and depends upon a Manichean structure of oppositions, too homogeneous a sense of intention, and too much continuity in orientalism. Other recent works in what is now called post-colonial theory have sometimes tended to apply Said's methods wantonly as a fixed set of responses to farflung and very disparate colonial situations or to essentialize the participants in what sometimes appears to be a colonial psychodrama.

There is a need now, as Nicholas Thomas has recently argued, to extend Said's ideas in different fields and to test and revise them in more historically specific accounts that 'avoid any polarization of material and ideal aspects': in other words, to study colonial projects rather than colonial discourse.[4] Thomas's definition of colonial projects has parallels with the approach taken in parts of this book. The idea is to draw together the imaginative and the instrumental, the work of self-fashioning and that of fashioning others, the particularities of agency and the broader networks of discourses. The word 'project' itself

> draws attention not towards a totality such as a culture, nor to a period that can be defined independently of people's perceptions and strategies, but rather to a socially transformative endeavour that is localized, politicized and partial, yet also engendered by longer historical developments and ways of narrating them.[5]

Finally, these colonial projects may overlap and compete with other projects and conflict with indigenous interests, and thus become sidetracked or compromised, projected rather than realized.

Said's work has both caused deep controversy in this field, and stimulated a spate of writing across literature, human geography, cultural studies and the history of art, but the debate about his ideas has only slowly filtered into consideration of the built environment and of the role architectural orientalism played in this larger cultural archive. While Victorian architectural writing may seem immediately susceptible to his approach, Said's definition of the essentially textual nature of orientalism casts some doubt over a straightforward application of his ideas to built form.[6] Moreover, the relevance of Said's critique of orientalism to the capital-intensive activity of architecture, even to colonial architecture in the Near East – that particularly powerful locus of orientalist thought for Said – has still to be properly understood. I will argue later in this book that it is precisely because this architecture was involved in direct and complex bonds and ties with local cultures on a range of institutional, practical and symbolic levels, that rather different problems are entailed from Said's field of enquiry. Disraeli's novel *Tancred* and John Frederick Lewis's harem pictures were not just different kinds of objects from a church in Jerusalem or an embassy in Istanbul, they were also only intended to be read and seen within the imperial culture of Britain to which they could present their own version of oriental authenticity. Said and his followers' choice of objects to write about has tended to sustain this idea of orientalism always and only having a western audience. 'None of the Orientalists I write about seems ever to have intended an Oriental as a reader', he claims. 'The discourse of Orientalism, its internal consistency and rigorous procedures, were all designed for readers and consumers in the Metropolitan West.'[7] British architecture in the Near East, whether orientalizing or not, was almost always intended to be seen and understood, in some way, by orientals. Also Said's recent acceptance of the limited effect of literature – 'a novel is neither a frigate nor a bank draft' – might be contrasted with the equally terse 'a construction site is worth a battalion' of Hubert Lyautey, French governor-general of Morocco from 1912 to 1925.[8] Lyautey believed that architecture might help to replace force with civility and governmentality. It should remain an open question whether architecture has more in common with canals, armies, advertising, and even frigates and bank drafts, than with novels, paintings and soup tureens.

In the informal empire architecture gave the British a means to establish and present themselves within a different host culture in a pointedly material way. Any preconceptions of the Orient might be forced into subordination, momentary or not, to this end as the temporalities of politics, war, inflation and slump took their toll on cultural artifacts. To put it another way, the Orient as an imaginary construction in writing might hinder the actual construction of real foundations, walls and roofs; consequently failure, contingency and incompetence have to be accepted into analyses of this architecture. It was the interaction of these two major factors – British attitudes and local realities – that shaped the history of British architecture in the Near East.

The issues of representation and meaning in architecture indicate important differences from those orientalist objects that were consumed in Britain and analysed by Said. As mentioned earlier, Said does not consider how orientalism may have been aimed at the East, yet, while we must not presume that orientalism was in any simple way imposed, accounts of architecture are incomplete without asking to whom buildings were addressed and how they were understood. This question of reception is especially significant in an imperial setting. The Dome of the Rock (AD 692) in Jerusalem, that archetypal missionary and imperial building, had its exterior covered with decoration and inscriptions directed by the new Muslim rulers at the local Christian population.[9] To take an example closer to this period, Lord Valentia defended Government House (1798–1803), Calcutta, from those who criticized its expense in terms that will become familiar in this book:

> They ought to remember that India is a country of splendour, of extravagance and of outward appearances; that the Head of a mighty Empire ought to conform himself to the prejudices of the country he rules over; and that the British, in particular, ought to emulate the splendid works of the Princes of Timour, lest it be supposed that we merit the reproach which our great rivals, the French, have ever cast upon us, of being alone influenced by a sordid mercantile spirit.[10]

Contrary to Said's idea that orientalism is aimed at western readers, what Valentia's statement immediately demonstrates is an anxious awareness of other audiences. As well as the regulation of space and the management of resources, the presentation of architecture – in this case a colonial Palladian residence but equally, as we shall see for example, a neo-Islamic church – is bound up with the gaze, the judgements and the interpretations of others; most especially, in this way of thinking, of other races. Under oriental scrutiny the building must perform the appropriate and recognizable functions and meanings of colonial identity. If it fails, or remains incomplete and unresolved, then British subjectivity is also incomplete and compromised.

Even if it were in my competence to do so, it is notoriously difficult to reconstruct the responses of 'native' informants.[11] Instead, and in accordance with the focus on British colonial projects, I prefer generally to see the public as 'a phantasy within the work and within the process of its production'.[12] In other words, whilst the users of British architecture in the Near East may be clearly defined, its public – the ideal target and prescience of its representations – was more various, more amorphous, and sometimes more imaginary. Nicholas Thomas warns against presuming too much here:

> It needs to be acknowledged that the discourse may not have impinged upon indigenous consciousness at all, or was at best indirectly related to discourses that were expressed at the site of colonization: to presume imposition is to overstate the importance and effectiveness of imperialism, to forget that imperialists were often arguing with each other or speaking narcissistically to themselves.[13]

There is nevertheless a need to recognize that the boundary between an ideal public and an actual audience is neither wide nor fixed, and that one can easily spill over into the other. Arguably, the conditions of informal imperialism required a consideration of even more numerous interests both in the host country and in Britain than the architecture built in a more formalized imperial context such as India. Architects working in the Near East might have to consider disparate groups in the British 'centre' – government, providers of funds, religious interests – as well as various concerns in the Near Eastern 'periphery', such as the local British community, other European powers, semi-autonomous local rulers, the Ottoman government, the objects of missionary work, and the anonymous representatives of certain gross ethnic divisions. Accordingly, within a complex environment of competing interests, these buildings attempted to interpellate or address and by addressing to identify, perhaps recruit, and certainly to anticipate responses from these different and perhaps contradictory groups, making of them one ideal public. To argue for this and to expect there to be different levels and intensities of address is simply to extend to architecture what missionary work, commercial ploys and tactful diplomacy, all of them housed by the architecture discussed in this book, are commonly accepted to be about. The public was ideal because meaning could not be produced by a dialogue with it as an entity, but must hopefully and thus perhaps incoherently be aimed in the direction where it might exist. (This asymmetry between projected public and actual users or audiences is reflected in this book; the focus of interest is upon the designs of the intruding culture.) And this question of a public, a community of subjects summoned forth within an ideal intercourse, was also considered to be bound up with style.

In Victorian Britain it was usually accepted that to build was to create meaning: architecture was 'phonetic', it had 'expressional character', and it exhibited 'particular moral or political ideas'.[14] Choosing a style implied choosing meanings, but what meaning might be ascribed to any particular style was frequently a contested matter in Victorian architecture. For this reason, and because of its informal imperial context, British architecture in the Near East cannot be understood according to the tools of some of the best recent histories of colonial architecture. Amongst these should be counted the templates of assimilation, associationism and urban apartheid that have proved so useful in accounts of French neoclassical and neo-Moorish architecture and urbanism in North Africa.[15]

In Britain a theorized and occasionally doctrinal eclecticism and revivalism formed the climate of debate in architecture. These were the products not only of acute historical awareness and of a search for the modern, but also of a new-found belief that the designer had the power to select and manipulate the

storehouse of historical material, sometimes irrespective of continuity in
workmanship and technique, drawing upon often minutely particularized and
synthetic attitudes to eclecticism. This fascination with eclecticism has curious
parallels with recent theoretical interest in hybridity; indeed, hybridity itself
was a Victorian obsession. Hybrid or eclectic architecture offered by turns a
fascinating or threatening object. One question that has to be addressed in this
book is whether this debate about meaning and style was any more resolved
or any better exposed amongst the apparently more polarized identities of the
informal empire, or if there was a further fragmentation of notions about an
appropriate public architecture, an architecture of civility.

This book is a close study of the discourse of orientalism in architecture as
well as architecture's role within colonial projects at a particular historical
period and in a particular colonial relationship. But I hope that its interest and
usefulness are not limited to these circumstances. Indeed, it is intended to
clarify the historical background to a range of more contemporary interests: the
understanding of modernism and modernization in non-European settings,
and their coexistence with customary or traditional practices; the development
of post-colonial theory, especially in terms of the built environment; the
similarities, already indicated in my description of eclecticism, between
Victorian and postmodern concerns; and perhaps even the problems and
opportunities of architecture in Third World societies under new forms of
colonialism today. These interests are reflected in a number of questions of
current importance raised by these Victorian concerns. Should western-
educated architects adapt their own styles to foreign lands? Should they adopt
local styles, and on what grounds? What can Third World architects find of
use in western architectural practice? How fluid are the possible political
readings of any style? When is upholding a national or local culture of
architectural design a parochial and exclusive gesture, and when is it a radically
preservative act of identification? This book cannot provide answers to these
questions but it can proffer historical parallels.

The book is organized into two parts. Three chapters in Part I deal with
Victorian concepts and debates about Near Eastern architecture; whilst four
chapters in Part II examine several building projects in the Near East.

In Part I the Victorian interpretation of Islamic and Byzantine architecture
is discussed, particularly in the work of John Ruskin, James Fergusson and
Owen Jones, but also through the evidence of travel reportage, visual records
and built imitations. Chapter 1 sets the scene, examining how the historical
frameworks by which Islamic architecture was understood before the Victorian
period related to the new and more rigorous approach initiated in the 1830s,
characterized here as the 'new orientalism', in which architectural orientalism

had finally emerged as a disciplinary object. Chapter 2 abandons the sequential approach in favor of extended and detailed forays into the concepts that structured Victorian representations of Islamic architecture, looking particularly at the role given to race in architectural history and theory. A balance has to be found here between attending to local differences and recognizing shared assumptions. For instance, Owen Jones's *Grammar of Ornament* (1856) may be the product of a philosophic radical and Ruskin's *The Two Paths* (1859) that of a quasi-socialist critic – both offer different kinds of challenges to the mainstream – but they share certain notions about Islamic culture, the determination of race, and the progressive role of the West. Extending their equally radical if different visions of British culture and society to imperial contexts left equivocal results, neither of which can easily be labelled more progressive or more liberal than the other. The geographically and historically overlapping architecture of Byzantium is the subject of Chapter 3. Although serious historical study of Byzantine architecture by British writers is usually thought to have started in the 1890s, here that judgement is reassessed whilst also arguing that it was precisely Byzantium's eastern location that gave it a strategic place in historical schemes. In both this chapter and in Chapter 2 several nineteenth-century controversies about attribution or affiliation are discussed: the real site of the Holy Sepulchre, the actual origins of the Dome of the Rock, and the possibility of Judaic sources for Byzantine architecture. It should be made clear now that my intention here is not to arbitrate in these disputes, but rather to show why they had such significance and what was at stake beyond claims to historical truth.

Part II does not attempt to survey British buildings in the Near East but instead looks at several key buildings and unexecuted building projects, mainly in Alexandria, Istanbul and Jerusalem. Architecture, as well as being an art of pleasure, instruction and shelter, is articulated as part of an ideological space and within actual locations, and carried out by means of systems of labour and their agents. Whilst architects are the primary focus in this account, there are other agents to be considered who helped enact the enterprise of empire building: missionaries, politicians, builders, official administrators and local intermediaries. Only a few of these buildings are orientalist in appearance; many, indeed, seem to turn their faces firmly away from any visual affiliation with the Orient, though this in itself may embody their particular position on orientalism. These buildings therefore have to be related to the changing townscapes into which they were inserted and against which they were to be partly understood. They also need to be related to other British buildings in the Near East, to the building industry in these localities, and to architectural practice and theory in Britain. It is only by weighing up all these factors that we can come to an understanding of how particular colonial projects came into coherence around these buildings. They have not been judged worthy of this attention on some scale of purely architectural achievement, but more because of their unique semantic content; they are eloquent rather than representative or exemplary.

Part I

ORIENTALISM AND ARCHITECTURE

1

USEFUL KNOWLEDGE

INTERPRETING ISLAMIC ARCHITECTURE, 1700–1840

•

The rest, whose minds have no impression but of the present moment, are either corroded by malignant passions, or sit stupid in the gloom of perpetual vacancy.

(Samuel Johnson, 1759)

An early nineteenth-century architect looking for recorded knowledge about Islamic architecture could have satisfied little more than the most short-lived curiosity. There was much on other forms of architecture. Since the mid-eighteenth century there had been various archaeological and rationalist projects to classify Greek and Roman architecture, and a similar attempt to understand Gothic began in the late eighteenth century after a long period of neglectful familiarity. But by contrast, the conquest of Islamic architecture by nineteenth-century scholars had little preceding it but the laconic images and reports of travellers mostly interested in other matters. Islamic architecture was seen as one of a range of natural sights and cultural artifacts. Travelogues, architectural accounts and espionage reports, therefore, often conveyed similar responses. Even the great inaugurating archive of Egypt, the *Description de l'Égypt* (1809–28), treated Islamic architecture as only one amongst many other subjects. Islamic culture was, anyway, regarded as a despised or lowly matter and there were few intellectual tools available to understand it.

The *Description* was made possible by military conquest. Likewise, the subsequent growth in knowledge about Islamic culture came about in tandem with the West's economic domination over the Ottoman Empire. Egypt and Asia Minor, especially Cairo and Istanbul, were particularly crucial areas for western interest and both had enormous strategic importance, not only economically and politically. Egypt had ancient claims as the birthplace of European culture; Istanbul could be seen as the point of its severance. Both became arenas for rival European influence, predominantly between France and Britain. Thus, in the understanding of Islamic architecture, knowledge and power were inextricable.

The main argument of this chapter is that it was only in the second quarter of the nineteenth century that architectural orientalism emerged as a distinctive cultural formation out of its two parent discourses. That this 'new orientalism' did emerge at this moment had something to do with the discarding of classical paradigms and Picturesque theory. But it had much more to do with the appeal of the new human sciences, particularly ethnography, and the operative conjunction of rationalism and modernization.

THE EIGHTEENTH CENTURY

Most pre-nineteenth-century western travellers to the Near East went there for reasons other than architectural, and foremost amongst these reasons were trade and diplomacy. Like travellers to India and China, they collected statistics on revenue, samples of merchandise and information on military assets. In the Near East, as in India, the European attempt to survey and quantify was accompanied by the establishment of rival trading posts in the seventeenth and eighteenth centuries. The exploitation of eastern markets within a world economy was thus set in train. British trade with the Ottoman Empire was supported at state level by the granting of a royal charter to the Levant Company in 1581, and to the East India Company in 1600. Such charters gave the government a share in profits as well as some regulation over company activities. In the next century agents based in Izmir, Istanbul and Aleppo organized a sizeable trade based particularly on the exchange of woollen goods for carpets, silks and consumables. With these firm connections came a spate of travel books on the Near East – the best known were the works of Grelot, Wheler and Spon, and Maundrell – many of which were collected by architects like Wren and Hawksmoor.[1]

Those travellers who went to the Near East for cultural reasons, or those who mixed cultural with commercial or diplomatic purposes, usually wanted to understand the geography and civilizations of the Bible (seeing oriental customs as a continuation of Biblical life), and to explore Egypt as a palimpsest still bearing the traces of European origins. In this sense, travelling a distance was also travelling in time, and the activity of description might well be a translation of the enterprise of natural history into an observation of the cultural past. Yet although aspects of Islamic society might be reported for the charm of their exotica, overall Islamic culture was identified as only a regrettable overlay: either stagnant or corrupt, historically fixed or decaying. This was confirmed by such contemporary historical accounts as Edward

Pococke's *Specimen historiae Arabum* (1650), the great collection of Arabic source material translated in Bartholomé d'Herbelot's *Bibliothèque orientale* (1697), or the 'Preliminary Discourse' written by George Sale as a preface to his translation of the Qu'ran (1734).

Outside this circle of vision few eighteenth-century travellers tried to forge a direct understanding of what they experienced or even to ask new questions of it. This was especially the case with Islamic architecture, where the canon of Graeco-Roman architecture guided the eye. In 1709 the poet Aaron Hill published *A Full and Just Account of the Present State of the Ottoman Empire*, based on his travels in the Near East from 1699 to 1703. Like many later accounts, this set out to be an all-embracing record of its subject: a source-book of useful knowledge about the area. Chapter 17 covered 'Publick and Private Buildings in Turkey' and there Hill described baths, *hans*, hospitals, houses, gardens and fortifications. He itemized the typical features of a generic mosque:

> *Spotless white* . . . stately *Cupola*, supported by a *double*, sometimes *treble* row of Pillars of a different Order each from other, yet without a Name whereby I can express them in the *British Language* . . . *four, six*, or *eight* tall *Turrets* . . . A stately *Portico* . . . tho' Images are disallowed, the compass of the *inner Wall* of all their *Mosques* is full of *Niches* . . . *Glass Lamps*.[2]

Clearly, the problem of naming was paramount for Hill, and his solution was to inventorize, applying the nearest equivalents out of a familiar vocabulary. The other problems were that Ottoman architecture was substandard by the canons that Hill applied, and that those canons could only be partially mobilized anyway. Hill recognized this:

> The *Turks*, unskill'd in ancient Orders of *Ionick, Dorick*, or *Corinthian Buildings*, practice methods independent on the Customs of our *European Architecture*, and proceed by measures altogether *new*, and owing to the Product of their own *Invention*.[3]

But despite Hill's interest in architecture, he published no plans and his illustrations show architecture as background to some aspect of local customs, the real interest of the image.

By contrast, Richard Pococke's even more compendious *A Description of the East* (1743–5) published schematic plans and generalized elevations and sections of several Islamic buildings: the Mosque of Amr ibn al-As, the Bab al-Nasr, and 'Joseph's Hall' (the now largely demolished Qasr al-Ablaq) in Cairo; the Dome of the Rock at Jerusalem (called the 'Mosque of Soloman's

PLATE 1 Richard
Pococke. Dome of the
Rock, Jerusalem,
1743–5. Plan and view.
(*A Description of the East*)

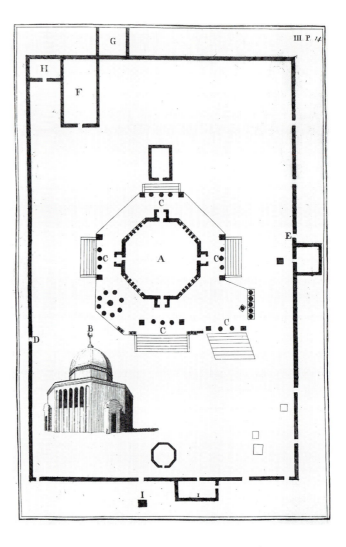

Temple') (Plate 1); and the Great Mosque at Damascus.[4] In the houses that he
visited Pococke was fascinated by the mechanical apparatus by which the
harem was separated from the rest of the house.[5] Otherwise his comments on
major buildings were brief and anecdotal, as we would expect of a writer-
traveller anxious not to delay his reader on the way to classical remains or the
monuments of ancient Egypt. Cairene monuments were illustrated in the first
volume, devoted entirely to Egypt. Here the chapter on architecture (others
were on government, natural history, customs and antiquities) was entirely
given over to ancient Egyptian monuments arranged in a sequence following
the course of the Nile.

    The most influential eighteenth-century work to illustrate Islamic
architecture was J. B. Fischer von Erlach's *Entwurff einer historischen Architectur*
(1721, translated into English in 1737). In his preface Fischer made his intent

clear: 'Artists will see, that Nations dissent no less in their Taste for Architecture, than in Food and Raiment'. Yet there were common verities: 'notwithstanding all these Varieties, there are certain general principles in Architecture ... Rules of Symmetry; that the Weaker must be supported by the Stronger, and the like'.[6] In pursuit of this variety within ruling architectural principles, the third part of Fischer's book was devoted to an extraordinary range of architecture: 'Buildings of the Arabians, Turks etc. and some Modern One's of the Persians, Siamese, Chinese and Japonese'. Amongst its fifteen plates were many unmeasured plans and perspectives, and some sections and elevations. Since Fischer never travelled outside Europe, he was dependent on the sketches and reports of travellers for these images. Of the Islamic buildings depicted, many were relatively accessible: a Turkish bath outside Budapest, the Mosque of Sultan Orcanus II in Bursa, the Mosque of Sultan Ahmet and the Suleymaniye in Istanbul. But there were also the rarely visited or totally inaccessible monuments: the Ali Qapu Palace and Maidan i Shah at Isfahan, and the mosques at Madinah and Makkah based on drawings by an Arab engineer (Plate 2). Fischer's inclusion of Islamic and other eastern buildings on a scale and with a degree of detail comparable to the illustration of more canonical ancient buildings, was to remain unique in the eighteenth century. Beyond its inevitable function as a book of illustrations to be

PLATE 2 J. B. Fischer von Erlach. Makkah, 1721. Perspective. (*Entwurff einer historischen Architectur*)

plundered for orientalizing garden buildings, it also indicated a new attitude towards these sources. The apparent equivalence in the status of these buildings opened up for architects the prospect of an eclecticism which was both historical and cultural, leavened by constant formal principles. But with Fischer we have moved far from the direct encounter with architecture of the eastern Mediterranean, and, because his influence in Britain was limited, far also from the particular conditions of British experience.

EARLY NINETEENTH-CENTURY ARCHITECTS IN THE NEAR EAST

Before the middle of the nineteenth century most of those British architects who travelled in the Near East did so with their eyes fixed on the remains of a classical heritage. It was the lineaments of Graeco-Roman civilization that filled notebooks geared to collecting necessary professional knowledge. The usual pattern was to include Asia Minor in a tour of Greece and Italy. But although architects visited Islamic lands, Islamic architecture either simply did not exist for them or it lay outside the classical paradigm; both amounted to the same thing. C. R. Cockerell, for example, whose travels lasted some seven years from 1810 to 1817, taking in Greece, Italy, Sicily and Asia Minor, made little mention of Islamic architecture in his journal, and then either disparagingly or as a scenic but otherwise unremarkable aspect of the townscape. Typically, of Istanbul he wrote:

> To architecture in the highest sense, viz. elegant construction in
> stone, the Turks have no pretension. The mosques are always copies
> of Santa Sophia with trifling variations, and have no claims to
> originality. The bazaars are large buildings, but hardly architectural.
> The imarets, or hospitals, are next in size ... but neither have they
> anything artistic about them.[7]

To some extent difficulty of access and the *ad hoc* nature of their trips may have helped to dissuade architects from studying Islamic buildings. (By contrast, far from the classical paradigm and under direct British company rule, in India the British began to commission detailed drawings of Muslim architecture from local artists.)[8]

For Cockerell and for many other architects who began to practise in the first two decades of the century, Islamic architecture was imbued with the associational values of the Picturesque. Picturesque theory in the arts had widened the range of the aesthetic, sanctioning choice from a plurality of styles provided they were associated with either the character and decorum of the building type, or the meaning of a particular site or narrative programme. Islam, in this way of thinking, could be a commodity like anything else, to be enjoyed for its novelty and, like fashions, discarded when the pleasure-seeking gaze tired. Much as other styles might imply moral or poetic ideas, so Islamic was often linked to pleasure, femininity and entertainment. The neo-Islamic buildings that had been designed in the eighteenth and early nineteenth centuries – among them a Turkish mosque and two Alhambras at Kew, S. P. Cockerell's Sezincote (1804–5) and John Nash's Royal Pavilion, Brighton (1815–23) – relied on the easy delights and connotations of Picturesque theory, which included remoteness as a value in itself. As such they could be designed from artists' images, travellers' impressions, or a book like Fischer von Erlach's; no painstaking or firsthand examination of the originals was required. William Chambers's mosque at Kew (1761) is a case in point (Plate 3). Two minarets, a crescent on the dome, and Arabic inscriptions over the doors are enough to establish its character. But the minarets are solid and without any means to reach their tiny balconies, and inside the mosque there is no *mihrab* and the ornament adopts a more familiar rococo manner, abandoning any pretence at Islamic inspiration.

When travelling, most British architects held before them the model of those seminal eighteenth-century architect-scholars who worked in the eastern Mediterranean: Robert Adam at Spalato, Wood and Dawkins at Palmyra and Baalbec, and Stuart and Revett in Athens. In part the aim of C.R. Cockerell and other architects of the new century was to find ways of contributing to the Graeco-Roman tradition. In this respect the travels of Sir Charles Barry, recorded in many detailed journals, were both exemplary and exceptional.

Barry left England in June 1817, travelled to Greece, Turkey, Egypt, Palestine, Syria and Sicily, as well as Italy and France, and returned in August 1820. Originally his plan had been simply to make the conventional tour of Greece and Asia Minor, but in Istanbul he met David Baillie, who invited Barry to accompany him as a draughtsman on a trip to Egypt. Barry was thus one of the first British architects to study ancient Egyptian architecture in Egypt, spending a considerable amount of time drawing and studying its monuments. Behind Barry's encounter lay a long history of western interest in ancient Egypt, expressed in Hermeticist and Neoplatonic traditions, in Freemasonry, Rosicrucianism and Pyramidology.[9]

Like many travellers to the Near East, for Barry cultural journey was also an opportunity for the gathering of a different kind of information. In Egypt he collected population figures and data on exports. He visited a cotton mill, noting that the machinery had come from Milan.[10] But on other fronts Barry was less inquisitive. His priorities are made clear even in incidental comments:

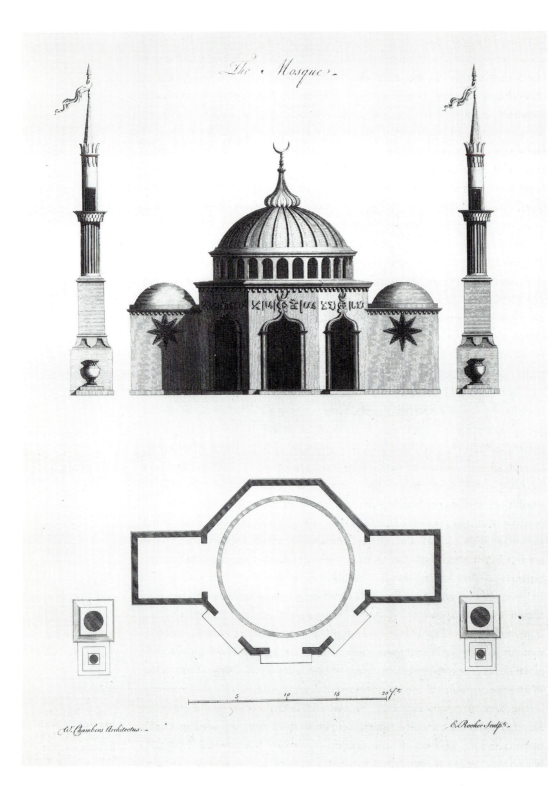

The Mosque

W. Chambers Architectus.   E. Rooker Sculp.

he praised an emir whom he met in Syria as a man of taste because he owned a volume of Palladio, whilst elsewhere he attacked the Turks for allowing Greek civilization to fall into desolation because of their jealousy and churlishness towards its antiquities.[11] He made only the occasional brief comment or sketch that acknowledged monuments dating to periods after the Muslim conquests. In Istanbul, where he spent a month in the summer of 1818 between his travels in Greece and Egypt, he admired 'the magnificence of some of the mosks, particularly Suleymani – which seems to me to be the most commanding of them all'.[12] In Cairo he noted 'bursts of Saracenic magnificence ... The mosks are very numerous. Some of them extremely beautiful and rare specimens of true Saracenic architecture'.[13] In Damascus he observed a house '[that] glows with oriental magnificence'.[14] Usually Barry delighted in this beguiling and Picturesque *frisson*, but the dazzled admiration expressed in these sporadic comments also reveals a pervasive incomprehension. While the Picturesque aesthetic allowed this facile appreciation, there were few intellectual tools to empower understanding and only a sketchy historical perspective to encourage it.

THE STUDY OF ISLAMIC ARCHITECTURE IN THE EARLY NINETEENTH CENTURY

Barry's incomprehension was more to be blamed on prejudice than on an absolute absence of western knowledge of Islamic architecture. But until the second quarter of the nineteenth century there was little in the way of theoretical or historical analysis of Islamic architecture. Those eighteenth-century texts that attempted an account of it had foundered over nomenclature, and few had much factual or descriptive content. Significantly, it was not until Egypt had been conquered by a modern European power that a more expansive and resourceful account could be made.

Napoleon's invasion of Egypt in 1798 was the product of the Egyptophile atmosphere of Revolutionary France and the geopolitics of military adventure. It was accompanied by all the paraphernalia of scholarly colonialism, and its most important production was the twenty-three massive volumes, fourteen of which were devoted to illustrations, of the *Description de l'Égypte* (1809–28). With these, as Edward Said has observed, 'the Orient as a body of knowledge in the West was modernized'.[15] Where Hill and Pococke, or the Abbé Le Mascrier (whose identically named *Description de l'Égypte* appeared in 1735), had attempted amateurish compendia of things Islamic and Egyptian, Napoleon's *savants* (including architects, engineers and surveyors) compiled what is properly regarded as an archive. The *Description* represented an

PLATE 3 William Chambers. Turkish mosque, Kew, 1761. Elevation and plan. (*Plans ... of the Gardens and Buildings at Kew Surry*)

apparently exhaustive record of all things Egyptian made into a library resource. Both conquests of Egypt, military and scholarly, had a symbolic function: France was to be regarded as assuming the mantle of western civilization and standing on the centre stage of world history. The justification for these claims was not anything that had happened in the previous thirteen hundred years in Egypt or its present-day 'barbarism', but a classical and ancient past understood as the source of what were seen as distinctively European cultural values.[16]

The *Description*'s illustrations of Islamic architecture were motivated by a cartographic imperative.[17] Just as D'Anville's 1765 map of Egypt had proved inadequate to France's army in Egypt, so Pococke or Le Mascrier were inadequate to its scholars. The enterprise was not openly interpretative but monumentally descriptive. Whilst ancient Egyptian structures were presented as the ideal and undecayed setting for imperial dreams, Arab buildings were seen as part of the 'État moderne', the topsoil over the real cultural strata (five of the *Description*'s volumes deal with the 'État moderne', as opposed to nine on 'Antiquités'). Nevertheless the properties of this deposit had to be known in order to reform the economy and industry of the country. The building industry was, of course, crucial here, especially when the French came to build their arsenals, tanneries, windmills and factories, and even more so with their own colonial institutions. It was thus that Islamic architecture slipped into the military and economic nexus.

Of all the articles devoted to the 'État moderne' in the *Description*, only one dealt with Cairo's architecture, and even there most of the text described population, health, industry or other more pressing matters.[18] However, Jomard's text did provide dates of buildings and Arabic terminology, and made use of an Arabic text for information about architecture. Cairo's monuments were traced through townscape views as well as plans, elevations and sections of buildings. Never before had so many illustrations of Islamic architecture been assembled, and never before had such care been taken over their accuracy. Here and there the other practicalities of the exercise were revealed: the first 'État moderne' volume of plates brought together maps of towns, plans of fortifications, and details of bridges. But the majority of its vast pages displayed the Islamic buildings of Cairo: tombs, fountains, houses, baths, five plates devoted to the citadel, and most plates of all given over to mosques, culminating in the seven magnificent plates depicting the Mosque of Sultan Hassan. One of the main points about the sheer unrelenting authority of these plates is the way that they replace the difficult realities of the streets of Cairo with a new and more easily grasped reality, one suited to the library. The elevation, sections and plans on one plate (Plate 4) are precisely related across the page, their volumes defined with the accurate tools

PLATE 4 Commission des sciences et arts d'Égypte. Mosque of Sultan Hassan, Cairo, 1809. (*Description de l'Égypte*, 'État moderne' plate volume 1)

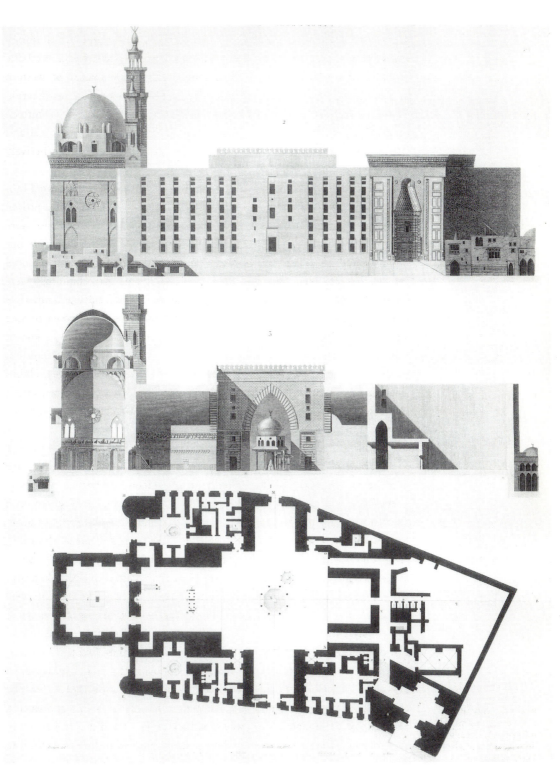

of the new descriptive geometry; the power of Enlightenment mathematics confidently meeting the demands of Islamic science and implicitly subsuming its divine orientations. France's intellectual prowess had made the mosque, as well as Egypt's other buildings, into something essentially reproducible.[19]

In the second 'État moderne' volume, which continued this inventorizing of contemporary resources, the population was also characterized by its representative types: the poet, astronomer, musician, sailor, Mamluk and dancer. Here an outline of Arab culture was made coherent by the authoritative sanctions of typology, mensuration, the accumulation of detail, and a cartographic-visual logic. An examination of Egypt's strategic position – its defensibility and its relation to India – had become complementary to an interest in both its ancient and modern history.

It was between the three images of ancient, medieval and modern Egypt that the study of Islam was to be stretched. Modern Egyptians were regarded as still medieval in their way of life, and yet pragmatic information about their country had to be gathered for the purposes of modernization. Ancient Egyptian civilization was still held to contain eternal verities, and yet the culture of its descendants seemed alternately time-bound or corrupt, resulting from the teachings of a false prophet. The dazzling and beguiling image of that medieval culture had somehow to be mastered or rationalized, and yet mastery of Egypt's past could perhaps only come about by mastery of her present.

After the *Description* western writers on Islamic architecture in Egypt, and by implication elsewhere, had the authority of the archive behind them. Without it, the work of Edward Lane and Owen Jones would not have been conceivable. It was a work that could hardly be physically surpassed, but it did inaugurate a deliberately scholarly attitude, extending the project of the Enlightenment, to encompass the Near East. Scholars had a sense of measuring their work against a monument, of filling in a newly outlined field. However, in terms of any acknowledged interpretation of culture, especially architecture, the *Description* offered little.

HAY'S GROUP AND THE NEW ORIENTALISM

By the 1820s a group of young British artists and architects had begun to look at Islamic architecture in a deliberately analytical way. They had two avowed aims: to try to find new explanatory categories but also, leading out from this, to search for principles that might guide their own work. With some licence their activity is here referred to as the 'new orientalism'. By this I mean that a new sense of urgency and intellectual enquiry had infected the study of

Islamic architecture – a kind of parallel to the 'oriental renaissance' of the late eighteenth and early nineteenth centuries when western scholarly knowledge of oriental languages and texts flourished. What had until then largely been either a textual study or, with the *Description*, an archival collation, now became concerned in this 'new orientalism' with the reading of artifacts, especially architecture, and a deeper consideration of their worth for contemporary production. Architecture and orientalism thus emerged as a serious coupling: the former as a newly instituted profession emerging out of a multifarious range of building and training practices; the latter as a discursive formation with its own specialists and a diffusive ability to thread its way through many different Victorian activities and interests. From this point distinct architectural concerns could be meaningfully articulated with the various discourses about oriental cultures mobilized by artists, travellers, missionaries, diplomats and others.

The linchpin of this new group was Robert Hay, but its most important thinkers were Edward Lane and Owen Jones. The group was initially brought together by the Egyptomania provoked by the publication of the *Description* and the discoveries of J.-F. Champollion and Vivant Denon. As before, the study of Islam was a by-product of the study of ancient Egypt.

Hay started to plan an expedition to Egypt in the early summer of 1824. In Malta, on his way out, he met the architects Frederick Catherwood and Henry Parke, who had recently travelled up the Nile with the antiquarian Henry Westcar and the architect J. J. Scoles.[20] Hay's project was more ambitious than mere travel. Over the next decade he organized two major expeditions: from 1824 to 1828, and from 1829 to 1834. His object was to study and record ancient Egyptian monuments, and to carry out this project Hay, who had recently inherited an estate from his brother, employed such artists and architects as Francis Arundale, Joseph Bonomi, Frederick Catherwood, J. J. Scoles, James Haliburton, Charles Laver, E. W. Lane, J. G. Wilkinson, G. B. Greenough, George Hoskins and Henry Parke.[21]

At this time the Egyptian government was eager to employ foreign technocrats to aid its economic transformation of the country, and several members of Hay's group had been employed in various capacities: Haliburton and Wilkinson had come to Egypt in 1821 at the invitation of Muhammad Ali in order to make a geological survey of the Nile, and Catherwood was employed as an engineer in the early 1830s to help repair the mosques of Cairo.[22] During these visits many of this disparate group became interested in Islamic architecture; indeed, Hay himself later published his *Illustrations of Cairo* (1840).

In 1833 Catherwood, Arundale and Bonomi made an expedition into Sinai and Gaza.[23] Catherwood's work is the most important; he made a detailed map of Jerusalem (published in 1835) and, with the help of a *camera lucida*, prepared a panorama of the city including all its major buildings. As an extension of these surveys he devoted himself to compiling the most extensive drawings yet made of the Dome of the Rock and the Aqsa Mosque. Catherwood certainly intended that these studies of buildings should be published in some form, but London publishers were indifferent. Although his drawings were lost they had a surrogate existence: they were given to James Fergusson in 1847 and used by him in his *Essay on the Ancient Topography of Jerusalem* (1847) and his *Illustrated Handbook of Architecture* (1855).[24]

The most influential member of Hay's group was Edward William Lane (1801–76). His work on contemporary Islamic society, *An Account of the Manners and Customs of the Modern Egyptians* (1836), went through four editions within a decade of its publication (the first edition sold out within a fortnight), and was the standard authority on its subject for over half a century. Hay, Bonomi, Haliburton and Wilkinson were already working in Egypt when Lane arrived in Alexandria in 1825. He lived in Cairo for the next three years until 1828, and during this time he made two expeditions down the Nile recording Egyptian monuments in obsessively accurate drawings, again, like Catherwood, using a *camera lucida*.[25] When Lane returned to England in 1828 he intended to publish a selection of his drawings as a 'Description of Egypt'. Although this never happened, perhaps because of the expense of reproduction, the chapters dealing with contemporary Egypt were accepted for publication on Lord Brougham's recommendation by the Society for the Diffusion of Useful Knowledge.[26] The elaborately indolent and docile Egyptians of Lane's account were exemplary antitheses for this Benthamite organization established to improve efficiency and promote the work ethic amongst Britain's labouring classes.

The *Manners and Customs* was finally published in 1836 after Lane had returned to Egypt for a further period of study from 1833 to 1835. Lane stated his intentions as 'to make some of my countrymen better acquainted with the domiciliated classes of one of the most interesting nations of the world, by drawing a detailed picture of the inhabitants of the largest Arab city'.[27] But Lane did not see his book simply as a correction of the Napoleonic *Description de l'Égypte*. Where that work had been monumentally descriptive yet distanced from contemporary culture, Lane's was to seek out the specific patterns of life and structures of meaning in Cairene society and, by implication, to disclose the constant and contingent features of humanity: his was to be a study of culture, in the German Romantic J. G. Herder's sense of that term. Lane's objectivity was to be vouchsafed by the accuracy and completeness of his examination of every aspect of Islamic society. Customs, religion and laws were foremost in this account, but there was also a particular kind of attention paid to the environment moulded by this culture.

In his introduction Lane took an elevated view over the city, from which he could grasp its total form. Yet, and despite Timothy Mitchell's use of this elevated view as part of his idea that Lane typifies the West's concept of the 'world-as-exhibition',[28] Lane did not publish a view or map of the city and he had no interest in locating or orientating his reader in the city. Apart from a mention of the citadel, no monuments are named or described and even the name of the city – Cairo – is rarely used. The description of the urban geography of the city is astonishingly brief. It is a metropolis located in a landscape, surrounded by walls with gates, and internally divided into quarters with narrow unpaved alleys. Lane's city is not just a place but an organism. His city is constituted out of its essential organic features (religion most especially) rather than the outward, inorganic and presumably contingent manifestations of them. It is, therefore, not so much Cairo but the generic 'Islamic city' that is pictured and constructed through Lane's text and images.[29]

Lane's text quickly moved into the city's domestic spaces. In the next twenty pages he described the private houses of the city, paying attention to the arrangement of rooms, materials and decorative details, and wherever possible providing the Arabic term for what was described, the function of each element of the plan and an explanation of spatial hierarchy (Plate 5). Later, in the chapter on religion, Lane did the same for the interiors of mosques, and elsewhere for shops and baths.[30] His illustration of a mosque (Plate 6) makes a pointed comparison with Chambers's picturesque mosque at Kew (see Plate 3). Both images are stripped and tend to the generic, but although Lane's illustration is unsubtle, it takes a view that deliberately encompasses most of the mosque's essential features: minaret, *mihrab*, *dikkah*, courtyard and *minbar*. Where Chambers had used such features they became decorative and entirely functionless adjuncts. Again, by comparison with the *Description*'s plate of the Mosque of Sultan Hassan (see Plate 4), Lane's mosque is crudely rendered. But what it offers is a different kind of resource and a different kind of reproducibility. In the *Description*'s mosque the absence of compass orientation and the preference for geometrical placement across the page seems almost deliberately flaunted. One knows how one might move through spaces, or better still how one might reconstruct them, but not why. By contrast Lane's illustration includes two praying positions and the text explains materials, orientation, opening times, mosque decorum, officialdom, and the gendered disposition of space. The mosque form seems an organic result of its internal functions and its larger cultural environment.

Lane's book could be used as travel literature or as an authoritative reference work. It supplied a battery of terms for future western students of Islamic architecture, but it did not provide, in any sense appropriate for its time, a

PLATE 5 E. W. Lane. 'A
Cka'ah', 1836. (*Manners
and Customs*)

description of Islamic architecture as a style of building. Lane was not a trained architect; he was writing a form of broadly accessible ethnography not intended for architects specifically. The nearest he came to a description of stylistic development is found in the second volume, where he berated the European influence in recent Egyptian architecture.[31] But the neglect of the designer's perspective seems to have benefited the description of Islamic architecture as the result of certain functional or ritual requirements; of usable places for inhabitants who held a common set of beliefs and customs. It is perhaps for this reason that it is difficult to find direct evidence of Lane's influence on specialist architectural discourse, although his architectural discussion certainly provided the living shell for Lane's authoritative picture of oriental life.

OWEN JONES

The 1830s witnessed closer links between British and French orientalism than had existed since the eighteenth century, and certainly closer than would exist

PLATE 6 E. W. Lane.
Mosque in Cairo, 1836.
(*Manners and Customs*)

later in the century. In a sense, the *Description* and other Egyptological work had provided a common scholarly source in both countries. As Edward Said has pointed out, whilst France and Britain were locked in imperial rivalry, their scholars could often regard orientalism as a joint venture.[32] There are many examples of this in architectural study. The French architect Pascal Coste sold many of his Egyptian drawings to Robert Hay, and was in close contact with Joseph Bonomi, T. L. Donaldson and even C. R. Cockerell and Charles Barry.[33] Bonomi was in communication with at least three other important French scholars during the 1830s and 1840s: Linant de Bellefonds, Jules Goury and P. E. Botta.[34] Charles Texier, the French Byzantinist, was later to leave most of his drawings of Ottoman monuments to the Royal Institute of British Architects.[35] But the most fertile of these Anglo-French contacts was that between Owen Jones and Jules Goury.

Owen Jones was the most dynamic figure in these loose-knit groupings of orientalists that formed in England. In 1825 he was articled to Lewis Vulliamy, who had travelled in Asia Minor from 1818 to 1822, and after his pupillage Jones travelled extensively in Sicily, Greece, Turkey, Egypt and Spain between 1829 and 1834. In Greece he met the French architect Jules Goury, who was working there with Gottfried Semper, and the two travelled together until Goury's death from cholera in 1834.[36] Their travels in Egypt were later the subject of *Views on the Nile* (1843), in which, as in so many travel books of the time, the Nilotic journey was the organizing narrative for a series of picturesque views. Like Vulliamy, Jones and Goury made serious architectural studies of several Ottoman buildings in Istanbul.[37] But the most productive part of their travels was the six months that they spent examining the Alhambra in Spain. It was on the basis of studies made in this period that Jones later published his seminal *Plans, Elevations, Sections, and Details of the Alhambra* (1836–45).

The depth of Jones's interest in one Islamic building had only been rivalled by Catherwood's sadly lost work on the Dome of the Rock. Unlike Catherwood, Jones was able to mobilize the mechanics of publishing, making important technical advances in chromolithography, to enable his work to reach a larger audience. As its title suggests, the book had the completeness of scope and quantity of detail that was usually only reserved for Greek temples. It was also provocatively rationalist in its approach: for example, there were demonstrations of how Moorish patterns could be geometrically developed from a simple grid, and of the geometrical basis of a *muqarnas* vault. But it was the colour of the Alhambra's ornament that most interested Jones. In this, and in his and Goury's interest in the polychromy of ancient Egyptian architecture, Jones was developing a recent archaeological and theoretical interest amongst continental architects. The key publication here had been

J.-I. Hittorff and K. L. Zanth's *Architecture antique de la Sicile* (1827–30), but it was preceded by significant discussions of polychromy, both as a newly discovered element in classical architecture and for its potential in contemporary architecture. Jules Goury had been present at these discussions, which enlivened Parisian ateliers during the 1820s,[38] and his and Jones's contribution to this current of theory was to use Islamic architecture, and in particular the example of the Alhambra, to find lessons for the development of design in their own day.

In 1835, after returning from his travels but before the beginning of the *Alhambra*'s publication, Jones delivered an important lecture to the Architectural Society entitled 'On the Influence of Religion upon Art'. Here, setting aside the useful lessons of Islamic design, Jones stated some more general attitudes towards Islamic culture. The lecture was an attempt to trace the connections between styles of architecture and religious institutions. Religion, imbued with certain racial notions, was seen as more important than such factors as climate or social organization. Jones argued that Islamic culture was formed out of three impulses: the reaction away from Christianity, the teachings of the Qu'ran, and, most crucially, the racial memory of architectural origins.

For Jones, the key difference between Islam and Christianity was the former's 'dread of idolatry':

> This dread of idolatry caused a singular feature … we find the temples of the Arabs decorated throughout as none others have been, unaided by the productions of nature, which they have copied, if at all, in a manner so distant, so changed by the fertility of their imagination, that we are quite at a loss to discover the traces of the originals. It would seem rather that the Arabs, changing their wandering for a settled life, *in striking the tent to plant it in a form more solid*, had transferred the luxurious shawls and hangings of Cashmere, which had adorned their former dwellings, to their new; changing the tent-pole for a marble column, and the silken tissue for a gilded plaster: whilst in their temples the doctrine of the Koran, written on every side, proclaiming the power of God, and impressing upon the believer respect for the laws and the love of virtue, produced a species of decoration as original as it was magical in effect.[39]

Unlike Lane, and even a very different contemporary architectural theorist like A. W. N. Pugin, Jones was not interested in how the rituals of religion shaped and, in their turn, were shaped by the givens and the contingencies of architectural environments. It was instead a memory peculiar to the Arabs that gave their architecture distinction: the transfer of the qualities and substances of tents and their decoration was actually a memory of nomadic dwelling, an atavistic bedouinism. In the very same year, Thomas Hope had described this kind of memory as a 'universal propensity to retrace, in the latter method of construction, the forms of the earlier materials. It was a manner of reminding the nation of its past origins, its earliest infancy, its primitive arts'.[40] This view itself built on the rationalist doctrine of apparent utility most influentially articulated in the mid-eighteenth century by the Abbé Laugier, but in fact dating back to Vitruvius.[41] Jones's insight was to attempt to use a doctrine that had been associated with classicism to give Islamic architecture distinct origins and parity of status. Usually any such interpretation had been curtailed by the belief that everything of any worth in Islamic architecture had come from the Graeco-Roman heritage. One of Thomas Hope's difficulties with Ottoman architecture, for example, was that this retracing or transposition of earlier practice could not be found in their buildings because they were 'designed for them by the Greeks, their new subjects, after their own fashion'.[42]

Elsewhere in Jones's lecture, the close identification of Islamic architecture with its religion was used in an attack on the present state of Christian architecture:

> Who that has stood beside the fountain of the Mosque of Sultan Hassan in Grand Cairo, or has trod the golden halls of the fairy palace of the Alhambra, has not felt the calm, voluptuous translation of the Koran's doctrines? Who amidst the aisles of a Gothic cathedral has not felt materialism wither away, and, awe-struck by the mysterious character of the building, cried out, – Here, indeed, is the dwelling-place of the Christian's God! Here may He be worshipped in purity of spirit? Who, once more I would ask, has attended the evening service of a Reformed Protestant Church, erected ... with every attention paid to the comforts of the creature and so little to the glory of the Creator in whose dwelling-place he is supposed to be; and has not had a feeling of regret and sorrow steal over him on viewing the evidences of wealth and luxury which surrounded him, to see so much was given to man, so little to God?[43]

Unlike Pugin, Jones was not interested in calling for a religious revival led by architecture. Instead the secularism of the new age had to be accepted; new works had to derive from a new trinity – 'Science, Commerce and Industry'. This was neither the first nor the last time that the example of the East was used to attack contemporary western society.[44] As always, such assaults are more informative about the subject attacked than the exemplary object. But the example of the East could also help architects with what they regarded as a pervasive conundrum, the problem of style. Explicitly, if a historical style was to be used, which one? If not, how could a new, modern style be created?

Owen Jones felt this dilemma as much as any architect. In the 1840s he experimented with applying Islamic ornament to conventionally planned houses.[45] By the 1850s he had found a more radical solution where, instead of concatenating stylistic forms, a new synthesis apparently not derived from historical forms was proposed. This was based almost entirely on a theory of applied polychromy inspired by Jones's study of the colouristic effects of the Alhambra. Jones found confirmation for this largely decorative solution in the chromatic researches of contemporary scientists, and he applied it to iron and glass structures such as the interior of the Crystal Palace (1851). Although this issue has been fully dealt with elsewhere,[46] for present purposes it relates to another important current in western attitudes towards Islam, which will be introduced here and then taken up later in this book.

The social and philosophical thought of the Comte de Saint-Simon and his followers had been imbibed by Jones through his friendship with Jules Goury and other French architects and theorists.[47] The Saint-Simonian belief in scientific progress organizing modern society implied a unification of the world through communications and the 'industrialization of the earth'.[48] Architects, engineers and artists were to play a key administrative role at the head of Saint-Simon's ideal society. Also, because they saw Egypt as the crucial link between East and West, Saint-Simonians were deeply involved in promoting its place as a laboratory of modernity within a 'système de la Méditerranée'.[49] There are telling similarities in this to the British utilitarian view of India, a view that dominated British attitudes towards the subcontinent in these same decades. In Saint-Simonian theory, as in Auguste Comte's related teleology of knowledge, history was divided into organic periods and critical periods. Egypt, and the East as a whole, were fixed in the first period: a metaphysical or abstract stage of history dominated by one creed; a stage preceding that of positivist or scientific modern Europe.

Clearly such beliefs were not directly transferable to Jones's architectural theory and practice, but there are links. When Jones called in his lecture of 1835 for a culture that accepted the new secular gods of 'Science, Commerce and Industry' he was calling for a new kind of architecture and voicing a basic belief of scientific materialism. There were also two underlying elements in common: first, the marrying of eastern effects and western technology, of the normative and rational to the exotic and 'feminine'; and second, and not at all contradictory, the opposition of the stasis of Islam to the dynamism of the

West (both excluded revivalism or historicism). By the middle decades of the century such ideas had great influence, indeed they were the basis of iron and glass structures like the Crystal Palace. These ideas could also provide a rationalization for colonialism in the Near East, or at least for quickening the speed of economic penetration.

2

SOUTH-SAVAGE

INTERPRETING ISLAMIC ARCHITECTURE, 1840–70

•

You will find that the art whose end is pleasure only is pre-eminently the gift of cruel and savage nations, cruel in temper, savage in habits and conception; but that the art which is especially dedicated to natural fact always indicates a peculiar gentleness and tenderness of mind.

(*John Ruskin, 1859*)

The one great fact, which it is essential to insist on here is, that if we do not take into account its connexion with ethnography, the history *of architecture is a mere dry, hard recapitulation of uninteresting facts and terms; but when its relation to the world's history is understood, when we read in their buildings the feelings and aspirations of the people who erected them, and above all through their arts we can trace their relationship to and descent from one another, the study becomes one of the most interesting as well as one of the most useful which can be presented to the inquiring mind.*

(*James Fergusson, 1865*)

Victorians usually judged Islamic architecture in much the same way as they judged its creators. This in itself was similar to any other cultural product or style, whether European, eastern or historical, but it was also an increasingly pressing issue, and one that was often political and usually racial in relation to Islamic architecture in the mid-nineteenth century. Here was a cultural expression that must be deemed oriental, one that was surely without the equivocations and confusions attending the placement of, say, Byzantine (as will be discussed in the following chapter). More seemed to be known about Islamic culture than before, more direct experience could be drawn upon, and there were pressing reasons to gather information and adjust hypotheses.

The quotations from John Ruskin and James Fergusson at the head of this chapter provide useful entries into these issues. To write any history of architecture in the nineteenth century was to make a study of cultural affiliations and differences. According to Fergusson this became a 'useful' work, something more than inert information, when the historian excavated or extrapolated architectural evidence of the bonds identifying and linking a group of people together. Architecture could then be seen as a part of world history and as an expression of the organic vitality of nations. Architectural history would also be instrumental in an assessment of origins and evolution, and help to form an explanation of the present. Criticism or justification of contemporary concerns would spring from the firm ground of history.

As the certainties of Ruskin's passage exemplify – 'You will find . . .', he says, 'pleasure . . . is pre-eminently the gift of cruel and savage nations' – architectural or artistic evidence could also uphold the way that national character was perceived. Even for a writer like Ruskin, a predetermined psychology – a graspable ordering principle – could be read back into the productions of nation, race, or people. The psychology would subsume and negate individual differences under the larger, and no doubt more useful, concern for differences between groups. In this scheme, however, the individual would return in the guise of the embodied psychology of the group. Thus for Ruskin the 'mind' of the nations of the North was characterized by a 'peculiar gentleness and tenderness', while that of those of the South was inevitably polarized as 'cruel and savage'. Yet their cultural forms were not indexed to these traits, but stood in a direct, metonymic relation to them: in Ruskin's formula, southern savagery created an art of pleasure, while northern gentleness produced a naturalistic art.

Between 1840 and 1870, following the impetus of the 'new orientalism', a large corpus of material devoted to Islamic architecture came to be gathered and made available to the privileged British architect or architectural historian who wished to study the subject without actually venturing out into the Islamic world. It was a corpus that consisted of weighty multi-volumed works purporting to be of archaeological exactitude, batches of measured drawings and sketchbook studies, historical and theoretical overviews encompassing the subject in a comparative framework, articles in a scholarly or journalistic mode in various periodicals, and even built imitations of Islamic buildings.

Rather than attempt a minute examination of these often repititious works, this chapter examines the role of racial theory and the place of Islamic architecture in the writing of four of the most important Victorian architectural commentators: E. A. Freeman, James Fergusson, John Ruskin and Owen Jones. In a sense, by the mid-century, all of these writers were distanced from their objects of study (even Ruskin, whose work on Venice was based on close empirical study, was writing about Islam from a distance) and all needed to be because their concern was with an historical and cultural overview and the placement of Islamic culture within that. These are accounts of Islamic architecture in which the mode of seeing is less as a sight passed on horseback and more as an object scanned by the telescope of a study. With all of them the very value of their historical and critical writing was bound up with its ability to make cultural differentiation meaningful through the deployment of discourses about ethnicity, in particular, whether derived from models in natural history, philology, the social sciences or religion. All of these writers aimed their work as much at readers outside the architectural profession as those inside it, yet their competence was mostly based, Ruskin being the great exception, on the assurance of professional disciplines as the basis of their writing. That knowledge of oriental architecture had to be both professional and popular is demonstrated in the final sections of this chapter, which look at a very public debate about the usefulness of Islamic design to the problems of modern style and western society, and then at the way exhibitions and other exhibitionary buildings presented Islam in material form and as part of a vision of global relations, historical and geographic.

FREEMAN

Racial frames of reference, often inherently contradictory and subject to continuous adjustment, enjoyed wide currency in Victorian culture.[1] Races were understood as scientifically established entities, to be recognized in the character and physiognomy, the inner and outer form of people. Conceptions of art and its history were not exempt. Since at least Winckelmann, histories of art had interpreted culture as representative of the spirit of a people, and Hegel had made this more pointed by separating 'historic' from 'non-historic' nations, the art of which would be determined on this essentialist basis. Early in the nineteenth century the Saint-Simonians and positivists were clearly imbued with this thinking. Art and architectural history in general were thus given a new impetus to relate cultural form to race and to define cultural difference by race.

It should be no surprise, then, that the writing of architectural history, particularly a history premised on the superiority of western architecture, regularly drew on contemporary racial theory and the linguistic and ethnographic assumptions and parallels with natural history on which that theory was based. Victorian architectural theory and history were therefore a part of larger discourses on race. Although for many recent historians this is merely an inhibition or distortion of its classifying accuracy, and therefore to be refined out of a more dependable cumulative knowledge, this racial element will here be seen as crucial to the persuasiveness of Victorian architectural thought at its time, a crucial element in its claim to be a relevant modern discipline. In the next chapter we will see this with Byzantine architecture, but if anything this issue was even more apparent in the interpretation of Islamic architecture (Islamic architecture was usually characterized and accorded its position in architectural classifications much as Arabs or Semites were judged and placed in racial groupings. The racial family could be seen as having its own cultural traditions that expressed qualities particular to itself.)

Often, though, these racial categories were not overt. The historian Edward A. Freeman's (1823–92) views on Islamic architecture represent a pervasive attitude. In his *History of Architecture* (1849), 'Arabian' architecture's value largely resided in the familiar opportunity it gave for the projection of associations, and it could not therefore be seen as the result of real labour:

> Its charm consists in the excessive richness and gorgeousness of its buildings, and in the romantic associations with which we invest the Moorish conquerors of Spain and the heroes of the Thousand and One Nights, which make their structures seem rather like fairy palaces than the creations of men like ourselves.[2]

More importantly for Freeman's historical scheme, Islamic architecture was also seen as unable to develop, static, entranced by its own sensuality, and incapable of high seriousness:

> [Islamic architecture] contained the lifeless seed, which, never destined to arrive at perfection in its native soil, grew up under more genial influence into the pillared forest of the Gothic minster ... A style of architecture which has possessed the pointed arch for twelve hundred years, using it systematically as a favourite form, and yet has not superadded one of the mouldings which can alone render it even tolerable to the eye, cannot be assigned a high place in a philosophical view of art.[3]

Crucially, the style to which it was compared here was Gothic, the dynamic product of 'northern genius' and a prominent stage in the development of western architecture.[4] Freeman's notion of history, like that of many High Church theorists, was clearly influenced by John Henry Newman's idea of accretive development in theology. 'Development' was premised on the existence of its Other, stasis. Comparisons with Gothic exposed the supposed lack of invention in Islamic architecture, an extension of the idea, not overtly stated by Freeman, that Semites were uncreative. According to this ritually repeated notion, if change was observed in Islamic architecture then this had to be attributed to outside forces: either to the races that were conquered by the Arabs or to an already established architectural style.[5] Otherwise, Islamic architecture was atrophied, without the capacity for autonomous development.[6]

Although Freeman admitted Islamic into his 'true history' of architecture, this was only because without it certain features of Gothic – such as the pointed arch – could not be understood; otherwise it would have been relegated to the position of other immature, ill-regulated, disconnected and semi-civilized cultures.[7] Freeman's understanding of Islamic architecture thus complemented the Gothic nationalism of the High Church movement in the 1840s, which, as will be shown in Part II, at this time advocated a faithful and uninflected northern medieval style whatever the colonial setting.

Like Thomas Hope and Owen Jones, Freeman believed that racial memory – the memory of what was taken to be the race's original building type – informed and guided all the architectural products of the nation. But the qualitative difference between some cultures and others depended upon the impact of events on these 'original types': events such as mechanical discoveries, political or religious revolutions, and 'revulsions' in taste.[8] History, for Freeman, thus operated by catastrophe and cataclysm, as well as by development.

Out of this synthesis of historical and ethnographic concerns came Freeman's belief in western superiority. Other cultures presented

> a long dreary catalogue of men without actions, or of actions without effects, and belong rather to the ethnological or philological enquirer, than to the historian or the moralist. What is the whole history of the East . . . but a barren catalogue of kings, and priests, and conquerors, when it is viewed side by side with one stirring page of Greece, or Rome, or mediaeval Europe? . . . And thus too with their architecture; all styles are not of the same merit, all do not equally contain a principle of life, all are not equally the expression of an idea; partly from these inherent differences, partly from external causes, all have not the same historical importance in influencing the art of future ages. It hence follows that all do not present the same facilities for an investigation of their pervading principles of construction, decoration, and symbolism.[9]

It was not that the West somehow had more history. The 'principle of life' betrays Freeman's belief in a determining factor that was deeper than either the influence of primeval building types or the accidents of history. The dynamic or 'stirring' quality of western history was a product of the inherent dynamism of Europeans. The spirit of the age, or what Freeman elsewhere referred to as the 'developments of some great philosophical and moral principles',[10] was simply absent outside the West. In fact, even principles – the capacity of the intellect to order matter – were absent elsewhere.

This theory was directly applied in Freeman's treatment of Islamic architecture. He claimed that the ability to evolve theoretical principles out of aesthetic and practical concerns was northern and utterly lacking in Islamic creation:

> Saracenic fancy … delighted in astonishing the eye with a vast superstructure raised on a support apparently quite inadequate to sustain it. The style is rich, wonderful, calculated to enchant at first sight; but it will not bear critical investigation … [It is] the exuberance of a fancy, vivid and fertile to the last degree, but uncontrolled by any law of taste or consistency.[11]

Its irrationality and fancifulness were, of course, feminine; or rather, the feminine complement of the male Norman or Gothic ancestor of Victorian muscular Christianity:

> [The Palace at Palermo] breathes the most thoroughly Arabian spirit, and calls up the same dreamy and romantic notions of Eastern splendour as the habitations of the Spanish Caliphs. One really feels that a stern-visaged, iron-clad Norman was out of place in such a light, sunny, lofty abode.[12]

Freeman thereby admitted Islam into his history more as an antithetical element than as an integrated or contributing force.

FERGUSSON

James Fergusson (1808–86) was not only a great expert on Indian architecture but also, through the scope of his synthesizing histories, one of the most widely read of Victorian architectural historians. Fergusson followed Freeman in his twofold division of architectural history, but where Freeman was unconcerned with what did not contribute to his 'true history' of western architecture, Fergusson devoted one half of his popular *Illustrated Handbook of Architecture* (1855) to this other history. While still retaining a belief in the inherent stasis of Islam, Fergusson's account of its architecture was far better informed than Freeman's, Fergusson casting his net more widely amongst contemporary Islamic specialists: drawing on Pascal Coste, Girault de Prangey and Catherwood, amongst many others.

Fergusson's account was also far more appreciative than Freeman's. He particularly admired the minarets of Cairo and the Maidan i Shah in Isfahan. The latter was 'a scene of gorgeous, though it may be somewhat barbarous splendour almost unequalled in the whole world', but its main interest

> rests on the fact of its being a modern reproduction of the style of the ancient palaces of Nineveh and Babylon, using the same thick walls of imperfectly burned bricks, and covering them with the same brilliant coloured decorations of glazed and painted tiles and bricks, carrying this species of decoration to an extent never attempted in any other part of the world.[13]

It was this innate refinement and obsession with the beautiful that was the essence not just of Islamic culture but of the whole East for Fergusson. For this reason Moorish and Ottoman architecture were less impressive due to the evidence of compromising influences from western sources. But with all these architectures, religious and other symbolic properties were neglected in favour of the formal.

Fergusson regarded early Islamic architecture as a style almost entirely transparent to the forms and methods that were indigenous to the different areas conquered or converted by Muslims. Where those areas were least affected by Roman or Byzantine culture, there the architecture was most distinct. In the Mosque of Ibn Tulun in Cairo (Plate 7), Fergusson found the moment of classic balance, the Chartres of this style: 'Saracenic architecture [is] here complete in all its details, every part originally borrowed from previous styles having been worked up and fused into a consentaneous whole'.[14]

For Fergusson, unlike Freeman and others, Muslims certainly possessed a fertile inventive capacity. The danger was their lack of discipline: 'The Mahometan nations were led by their exuberance of fancy, and impatience of all restraint, to try every form, to attempt to fix every floating idea, and to take advantage of every suggestion either of nature or of art'.[15] Fergusson concluded that Islamic was deficient in the 'higher qualities of art' such as order, repose and rationalism that he found in Gothic, Greek and ancient Egyptian architecture.[16] In his fascinated equivocation Fergusson's work has similarities with that of James Wild (to be discussed in Part II). With both there was the same desire to introduce Islam seriously into the arena of

PLATE 7 Pascal Coste.
Mosque of Ibn Tulun,
Cairo, 1839. (James
Fergusson, *The
Illustrated Handbook of
Architecture*, 1855)

deliberation, but in terms of an aesthetic valuation rather than a social or religious one. (It was for this reason that both Wild's work at Alexandria and Fergusson's Holy Sepulchre theory, to be discussed in the next two chapters, contravened the moral ordinances of British High Churchmen.)

Fergusson developed a more ambitious outline for his ideas, based on a theory of race, in the introduction to his later edition of the *Handbook*, renamed *A History of Architecture in All Countries* (1865). Here he asserted that because races left distinctive traces in their buildings the study of these racial records was essential: 'Ethnology, based merely on Language and Physiology, is like Geology based only on Mineralogy and Chemistry'.[17] In other words, just as geology needed palaeontology, so ethnology needed archaeology (by which Fergusson meant the study of architectural remains). Architecture should be taken as equal in evidential value to language in the study of races. A comparative study of architecture, as comparative grammar had done for language, would throw light on the genealogy of architectural styles. Having established this, Fergusson then defined the typical features of what he described as the four great building races: the Turanian, Semitic, Celtic and Aryan.

This schematic breakdown and its terminology were reliant on the models devised by comparative philology and its extension of linguistic groups into racial classifications. In his 'Lecture on the Science of Language' (1861) Max Müller, the German philologist and Oxford professor, had divided languages into three main families: the Aryan, Semitic and Turanian, each with its own subdivisions. But where Celtic was a subdivision of Aryan in Müller's scheme, Fergusson raised it into a family of its own, probably to enhance the distinction between western Europe and India. Furthermore, Fergusson invested his scheme with other forms of armature. Thus the racial categories conformed to synchronic and diachronic patterns. In total they described a historical sequence from the Stone Age (Turanian), through the Bronze Age (Celtic), to the Iron Age (Aryan and, outside Europe, Semitic). Fergusson thereby adopted the genetic analogy of the German *Altertumswissenschaft* historians and their English followers, although now, instead of one race having a lifecycle, the races of the world were placed in evolutionary sequence. Again this has a parallel with a German philologist working in England, for Christian Bunsen had arranged language groups in a similar sequence in his book *Egypt's Place in Universal History* (1848–60). But Fergusson's racial categories also stood for unchanging cultural and psychological characteristics. Semitic, for example, entailed stasis, belief in the unity of God, patriarchal government, poetic temperament, and little interest in architecture.[18] Aryan cultures were seen as having monogamous morals, self-government tending towards republicanism, expertise in industrial and practical sciences, overly literary art forms, and an architecture primarily concerned with convenience.[19]

For Fergusson, Greek and Roman architecture was Aryan; most contemporary European architecture was Celtic; Islamic and Jewish architecture was Semitic; and Turanian was the catch-all for everyone else including Buddhists and Turks (whose failing contemporary rule was seen both as racially inevitable and, simply because it had lasted, as historically aberrant).[20] Part of his interest in ancient Indian architecture was due to his belief that the underlying, inevitably rational principles of a purer Aryan architecture could be an example to modern European architects. Indian architecture had declined when this racial stock was mixed with the incoming Turanians, whose faith was Buddhism. In fact for Fergusson it was only through self-purification, returning to the essential qualities of one's racial category, that architectural improvement could come about.[21] In this, of course, he was not far from Owen Jones's interest in the racial memory of building types; both men believed in scientific materialism and both believed that the East could provide models of rational processes.

Although Fergusson described his categories as forming sequentially, he also believed that they continued into the present. Here he was consciously modifying the historical approach of the positivist Auguste Comte: 'Nations, in the states which [Comte] calls the theological, the metaphysical, and the philosophical, exist now and coexisted through all the ages of the world to which our historical knowledge extends'.[22] Unlike Comte, for Fergusson there was no single line of development from one to another of these stages of knowledge. Instead race predetermined the stage at which culture was set and, because there were many races, many stages could be found at any one period. Thus there was a hierarchy of relative advancement amongst Fergusson's racial categories, but progress could only occur through the activities of the intellectual and scientifically minded Aryans, the authors of modern industry and empire.

Fergusson was not guided by a theory of history or culture here, but a theory of nature. Achievement, both relative and absolute, was not just the result of an accretion of knowledge within any category, but was brought about by the sliding and locking into place of a genetically granted superiority:

> Progress among men, as among the animals, seems to be achieved not so much by advances made within the limits of the group, as by the supercession of the less finely organised beings by those of a higher class ... [accomplished by] the successive prominent appearances of previously developed, though partially dormant creations.[23]

The metaphor that seems suppressed here was more explicit in other comments in Fergusson's Introduction. The Turanians, for example, were 'like the primitive unstratified rocks of geologists', in that they 'form the substructure of the whole world'.[24] Indeed, Fergusson's scheme was haunted by such geological metaphors: 'Race has succeeded race', he wrote, 'all have been disturbed, some obliterated – many contorted – and sometimes the older, apparently, superimposed upon the newer'.[25] The analogy or model used here was not Darwinian evolution but the slow and ceaseless movement from rudeness to refinement that was described in the influential geological theory of Charles Lyell. The uniformitarian theory described in Lyell's *Principles of Geology* (1830–3), taken in a metaphorical sense as a record of the progress of rationality, itself echoed the historical vision of Comte and the Saint-Simonians.[26]

If Freeman's view of architectural development combined catastrophe in human affairs with development in western architectural matters, Fergusson's was more monolithic; one might say uniformitarian. It encompassed all history, grading its racial expressions not in Freeman's bipolar manner but according to a hierarchy that was both inherent and successive.

I have attempted to relate Fergusson's theories of architecture and race to their intellectual sources, but to understand what strategic positions they had within Victorian racial discourses it is necessary to locate them within the debates and researches conducted by those who regarded racial study as their prime métier. An insight into this can be found in the hostile reception given to Fergusson's work by the Anthropological Society. Newly founded in 1863, the Anthropological Society represented a split from the Ethnological Society (founded in 1843). In today's parlance this might be seen as a rightward movement away from the older society, for instead of its close connections with the scientific establishment and its belief in monogenesis and diffusion, environmental explanations and developmental models like Darwinism, the new society upheld a more virulently racist set of beliefs. Its members were preoccupied by the anatomical aspects of physical anthropology, such as craniology, and used these to fill out a belief in an extreme form of polygenesis, including the notion of different species of humanity.[27]

When the new society's journal reviewed Fergusson's writing on ethnology and architecture,[28] it came to it from a pugnacious and newly established position on the extreme end of British racial theory. Given that from this position 'ethnology' was itself a taboo word, it is not surprising that the *Anthropological Review* found Fergusson's ideas wanting. What is also noteworthy is how, ironically from a group on the margins of the contemporary scientific world, Fergusson's work was largely criticized for its unscientific assertions and 'ill-informed speculation'.[29] Their reviewer agreed that ethnicity was essential to the understanding of 'all human manifestations' – few Victorians would not – but Fergusson's ideas were hopelessly trammelled by their reliance on monogenesis. Furthermore, Fergusson had taken on a nomenclature and classification system peculiar to himself and surely born out of 'misconception and misstatement'.[30] He had misconstrued the Turanians and failed to include Arabs within his conception of Semites; indeed, the Arabs, because of their 'finely arched crania', were the highest form of Semite, hence their capacity for fine architecture. It followed that if Fergusson had possessed the 'scientific' capacity to understand race by organic type then both his classifications *and* his judgements of architecture might have been truer.

In the light of these criticisms from the Anthropological Society, Fergusson's views on race and architecture can only seem moderate, even dusty, in their reliance on philological rather than physiological models of race. This, together with his use of Lyell's developmental model of natural change (unnoticed by the reviewer), places him in spirit close to the liberal establishment position in the 1860s.

If the theoretical pronouncements of the 1865 Introduction were not explicitly enlarged upon in the main body of the text of *A History of Architecture in All Countries*, nevertheless, their implications were evident. They provided Fergusson with a theoretical rationale for his lifelong interest in early Indian architecture. They offered a chance to organize and evaluate architecture and history according to racial groupings. Above all, they gave a point of origin for those rational principles of form, organization and structure – as well as a model for the integration of all elements of society – that he wanted to see resumed in Britain. But in terms of Islamic architecture these same groupings entailed a reinforcement of the belief that it had a lowly and largely irrelevant position in the scheme of things.

RUSKIN

Race and nationhood were key issues for John Ruskin (1819–1900), who came to believe that architecture and race were primarily emanations of geography – the national landscape – rather than indexed to language. Although he once speculated that he might have written 'the histories of the first Caliphs of Arabia' if he had worked in Spain as a partner in his father's wine business,[31] Ruskin never travelled to an Islamic country, he never saw an Islamic building, and direct discussion of Islamic culture in his writings was marginal to his major interests. But for an important period Islam formed a significant element in his thought, as representative of the opposite pole in the paired series that structured much of his writing on architecture: North and South, Christian and non-Christian, naturalism and conventionalism.

It was Venice that provided Ruskin with most of his opportunities to comment on Islamic architecture. Indeed, in *The Stones of Venice* (1851–3) Islam was a key ingredient in the cultural synthesis that Ruskin described and one that, together with the role of racial ideas in his architectural writing, has been consistently neglected by commentators on Ruskin. His attitude to Islam at this time was generally positive. Just as with western religion, the metaphysical quality of western architectural form had been introduced by Semites:

> Those old Greeks gave the shaft; Rome gave the arch; the Arabs
> pointed and foliated the arch. The shaft and arch, the framework and
> strength of architecture, are from the race of Japheth; the spirituality
> and sanctity of it from Ismael, Abraham, and Shem.[32]

Like Freeman and Fergusson, Ruskin also saw Islamic architecture as a mirror of the stock character of its makers. Without a 'framework and strength', it was instead excessive and sensuous:

> In his intense love of excitement [the Arab] points the arch and writhes it into extravagant foliations; he banishes the animal imagery, and invents an ornamentation of his own (called Arabesque) to replace it ... bars his surfaces with horizontal lines of colour, the expression of the level of the Desert. He retains the dome, and adds the minaret. All is done with exquisite refinement.[33]

This kind of national and geographic determinism had been an essential feature of Ruskin's early essay, 'The Poetry of Architecture' (1837–8). There he had described how architecture was linked both to the mind of a nation and to its landscape. Following the Romantics, Ruskin believed that nations were deeply characterized by the landscapes they inhabited, and that architecture was the expressive locus of this conjunction. The cottages of England, France and Italy, for instance, were at their best when they took on the character of the landscape, thereby expressing the character of the nation. But Ruskin also suggested how the environment might affect national character in Egypt:

> [In Egypt] we find a climate inducing a perpetual state of heavy feverish excitement, fostered by a great magnificence of natural phenomena, and increased by the general custom of exposing the head continually to the sun, so that, as in a dreaming fever, we imagine distorted creatures and countenances moving and living in the quiet objects of the chamber.[34]

Much later, in the fifth volume of *Modern Painters* (1860), Ruskin elaborated his sense of the importance of this subject by dividing the world into five climatic areas, each of which had a different effect on art. For example, the tropical forest considered typical of India did not help the growth of the mind and therefore only a savage, grotesque art could be made, while in the 'sand-lands' were to be found peoples with a high intellect producing a religious art. The ideal circumstances were those of the 'grape and wheat lands' such as Italy, where the highest intellect and the most perfect art were to be found.[35]

In *The Stones of Venice*, this determinism of education by landscape was extended to Islamic architecture. There, however, despite Ruskin's enthusiasm, a problem of pathology was detected:

> Much [the Arab] achieved; and yet in the effort of his overtaxed

invention, restrained from its proper food, he made his architecture a glittering vacillation of undisciplined enchantment, and left the lustre of its edifices to wither like a startling dream, whose beauty we may indeed feel, and whose instruction we may receive, but must smile at its inconsistency, and mourn over its evanescence.[36]

Every descriptive word or phrase here reiterated the notion of an insubstantiality endemic to the race. Elsewhere Ruskin defined this problem specifically as a matter of temperament and blood, contrasting his Arab type to Byzantine and Lombard types:

[Byzantines have] exquisite perception of grace and dignity; the Arab, with the same perception of grace, but with a restless fever in his blood; the Lombard, equally energetic, but not burning himself away, capable of submitting to law, and enjoying jest.[37]

Although Ruskin's racial distinctions were not always consistent, some patterns are discernible. When he referred to the Orient or the oriental mind he generally meant the Byzantine culture of Constantinople or Ravenna (which he had only come to appreciate fully after the publication of the *Seven Lamps of Architecture* in 1849), whereas the South or 'south-savage' was a combination of Byzantine and Arab. Ruskin seems to have preferred the North/South polarity to an East/West one because it accentuated his interest in climatic and geographic differences. Sometimes, as in *Ariadne Florentina* (1872), Ruskin made these distinctions explicit:

All north-savage I call NORMAN, all south-savage I call BYZANTINE; this latter including dead native Greek primarily – then dead foreign Greek, in Rome; – the Arabian – Persian – Phoenician – Indian – all you can think of, in art of hot countries, up to this year 1200, I rank under the one term Byzantine.[38]

In *The Stones of Venice* Arabs and Byzantines could be identical, or they could occupy different strategic positions, with little apparent reason for either configuration.[39] Individually they could be overly static (Byzantine) or overly energetic (Arab). The terms that Ruskin most commonly used to define Byzantine art were 'contemplative', 'mystic', 'mythical', and 'symbolic'; it had 'constancy', 'want of freedom', 'petrifaction', 'formalism', and 'monotony'. By contrast, Islamic was described by words such as 'exquisite', 'ardent', and 'fantastic'; it had 'excitement', 'enchantment' and 'evanescence'. Together Byzantine and Islamic (or Arab) were said to share a feeling for rich and fanciful ornament. More importantly, they formed a close relation of linked terms which was distinct from the character of the West (or North). Accordingly Ruskin could argue that from the ninth to the eleventh centuries, the architecture of Venice was almost identical to that of Cairo; both could be called Arabic or both Byzantine. Yet Cairo, unlike Venice, was not regarded as a meeting-point.[40]

A typical piece of Ruskinian taxonomy is a plate in *The Stones of Venice* illustrating 'The Orders of Venetian Arches' (Plate 8). This implicitly demonstrates the mixture of cultures that fascinated Ruskin in Venice. It is based on a set of telling architectural details pursued across many buildings, sketched, and then given classified form and comparative value by their tabular grouping. Here in the very centre of the plate, equidistant between Byzantine arches of the eleventh and twelfth centuries and late Gothic arches of the fifteenth century, are rows 4 and 5 illustrating 'pure Gothic' of the thirteenth, fourteenth and early fifteenth centuries. Yet this purity was certainly not equated by Ruskin with cultural or racial purity, but rather was seen as a point of complex balance or consummation between various influences and various races.

The greatest example of what Ruskin saw as the coming together of northern and southern cultures was the Ducal Palace, Venice. In Ruskin's words that building was a glorious ethnic hybrid:

> Opposite in their character and mission, alike in their magnificence of energy, they came from the North and from the South, the glacier torrent and the lava stream: they met and contended over the wreck of the Roman Empire; and the very centre of the struggle, the point of pause of both, the dead water of the opposite eddies, charged with embayed fragments of the Roman wreck, is VENICE. The Ducal palace of Venice contains the three elements in exactly equal proportions – the Roman, the Lombard, and Arab. It is the central building of the world.[41]

The notion of medieval Italy as a stage for a mighty racial struggle was not new to Ruskin; indeed, he later acknowledged Edward Gibbon's influence for this very idea.[42] Ruskin's geological metaphor, which is noticeably more active and dramatic than Fergusson's slow layering and unfolding, was also carried over into his view of Islam's more extended influence on western architecture. It provided far more than one or two flourishes in Gothic architecture:

> The lava stream of the Arab, even after it ceased to flow, warmed the whole of the Northern air, and the history of Gothic architecture is

PLATE 8 John Ruskin. 'The Orders of Venetian Arches', 1851–3. (*Works*, 10)

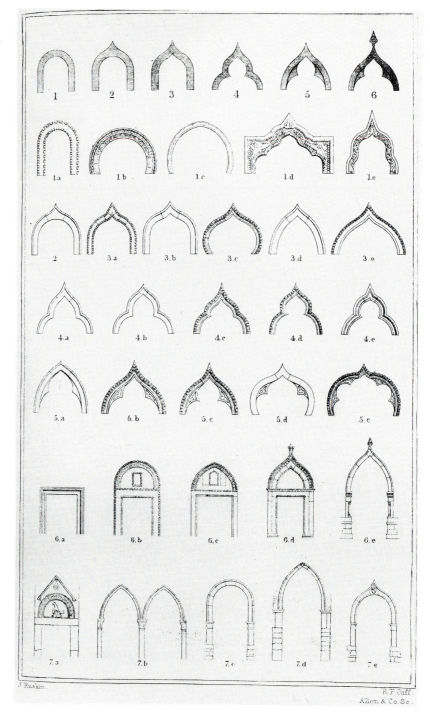

the history of the refinement and spiritualisation of Northern work under its influence.[43]

Above all, what seems extraordinary about these passages, apart from their language, is the way that the geological metaphor smuggles in the idea of racial mixture or hybridity, as the very source of architectural achievement.

From the 1840s the problem of hybridity had become a standard focus for discussion of race and natural history, and writers on English racial identity were not averse to describing it as hybrid. Thomas Arnold's Inaugural Lecture at Oxford, delivered in 1841 during Ruskin's intermission from his Oxford studies, had argued that the dynamic quality of the English in European history had derived from their racial hybridity.[44] For Ruskin the city of Venice itself was the progeny of a coital struggle between races, and its most representative building, the Ducal Palace, was a mongrel refinement and fusion of all that was best in its threefold parentage. The typological role of Venice was clearly established by Ruskin in the opening sentences of *The Stones of Venice*. It had a historical analogy with nineteenth-century Britain, whose empire based on seaborne power and trade might be threatened, in the wake of the continental revolutions of 1848, as much by internal as by external forces. Ruskin seems then to be offering an imperial model for architecture in his 'central building of the world', the Ducal Palace. And that model was to embrace a commingling of racial and historical elements.

Despite the interest in racial pathologies and landscape determinism, there is no doubt that, when he wrote *The Stones of Venice*, Ruskin's view of Islamic culture was a positive one that could emphasize both its deep seriousness and its vibrancy.[45] After all, the point of the energizing metaphor of the Arab lava stream was that it illustrated the contribution that Islamic forms and crafts had made in reviving a wrecked empire. It is important to emphasize that Ruskin saw this as a fusion, or at the least an infusing, rather than the violent dialectic of Aryan and Semite that was a more common idea in Victorian and modern fascist racial thinking. No doubt there was much of Ruskin's indirect influence in the encouragement of a mixed northern and southern Gothic style for the Crimean Memorial Church competition (to be discussed in Chapter 5). Istanbul could, after all, be seen as another city of confluence. But, as we shall see evidenced by the careful interdictions of the competition rules as well as the reactions even to Burges's winning design, few commentators had Ruskin's robust inclusiveness at this time.

RUSKIN v. JONES

However, within a few years of the publication of *The Stones of Venice*, Ruskin was striving to separate western culture from any contaminating contact with eastern. This repudiation of positive influences from the East was bound up with the continuous public conflict between Ruskin's views on ornament, design, art education and manufacturing, and those of Henry Cole and Owen Jones, both instrumental in the government-run Department of Practical Art (established in 1852) and the South Kensington Museum (opened in 1857). To strengthen his position on these topics, Ruskin reinfused issues of race and cultural superiority into his judgement of the Islamic sources that had been apparently rationalized and made an important facet of the work of Owen Jones and the Cole group.

Cole set out thoroughly to reorganize design education guided by the Benthamite cults of material progress and hard, means-for-ends rationalism. Inspired by Pugin's doctrines of good design, Cole and his circle judged that the European exhibits at the Great Exhibition were meretricious machine-made displays of naturalistic ornament inappropriate either to material or function. By contrast, the hand-made, non-western goods seen there, and particularly the objects sent from Islamic countries, offered a model of functional aptness; most importantly, of flat ornament rationally devised and carried out and therefore supposedly more suitable for modern technology.

As discussed in the first chapter, Owen Jones was a key figure in devising a new, more positive and investigative approach to Islamic culture. By the early 1850s, following his study of the Alhambra and the lessons of the Great Exhibition, Jones had evolved what might be termed a utilitarian theory of design based on the principles he discerned in Islamic art and architecture. Unlike Ruskin, who had little direct interest in the Islamic cultural matrix, Jones radically revised views of Islamic architecture. It was now worthy of comparison with the other great monuments of the past precisely because of its expression of religious feeling and its progressive development:

> Arabian art ... was constantly in a state of progression – was never stationary for a day; every building of importance, which required time for its construction, exhibits in its complete state the various phases which art underwent during its progress. This is as true of the temples of the Pharaohs as of the Gothic cathedrals, the Parthenon, and the Alhambra. Each primary style arose with the civilisation which created it, and was more especially the result of its religious institutions. Religion was the teacher, the priest, the artist.[46]

The lessons extrapolated by Jones were not to do with architectonic form but with the decoration of flat surfaces. This theory was formulated in a series of lectures given in 1852, and its principles were quickly taken up by Cole's Department of Practical Art.[47]

Yet an appreciative understanding of oriental culture was not typical of utilitarians. In the first half of the nineteenth century British policy in India was dominated by the 'Anglicist' ideas of utilitarians and evangelicals, imposing English culture as the superior medium.[48] Typically, James Mill, despite neither travelling to India nor learning any of its languages, had argued in his *History of British India* (1818) that Indian culture was worthless and should be totally replaced by British institutions; Thomas Macaulay had dismissed vernacular studies and imposed English as the language of education in India; and British utilitarians had even proposed the demolition of the Taj Mahal in 1828 on the grounds that the sale of its marble would be more profitable.[49] Generally speaking, utilitarian attitudes had stymied rather than stimulated oriental scholarship.

Jones's attitude was new, then, and furthermore his theory was popularly and widely disseminated in his book *The Grammar of Ornament* (1856). Here he published examples of ornament from a multitude of cultures (many from the collection acquired from the Great Exhibition and displayed at Marlborough House), including much material that would have been considered primitive by his readers. This exemplary grammar was presented in the form of details, often grouped in a grid across the folio pages, reliant on the text for information about their material and setting (Plate 9).[50] These examples illustrated some thirty-seven propositions or laws for the arrangement of form and colour in good design. For instance, Proposition 5 followed Pugin in stating that 'Construction should be decorated. Decoration should never be purposely constructed'. Proposition 8 laid down that 'All ornament should be based upon a geometrical construction', while Proposition 13 demanded that 'natural objects should not be used as ornaments, but conventional representations founded upon them sufficiently suggestive to convey the intended image to the mind'. Such principles could be found in what Jones called 'Oriental practice', particularly in the arts of the Islamic world.

Thus Islamic ornament (most of it taken, as we shall see, from the studies that had been made by James Wild and Joseph Bonomi in Egypt) was heavily represented by five of the twenty chapters in the *Grammar*, in stark comparison to the single chapter devoted to western medieval ornament. Islamic design was largely seen as a rational, geometrical ordering of flat surfaces, and a use of colour that bore out the scientific findings on which Jones based several of his propositions.[51] This notion of a purposeful conceptual basis in Islamic and other non-western design – in effect, implying

PLATE 9 Owen Jones.
Arabian ornament,
1856. (*The Grammar of
Ornament*)

that its designers were reflective – was the most challenging aspect of Jones's work. It was combined with the more common idea that Islamic culture was pervasively religious. Jones, as in his 1835 lecture, saw Islamic ornament as deeply wedded to this primary cultural condition:

> [Muslims practised] an art which had grown up with their civil-
> isation, and strengthened with their growth. United by a common
> faith, their art had necessarily a common expression, this expression
> varying in each according to the influence to which each nation was
> subject.[52]

Apart from its principles, therefore, there was the quasi-Puginian example of its religious integrity to be found in Islamic art. Its ornament had a unity, propriety and purpose that expressed the principles of its religion. Pugin had founded his influential theories on a belief in a similar harmony between Gothic architecture and medieval religion, but where Pugin disliked what he saw as the excessive or voluptuous aspect of eastern design and had no interest in Islam, Jones adopted both of these in order to advocate Puginian principles through a new and supposedly ahistorical source, a source that could exemplify the benefits of geometry and the scientific understanding of colour, and thus be a fit model for the modern secular religion of science.

Jones's teaching was disseminated by the group around Henry Cole at the Department of Practical Art as well as through the Government Schools of Design and the new South Kensington Museum.[53] It was also reflected in several popular guides which used Islamic sources to advocate idealizing or abstracting from nature for manufacturing purposes: such was John Gardner Wilkinson's *On Colour and on the Necessity for a General Diffusion of Taste among all Classes* (1858).[54] And it was the diffusion of this taste that particularly concerned Ruskin.

Ruskin had long extolled an art whose primary inspiration was nature; by which he meant both the material world of landscape and the divine force that he believed had made and directed that world. In the late 1840s, following the French Catholic art historian Alexis-François Rio and his English disciple Lord Lindsay (as we shall see in Chapter 3), Ruskin had come to believe that the appreciation of art should be based on the apparent depth of religious feeling expressed in the representation of nature, and not on the perfecting of forms abstracted from nature or supposedly standing for its essence.[55] As Ruskin argued in *The Seven Lamps of Architecture*, the study of nature was exemplary because it was the study of the abundance and variety of God's design. Accordingly the designer should only conventionalize nature where it was appropriate to materials, to position, or to certain techniques. Naturalistic ornament should be inventive and in accord with its architectural frame. It should be neither regardless of this framework nor merely a servile addition to it. Thus natural ornament praised God and gave expression to labour.

Broadly speaking, in terms of religious art, the 1840s in Britain had seen both a Catholic interest in archaicism and symbolism, and a Protestant interest in naturalism. However, often these used the same historical examples. Where Rio had placed his emphasis on the expressive abstraction of medieval Christian art, Ruskin stressed its 'savage' naturalism and objected to its severe conventionalism. In his chapter 'The Nature of Gothic' in *The Stones of Venice*, Ruskin had argued that it was this love of fact that made Gothic work superior to that of the 'rich fancy' of Byzantine, for example.[56] In that chapter and elsewhere Ruskin insisted that this same love of fact had been lost during the Renaissance 'in turning away the eyes of the beholder from natural beauty, and reducing the workman to the level of a machine'.[57] Ruskin's position had led him to defend the Pre-Raphaelites as naturalists reviving a Protestant tradition, steering clear, however, of their more symbolical and therefore Tractarian interests. He believed that an art inspired by nature was representative of a progressive but natural people.

Ideologically, the polemical form taken by Ruskin's naturalism was not just a way of separating Protestant from Roman Catholic expression; more importantly it also provided a polarized model for defining and separating civilized from primitive cultures, and the West from the East. This can be seen to stem from the notion of geographical determinism articulated in 'The Poetry of Architecture' and *The Stones of Venice*. It had seemed, for example, that the 'dreaming fever' brought on by the landscape of Egypt, which in turn had led to the 'startling dreams' of Islamic art, was simply the inevitable results of an unfortunate geography. But by the late 1850s, Ruskin was not so much explaining Islamic art as charging it with neglecting nature altogether. Furthermore, it was no longer something that could fuse with or even be an accepted component of Gothic or Byzantine; it was now clearly placed in the opposition camp.

This was the stance articulated in Ruskin's direct reply to the teaching of the Cole group, a series of five lectures delivered between 1857 and 1859 and published as *The Two Paths* (1859). In the first of these (the second in time of delivery), 'The Deteriorative Power of Conventional Art over Nature', given as an inaugural lecture at the South Kensington Museum in January 1858, Ruskin elaborated his most extended and extreme views on race and culture. Taking his cue from the museum's collection of Indian art, which had been singled out for special praise in Jones's *Grammar*, Ruskin opened his lecture with a comparison between Indians ('rejoicing in art' and endowed with a gift for it) and Highland Scots ('careless of art' and incapable of it).[58] There was a conundrum here. Although the art of Indians was by far the more admirable, its creators – especially its Muslim creators – had also perpetuated the horrors of the Indian Mutiny then being gruesomely reported in the British press, while the Scots, who had been foremost in suppressing that rebellion, excelled in their 'energy of virtue':

> Out of the peat cottage come faith, courage, self-sacrifice, purity, and piety, and whatever else is fruitful in the work of Heaven; out of the ivory palace come treachery, cruelty, cowardice, idolatry, bestiality, – whatever else is fruitful in the work of Hell.[59]

So often art seemed to have been used for the 'exaltation of cruelty', not just through the media of war-paint, weapons and soldiers' uniforms, but also, and more importantly, through an all-pervasive principle. There was one thing common to the art of all cruel nations, and perhaps Islam in particular: 'it never represents natural fact . . . It thus indicates that the people who practise it are cut off from all possible sources of healthy knowledge or natural delight'.[60] By contrast, the Scots' outlook and morality were derived straight from the landscape of their country. Ruskin concluded that art,

> Followed as such, and for its own sake, irrespective of the interpretation of nature by it, is destructive of whatever is best and noblest in humanity; but that nature, however simply observed, or imperfectly known, is, in the degree of affection felt for it, protective and helpful to all that is noblest in humanity. You might conclude farther, that art, so far as it was devoted to the record or the interpretation of nature, would be helpful and ennobling also.[61]

Ruskin thus argued that a culture declined when it based its art on convention and was driven by the search for pleasure alone. Losing touch with nature was a sign of losing touch with morality. Nature was a moral guide since it was God-created, whereas the man-made principles that controlled conventionalized ornament succeeded only in dividing faculties and fracturing nature's unity. To represent nature was to restore the harmony lost at the Fall, lost again during the Renaissance, and never present in the Islamic East.[62]

The extreme determinism of this theory was turned inside out when Ruskin argued that the production of art, and by extension the production of architecture, could itself actually form individual, and thereby social and national, mentalities. That art which was solely concerned with its own properties – where 'the delight of the workman is in what he *does* and *produces*, instead of in what he *interprets* and *exhibits*' – such art would seriously affect the capacities of its creators, leading to 'the *destruction both of intellectual power and moral principle*'.[63]

Yet however crude and almost self-parodic this seems, and however explicable given the polemics of the debate, the location of the lecture, and the recent events in India, it was only after all the logical extension of the more persuasive cultural critique – aimed at modern industrial civilization and often sympathetically recycled by modern writers[64] – presented in 'The Nature of Gothic'. The kind of interpretative naturalism that Ruskin was calling for, both in that chapter of *The Stones of Venice* and in his 1858 lecture, depended for its reasoning on a series of oppositions whose intended universal application was made blatantly explicit in the lecture. While, in the earlier work, naturalism was opposed by conventionalism, and the slavishness of industrial production was opposed by the freedom of medieval craftsmen, in the later work not only was Ruskin's notion of 'design' contrasted with that of the Cole group, but also the admired schools of Florence and Venice were opposed by

by developing architecture further you further degrade society by moving it further away from nature

the arts of India and the Islamic East, and the virtue of Scots by the cruelty of eastern races.

But these oppositions go back even further than this. In the second volume of *Modern Painters* (1846) Ruskin set up a dichotomy between 'aesthesis' and 'theoria': the first was a 'mere sensual perception'; the second was a response involving moral perceptions and sensibilities and could best be found in an art that was guided by a sense of natural theology.[65] An art that depended only on aesthesis acted as a moral and spiritual narcotic. This, of course, is the argument underpinning Ruskin's later strictures on oriental culture. To say this is not to deny the oppositional stance of Ruskin's work in British society, or its later influence upon anti-imperialists like J. A. Hobson and M. K. Gandhi. But these thinkers set aside the racial element in Ruskin's work and applied his critique of industrialism in the West to its expansion into non-western societies, a move of which Ruskin was incapable.[66]

The overt racism of Ruskin's position in the late 1850s is also borne out by an arresting detail in the second lecture of *The Two Paths*, on 'The Unity of Art'. There Ruskin clarified what he meant by his reference to the 'detestable' ornament of the Alhambra in *The Stones of Venice*. It was, he said, intended to refer to the racial qualities of the makers of the building.[67] Furthermore,

> All ornamentation of that lower kind is pre-eminently the gift of cruel persons, of Indians, Saracens, Byzantines, and is the delight of the worst and cruellest nations, Moorish, Indian, Chinese, South Sea Islanders, and so on. I say it is their peculiar gift; not, observe, that they are only capable of doing this, while other nations are capable of doing more; but that they are capable of doing this in a way which civilised nations cannot equal. The fancy and delicacy of eye in interweaving lines and arranging colours – mere line and colour, observe, without natural form – seems to be somehow an inheritance of ignorance and cruelty, belonging to men as spots to the tiger or hues to the snake.[68]

Ruskin's choice of cruel nations was made carefully, for it was exactly the arts of India, Islam, Byzantium and the South Seas that had received the most sympathetic treatment in Jones's *Grammar of Ornament*. Where, in *The Stones of Venice*, the racial argument had mostly been beneath the surface, in *The Two Paths* it became the foremost element of Ruskin's polemic, by which he could persuade his audiences that the issue was not one of mere difference in design philosophies and attitudes to industrialism but one that bore on the very survival of the nation through its power over other peoples. At the least it was a question of the survival of history and culture in the face of positivist and utilitarian policies. This was, then, not only a local debate about the best method of educating craftsmen and designers, but an articulation of a broader attitude towards cultural identity and colonial power. Accordingly, Ruskin's notion of uncivilized conventionalism was to play a crucial role in the development of theories of primitivism towards the end of the century.[69]

By the late 1850s Ruskin's theory was pointing to and opening up a kind of gap within British colonial culture. In the Near East, as we shall see, there were attempts to retrain local workforces as British influence spread, and there was an increasing importation of labour and finished goods from Britain. Buildings had been designed in neo-Islamic, classical and Gothic Revival styles. But none of these styles or strategies were suitable for Ruskin: both neo-Islamic and classical were dangerously distant from his conception of nature and, despite their passing interest in local skills, Gothic Revivalists exerted too strict a control over their buildings. It was not until the 1870s, and then in India, that educational and architectural projects attempted to fill this gap.[70]

COPIES AND COMMODITIES

The links that Ruskin perceived between the empire, the education of the designer and the role of art (whether conventionalized or naturalistic) within manufacturing had already been displayed to different purpose in the Great Exhibition of 1851. The debate between Ruskin and the Cole group was fuelled by disagreements about what constituted Islam, as well as its worth, and these in turn were based on such 'truthful' representations of Islamic art as could be seen within that exhibition and in the Crystal Palace when it was moved to Sydenham in 1854. My argument here works in parallel with Timothy Mitchell's in his *Colonising Egypt* (1988). Mitchell's thesis was that a certain ordering principle, 'the world as an exhibition', was displayed and promoted at these international expositions as a way of rendering global capitalist relations in terms of lucid relations of commodities. This principle was also, Mitchell suggested (and here, as Part II of this book will show, I am less comfortable with his argument), the armature for the modernization and radical transformation of Egyptian society.[71] For this to work certain assurances of detachment and objectivity had to be provided. Imitations or pastiches of Islamic architecture were built in most of the international expositions, as well as in many museums. These exhibitions and institutions were sites of education and entertainment, places where knowledge of Islamic culture would be differently consumed from its more disciplinary presence in academic and professional sites. They were places where, in a sense, knowledge was exchanged and recodified between classes, but from which the conditions of commodity exchange, largely absent with most displays, returned in a curiously abstracted and theatricalized form for the oriental displays.

In these British venues Islam was usually represented by its own products and by mock-up Islamic environments. At the Great Exhibition Henry Cole devised a classification by nation, rather than as previously by stages of production.[72] Here, the material culture of other nations was displayed in settings metonymically associated with their origins, though still dominated by the iron structure of the Crystal Palace (itself the result of the marrying of eastern effects and modern technology). Thus, for example, the products of Egypt and Turkey were seen in draped spaces decorated with small domes and crescents (Plate 10), while for Tunis a tent made of animal skins was the centrepiece. Islamic objects became both specimens and commodities, displayed in spaces that were part-museum, part-bazaar. Gustatory and visual exoticism were closely allied. In the Turkish Court there were hookahs, narghiles, horse-cloths, silks, embroidery, coffee sets, Turkish Delight, Egyptian rose-water, and brushes made of date fibre. The contents of the Tunisian Court, fitted as a shop and with an attendant to haggle over prices, were described as 'An Arab hair tent, carpets, bags for feeding horses, martingales, Arab guns and swords, bornuses (Moorich cloaks), mantles,

PLATE 10 Crystal Palace. Turkish Court, 1851. (W. Dickinson, *Dickinson's Comprehensive Pictures of the Great Exhibition of 1851*, 1852)

joubbas, and ostrich skins with feathers'.[73] And around these spaces the arabesques of ironwork, the large hangings dividing up the upper level and the glittering effects of Jones's colour scheme diffused a more abstract orientalism.

When the Crystal Palace was moved to Sydenham these exhibits were dispersed and replaced by architectural courts. Owen Jones suggested that one of the courts should be Islamic, and chose the Alhambra as his model; amongst its rivals were the Byzantine Court (by M. D. Wyatt) and the Abyssinian Court (by Austen Layard and James Fergusson).[74] Each court was to exemplify an architectural style. Some provided a digest (as with the Byzantine Court, assembled from sources in Cologne, Ravenna, Venice, Rome and Sicily), whilst others were abridged copies of particular buildings. They were grouped in two rows facing onto the main nave of the building and in a sequence that recognized both stylistic and geographical affinities; so that, for example, the Alhambra Court (Plate 11) was placed between the Roman Court and a copy

PLATE 11 P. H. Delamotte. The Alhambra Court, Crystal Palace, 1854. Photograph. (V&A X8A)

of Abu Simbel's tomb, and opposite the Byzantine Court. The official guidebook was careful to point out that the arrangement was not smooth at this point: 'The architectural sequence is now interrupted. We have arrived at one of those offshoots from a parent stem which flourished for a time, and then entirely disappeared'.[75] In the Crystal Palace itself, this representation of Islam and other cultures was but one part of a range of linked disciplines including natural history and its cognate, ethnography.[76] Education, as the declared first aim of this complex, was considerably enhanced by the entertaining *frisson* of sudden juxtaposition; scholarly findings were the basis of a popular entertainment complex.

Providing a historical and architectural explanation of the Alhambra Court, Owen Jones's guidebook was typical of the way in which scholarship was presented in an accessible and authoritative form. Here Jones repeated his innovatory views on Islamic architecture and summarized his study of the real Alhambra, providing plans and translations of inscriptions. The Alhambra Court was an aid to this account, an abbreviated and edited model, or 'fragmentary reproduction', of the real building.[77] The ornaments were full-size reproductions, but their arrangement, as well as that of the whole court, differed considerably from that of the original. The court condensed the Alhambra into three reduced versions of its most significant rooms: the Court of Lions, the Hall of the Kings, and the Hall of the Abencerrajes. But the most immediate difference, and one to which Jones drew attention, was that the facade of the court which fronted the busy main nave of the exhibition building was richly ornamented, providing the honorific exterior presence that was felt to be absent from the real, inward-looking and even reclusive, Alhambra. This invented facade was an assemblage of ornamental details from various parts of the original complex: a *muqarnas* cornice from the internal facade of the mosque, a facsimile of the entrance to the Court of Lions, diaper decoration from the walls of the Sala de la Barca, and a mosaic dado from the Patio de la Alberca.[78]

Using these examples of ornament, Jones compiled a list of principles that were intended to guide the proper application of colour and the arrangement of forms on flat surfaces.[79] It was in these principles, later repeated in the *The Grammar of Ornament*, that the pedagogical focus of Jones's endeavour lay, and it was their rationalist approach, as we have seen, that was to be fervently opposed by Ruskin.

The court and its guidebook can be seen, then, as part of the Crystal Palace's attempt to exhibit a panoramic scope of world culture, but also as having specific value in a more local debate. They popularized a certain kind of knowledge about the Orient, not by intentionally deceiving the viewer into assuming that the court was the real thing, but rather by saying that reality elsewhere was already understood and objectified, and therefore could easily be comprehended by the exhibition visitor. Jones was anxious to show precisely where his court was different or inadequate as a reproduction, assuring the viewer both of his mastery and of his distance from Islamic culture. His authoritative exposition of the Alhambra, at Sydenham and in his earlier book, made it into the most representative Islamic building, both popularly and in architectural circles.

The majority of the Islamic articles exhibited at the Great Exhibition were not moved to Sydenham but purchased for a new Museum of Ornamental Art at Marlborough House, and later transferred to the South Kensington Museum, where orientalists like James Wild became involved in acquiring more of them. The original exhibits had been dispatched to the Crystal Palace by the participating countries and although the individual objects were not for sale their display symbolized the absorption of non-European nations into a global commodity culture. Such items could also fill a pedagogical role in the hands of British orientalists, as was shown by Owen Jones in his *Grammar of Ornament*. Here the work of education and the trade in Islamic goods were synonymous.

The Crystal Palace was only the largest and most obvious site for understanding Islam; in fact, detailed imitations of Islamic architecture became especially popular in its aftermath. Four of them should be mentioned. In 1854, on the back of popular interest in Turkey at the beginning of the Crimean War, the Oriental and Turkish Museum was established at St George's Gallery, Hyde Park Corner – a gallery with a reputation for exotica – and then by 1857 moved to Leicester Square. The organization of this popular private enterprise evoked the spaces and fittings of everyday Turkish life, with wax figures staffing bazaars, a harem (Plate 12), smoking divan, baths, coffee shops, and a carriage made in Istanbul especially for the museum. Its proprietors saw the display as 'less a copy of life than life itself brought to stagnation', and hoped that 'the great sympathy now felt by the British public for the Turkish nation' would ensure its success.[80] Also in 1854 the Royal Panopticon opened in Leicester Square (Plate 13). Designed by Thomas Hayter Lewis (who was regarded as one of the leading experts on Islamic architecture) in an 'Egypto-Saracenic' style using minarets and other motifs from Cairene mosques, its dome, fountain, and alabaster and mosaic walls furnished a popular science centre, housing exhibitions, new inventions, and a lecture hall (it was said to have so impressed the Khedive of Egypt that Lewis was asked to provide a replica for Cairo).[81] In 1855 Matthew Digby Wyatt modelled his conversion of a room in the otherwise neoclassical East India House, Leadenhall Street, on the Diwan-i-Khas in the Agra Fort (much of which, ironically, was to be destroyed in anti-Indian vandalism after 1857).

PLATE 12 Oriental and Turkish Museum, London. A harem, 1857. (*Catalogue of the Oriental Museum*)

PLATE 13 Thomas Hayter Lewis. Royal Panopticon, Leicester Square, 1854. Interior. (*Builder*)

Opened in 1858 (Plate 14), the new Islamic room was needed to house the large number of Indian products that the East India Museum had acquired after the Paris International Exhibition of 1855.[82] Finally, in 1864 Owen Jones designed an Oriental Court for the South Kensington Museum, most of which was inspired by the Alhambra.

These imitations were quite distinct from other buildings designed in a neo-Islamic style. They attempted neither to adapt the style to the exigencies of particular formal problems (as Wild and Jones, elsewhere, had done), nor, as in the Picturesque tradition, to spice the function of the building (particularly baths or garden pavilions) by evoking associations with the East.[83] Their intricate simulations of Islamic environments gave authority to the objects and knowledge that they displayed, establishing the truth of the representation and its status within the evolving middle-class leisure industry. Although it did not display oriental objects, through its very name the Royal Panopticon signalled the aim common to all of them. As the *Builder*'s editor noted:

> The name [Panopticon] was originally given by Jeremy Bentham to
> a prison on the radiating system designed by his brother wherein the

PLATE 14 Matthew D. Wyatt. East India Museum, London, 1855. (*London Journal*, 1858)

inspector could see the prisoners without being seen himself. We hope the Panopticon of our day will prove one of those educational levers which will gradually lessen the necessity for bestowing thought on any prisons at all.[84]

Its promoters 'felt persuaded that the time had arrived for the establishment of some additional, but more energetic, source of diffusion of knowledge'.[85] In this diffusion of a more disciplinary knowledge, Islamic style would conjure up and compress several allusions: it demonstrated knowledge – a 'perfect completeness of detail'; it exemplified historical respect for knowledge, for the Saracens had 'cherished [the sciences] with an ardour and success worthy the imitation of the present advanced age'; and it offered escape through knowledge, for the Panopticon was 'an enchanted palace in a city of the sternest realities'.[86] Driven by varying degrees of public benevolence, all these imitations combined the attraction of novelty (the Royal Panopticon's style was also seen as an attractive billboard to draw crowds in),[87] the presence of the real and the chance of self-improvement. In this synthesis they were little brothers to the larger, more evidently commercial, and more panoptic international expositions.

The great series of international expositions launched by the Great Exhibition might be seen as Saint-Simonian models of the world,[88] typifying the way that Europeans related other cultures, particularly those of the East, to their world-view. As one official guidebook explained, 'To make the rounds of this palace means literally to circle the earth. All peoples are come together here, and those who are enemies, here live side by side'.[89] Yet this macrocosmic harmony was also marked by the inscribed differences necessary to a sense of national and imperial identity. All peoples were not equally privileged. At the Great Exhibition, for example, half of the space was given over to British and British Empire exhibits (with the Indian section acting as the border and link with those of the rest of the world), and in the French exhibitions a display of French work usually dominated the centre of the exhibition. Furthermore, after the Paris Exposition Universelle in 1867, there was a clear distinction established between the peoples whose products could be shown in pavilions and those whose representatives were displayed as attractions in 'native villages'. Following from this the Centennial Exhibition in Philadelphia (1876) established the practice of arranging pavilions by racial groups. As Tony Bennett has argued, 'the effect of these developments was to transfer the rhetoric of progress from the relations between stages of production to the relations between races and nations'.[90] Nevertheless, Bennett is wrong, at least with key figures like Jones, also to argue that oriental cultures were always allotted an intermediary and inferior position in evolution. In the Great Exhibition and at Sydenham the exposure of differences could aid the design aims of reformers like Jones in their argument against the faults of dominant western production. That there was an inconsistent shift between their belief in western modernity (and the clear endorsement of that in these exhibitions) and their use of Islamic culture was not to be exposed. On another level Jones's approach could still help to promote the circulation of imperial products. (It should be said that Ruskin's work, despite its support of racial supremacy, simply did not lend itself to the kind of universalizing knowledge that Jones's work fitted so well within.) More widely, the exhibitions not only provided a sense of national unity and a naturalization of imperial power, but also helped to acquaint and educate all classes in the discriminatory knowledge necessary for imperial rule.[91]

Where architectural imitations and actual artifacts had been largely separate in the Crystal Palaces at Hyde Park and Sydenham, they were brought together in an increasingly seamless union in the later exhibitions. In Paris in 1867 nations were invited for the first time to construct their own pavilions, and those that did – including Egypt, Turkey, Tunisia and Morocco – built national houses which were taken to be typical of their national styles.[92] In 1878 these became separate pavilions in the grounds of the exhibition. Then, back in London, the Colonial and Indian Exhibition in 1886 imported craftsmen from India. Finally and most famously, in Paris in 1889 a complete urban stageset, a *rue du Caire*, was created with its own imported Egyptian donkeys, Cairenes, and other peoples in moving *tableaux-vivants*.[93] From the beginning, with the employment of Owen Jones for the Alhambra Court or Fergusson and Layard for the Assyrian Court at Sydenham, orientalist expertise had been brought in on every occasion to aid the authenticity of the venture. In the 1889 exhibition this was taken one step further when Egyptian craftsmen were imported to construct the buildings from recycled fragments under French superintendence.

Thus scholarly expertise, promotional skill, the gimmickry of popular entertainment, all had their place in these bazaars. They were places where people moved amongst the spectacle of curiosities, marvelling at both the 'universe of commodities' and at the power and knowledge that could organize such a display.[94] Other cultures, and Islam in particular, were an essential part of these festivals of consumption.

But these exhibitions were not just superficial entertainments. The teeming variety of objects was arranged through an individualizing and disciplining form of display: disciplined by their clearly demarcated place in a rank of equalized cultures; individualized by the various expertises brought to bear on their choice and explication in order to show their differences to best effect. There was no concealment of the rule of imperialism. In fact the clarity of the displayed order made it seem more a matter of fact, less a matter of those confused intentions and contingent realities that were, as Part II of this book will argue, displayed differently and often inadvertently in those British colonial projects of which architecture in the Near East was a part. To re-employ Marx's formulation, within the clarity of the exhibition Islamic objects and even Islamic architecture became commodity fetishes: mere hieroglyphics of a culture divested of the real conditions under which they were made; cyphers for the magical property of orientalism whereby people and objects were to be subject to the pyschology of consumption; to be able to possess the powers of possession.

———

Fergusson, Freeman and Ruskin all wrote about Islamic architecture from a distance. Similarly, the exhibition and imitation of Islamic goods or buildings were distanced creations: abbreviated, edited, reinterpreted and sometimes even wrenched from their settings; items of pedagogy, entertainment or exchange; records of association or subjugation; object-impresarios of a mediated Islamic world to a British public. The circulation and reiteration of similar statements about Islam between popular, specialist and official public domains (from the RIBA, to the Crystal Palace, Leicester Square, and the South Kensington Museum), around different modes of writing (the travelogue, the guide, and the academic folio volume), or between amateur and professional orientalists, demonstrate its discursive power in the mid-nineteenth century and its close involvement in the ideology of progress and empire well before the height of the Age of Empire in the late nineteenth century.

Like knowledge of other forms or styles of architecture, Islamic architecture could be aesthetically useful within the terms of eclecticism or of conventionalism. It could enhance or inflect the meaning of a new building and principles could be derived from its forms. But unlike the various Gothic or classical styles, Islamic architecture embodied ways of life and religion that continued into the present. It was the most potent sign of Islam, and thus its study was an integral part of the attempt to penetrate and control that culture. Europeans were seen to describe, interpret and even measure this architecture, in keeping with the notion that its own culture was mute and impotent.

At first Owen Jones's rationalist insights appear to be the exception, seeming to challenge the notion that the West alone was marked by rationalism. Yet Jones's analysis, without any sense of changing Islamic history, was undoubtedly instrumental in increasing the commodification of Islamic goods. Certainly it tried to make a flat, geometrical approach to, and taste for, design more widespread. It is here, of course, that Jones and Ruskin are opposite sides of a coin, for while Jones was seeking in the East a confirmation of rationalism and Protestant iconoclasm, Ruskin found in the Venetian East (as we shall see especially with his writing on Byzantine architecture in Venice) an escape from or alternative to Enlightenment notions of aesthetic order. When Islamic art seemed taken over by such thinking, and contaminated by events like the Indian Mutiny, Ruskin abandoned it, deploying an overtly racial argument against it. It should also be said that Jones's differences with Ruskin were still contained within the unquestioned parameters that, as Edward Said has argued, limited all statements about Islam: that there was an entity known as the Orient, that its culture was bound by its religion, that race had a determining role in cultural work, and that development and the drive to expand was the preserve, even the duty, of the West. We shall see in Chapter 5 how these ideas about the conventional and repetitive nature of Islamic art led Burges and Street to believe they could simply assimilate it to their rigidly divided and specified methods of building and contracting.

These general notions about the Orient were not substantially different from those held immediately before this period. What can be said is that they were now more often deployed, that they were accompanied by a growing body of suitable evidence, and that the knowledge within which they were integrated was now increasingly regarded as an essential part of the colonial relationship.

3

ORIENTAL BYZANTIUM

INTERPRETING BYZANTINE ARCHITECTURE, 1840–70

•

In Europe a more marked distinction exists between the Teuton, the Celt, the Slav ... than can be found in the East between the primary divisions of the human race. It is a character fixed, staid, and immutable; it is not Persian or Arabian, not even Caucasian or Mongolian: it is not ancient, modern, or mediaeval; but, a term of all ages and races, it is Oriental ... Such an Oriental character the Byzantine empire had from its very beginning.

(E. A. Freeman, 1849)

As a term 'Byzantine' still presents problems to architectural historians. Whether it defines the architecture linked to a political identity (the eastern Roman Empire), the architecture of a religion (eastern Christianity), or a closely characterized style, are still unsettled questions.[1] Located mainly in the East and yet born out of Rome, Byzantine architecture presented especially acute problems for Victorian architects and historians. Most immediate under Ottoman rule was the difficulty of access, either to the original monuments or to reliable accounts of those monuments. But as histories and descriptions began to multiply in the mid-century, more complex and critical problems emerged. How was Byzantine culture in general to be understood and placed using those historical frameworks based on notions of racial development that we saw deployed for Islamic architecture in the last chapter? What practical or professional justification could there be for studying the architecture of Byzantium? If Islam could represent, in abstracted or inverse form, an example to the modern West, what examples might Byzantium provide? And how could the drive necessary for its organized study be generated by geopolitical concerns?

It was out of these problems, I will argue in this chapter, that a peculiarly British interpretation of Byzantine architecture developed, one which was interested less in, say, those ideas about an exemplary structural rationalism that the French had found in it, and far more in the meanings of its cultural synthesis. Victorians found those meanings primarily in the forms of Orthodox Christianity, in the racial character of Byzantium, and in its bridging geographical location. It is for these reasons that Byzantine historiography was both closely and dialectically related to Victorian understanding of the Ottoman Islamic Near East.

BYZANTINE STUDIES

Until the middle decades of the century, the serious study of Byzantine culture was the preserve of German and French scholars. Their interest in it can be traced to the Romantic fascination with periods of historical transition as a source for a modern eclectic style. The term *Neugriechisch*, synonym for Byzantine, had first been brought into currency in the opening decades of the century, interchangeably with *Néo-Grec*, by a group of young German and French writers and architects, including Ludovic Vitet, Friedrich Schlegel and Sulpiz Boisserée.[2] The terms themselves graphically demonstrate that the interest in Byzantine was inspired by a new sense in which its Greek associations could become relevant. To pick up and follow a Greek current upstream through Romanesque and Byzantine also offered the prospect of channelling national medieval architecture back to a Hellenistic source. This had implications for both the direction of scholarship and the production of architecture.

For their scholarship, the most prominent amongst German publications were Ferdinand von Quast's comprehensively illustrated *Die alt-christlichen Bauwerke von Ravenna* (1842), and W. Salzenberg's Prussian government-funded *Alt-christliche Baudenkmale von Constantinopel* (1854). In France, A. N. Didron was one of the first to pioneer a serious scholarly interest in Byzantine art, visiting Greece and Istanbul in 1839–40 and publishing his *Iconographie chrétienne: histoire de Dieu* in 1843. From 1833 to 1835, Charles Texier made an extensive survey of Byzantine monuments in Istanbul, and for the rest of his career studied the Byzantine and Islamic monuments of Turkey and Persia, much of this work being financed by French government missions.[3] In 1840 Albert Lenoir published a series of articles on Byzantine in the *Revue générale de l'architecture*, and his *Architecture monastique* of 1852 illustrated the Byzantine buildings of Turkey and Greece. There was also a continuing French interest, spearheaded by Félix de Verneilh, in the connections between Byzantine and a group of Romanesque buildings in Aquitaine.[4] This French and German dominance of the field was only interrupted by Gaspard Fossati, a Swiss architect practising in Istanbul (including restoration work), who published *Aya Sophia, Constantinople* in 1852.

Byzantine was also examined for its possible contribution to contemporary architectural issues. German interest in Byzantine was an element in the development of the *Rundbogenstil*, the attempt to establish a round-arched modern style. But French architects were possibly more influential in their Byzantinism. Henri Labrouste, Ludovic Vitet, Léon Vaudoyer, and other Néo-Grec architects and critics, following the Saint-Simonians, had divided the architectural past into alternating synthetic and organic periods. The latter (for example, Greek and Gothic) were moments when social and aesthetic forms were harmoniously interlocked. The former, as periods of change and a critical spirit towards the assimilation of different traditions, were regarded as more appropriate models for the present. Furthermore, the supposed structural flexibility of such synthetic styles and their freedom from codification meant that they might be a spur to experimentation and more adaptable and responsive to modern conditions. The Byzantine Empire and Romanesque Sicily were especially important examples of these synthetic periods for this form of Romantic rationalism.[5] To Vitet, for example, both embodied the expression of Christianity through Greek rationalism.

How much, if any, of this French and German interest in Byzantine architecture, especially the critical spirit of the Néo-Grecs, was taken up by British architects? There was no indigenous link with Byzantine architecture to stimulate curiosity, although there seems to have been some acceptance that, architecturally speaking at least, the second quarter of the nineteenth century was a period of transition, and that Byzantine was a transitional style, even if the two were rarely related. As will be shown in Chapter 4, the architect James Wild was certainly aware that what some saw as the transitional nature of Byzantine architecture might lend itself to the present day, although he rejected its wholesale use in his own work. Similarly, in his *Preliminary Discourse* (1842), T. L. Donaldson claimed 'We are all in fact in a state of transition', but he advocated a contingent eclecticism rather than the use of any one historical style.[6] Other writers – particularly Henry Gally Knight in his *The Normans in Sicily* (1838) – followed the French interest in the architecture of Sicily, echoing their sense of its exemplary synthesis, although without their acute stylistic analysis.

In the mid-century British writers still found Byzantine a slippery object of study. In 1842 Edmund Sharpe read a paper to a meeting of the Cambridge Camden Society on 'The Early History of Christian Architecture'. Sharpe was obviously in some difficulty about what terms he should use to designate the styles of Christian architecture before 1200. Having settled on Byzantine and Romanesque he proceeded to survey the nomenclature adopted by recent writers:

Mr. Gunn called *all* Christian Architecture previous to the rise of the Gothick, Romanesque: German writers to this day call it with equal generality Byzantinisch. Professor Whewell, the reviver of the term Romanesque, does not appear to recognize a distinct Byzantine style. M. de Caumont designates the whole period as *Romane*. Mr. Hope used *Byzantine* without sufficient definition; and when contrasting it with *Lombardic*, must be supposed to use the latter term as equivalent to *Romanesque*. Wiebeking proposes to use *Neu Griekisch* instead of *Byzantinisch*. De Lassaulx adopts *Romanisch* as equivalent to the English *Romanesque* and the French *Romane*.[7]

Sharpe was clearly conversant with the work of continental scholars, yet he seems to have been unaware of any theoretical account of the style. For him the scarcity of information on eastern churches meant that they must remain inert historical matter. Writing in the same year, George Godwin was also aware of continental work – particularly that of Vitet – and had found that a multitude of terms was employed to describe the style. But, like several other English writers at this time, Godwin was only interested in the style in so far as it could be seen to have influenced later medieval architecture in France and England.[8]

The fluidity of terms for pre-Gothic medieval architecture was to linger on into the 1860s. The problem seems to have been at least twofold. First, writers felt the need for a label denoting a post-classical round-arched style, and either Byzantine or Romanesque might be used for this. Second, if geographical distribution was to be regarded as foremost, then the pairing was of unlikes: Byzantine was still essentially a political label, while Romanesque was a stylistic one. More had to be known about Byzantine to characterize it as a distinct style, and it seemed inevitable that much of that distinctiveness was to derive from its associated religion and its relatively eastern location.

The group of High Church architects and historians associated with the journal *The Ecclesiologist* were particularly interested in the way Byzantine kitted out the Orthodox liturgy. One of the first books devoted solely to Byzantine architecture had been André Couchaud's *Choix d'églises bysantines en Grèce* (1842). Couchaud, a pupil of Labrouste, argued that Byzantine was a continuation of Greek genius through Christian forms. Writing about this book, *The Ecclesiologist*'s reviewer noted his amazement at 'the notion of a French architect at Athens deserting the Parthenon ... to detail and publish mediaeval churches', which could only be 'significative of a new growth of European feeling'.[9] However, his reaction to Couchaud's subject was still wearily predictable. After Hagia Sophia, Byzantine 'became too often a lifeless, unimproving thing', the reviewer opined, and even Couchaud's text asserted that he could just as well have fixed the limit of his subject at the Greek revolution as at the Ottoman conquest, so changeless was the style.[10] Yet Couchaud did describe a historical development, dividing his subject into three periods, as well as providing plans and drawings of previously unpublished monuments.

Couchaud's reviewer looked forward to further work in what he called 'Oriental Ecclesiology', and what he envisaged was probably something like the 'Description of a Cathedral of the Oriental Church', published by the *Ecclesiologist* earlier in 1845. This purported to describe part of an unnamed although presumably canonical Byzantine church, but what it actually tried to demonstrate was that the Ecclesiologists' principle of clearly expressing the different liturgical units of a church was also true of Byzantine architecture. Over and above the peculiar indulgences necessary for the eastern rite was something more important:

> the spirit of this arrangement is precisely the same as that of the Western Church: all that we have ever called essentials, – the distinct and spacious chancel, the rood-screen, and the porch, – are retained by the Oriental, as well as by the Latin communion.[11]

The author of this was probably John Mason Neale, who, in 1850, published one of the longest and most positive English accounts of Byzantine architecture in his *Ecclesiology of the Holy Eastern Church*. Although not rating it as high as Gothic and not regarding it as having the capacity of continual development, Neale sought to save Byzantine from its misinterpretations:

> It seems to be regarded as a stiff corruption of heathen art; a 'Jacobean' imitation of Grecian loveliness. That it has in itself the breath of Christian life; that it worked out its own developments; that piety of the deepest fervour, and genius of the highest order, were poured forth on its thousand temples; that the sublime dome was its own, that shrine raised to the Almighty above the din and bustle of the earth, of which perhaps we have not yet seen the full development; all this is unknown or forgotten.[12]

His argument was largely based on Couchaud's 'systematized view' of Byzantine, which Neale combined with a typical ecclesiological interest in the rituals and symbols of Orthodox liturgy. Although the intent was one of recuperation, its measure was still the Ecclesiologists' ideal of Gothic architecture. The stock response of *The Ecclesiologist* to Byzantine as a stylistic resource was to contrast what one writer called 'the infinite capacity for developement and expansion by which Pointed Architecture is distinguished' with 'the immutable and not over-elegant character of Byzantine Architecture'.[13] Furthermore, the undeveloped form of Byzantine architecture was identical with the suspicious practices of Orthodox Christianity, and as such it would evoke inappropriate meanings.[14] All this indicates a slower, more hidebound and more religiously resistant attitude in England towards Byzantine architecture. Soon, however, this was not to be the only approach.

LINDSAY, FREEMAN AND FINLAY

By the late 1840s a group of writers, strongly influenced by the idealist currents in German historiography and philosophy, began to place Byzantium within new intellectual frameworks and principles of history, sometimes also taking a more positive attitude towards it. One of the most notable of these British Byzantine pioneers was the Scottish art historian and connoisseur, Lord Lindsay, whose *Sketches in the History of Christian Art* (1847) has been described as 'the main work of Hegelian art history published in Britain'.[15]

Lindsay set out to demonstrate the superiority of Christian over pagan art since the foundation of the Byzantine Empire. His interest in Italian medieval art can be seen as part of a cultural movement of the 1840s that was strongly influenced by the work of Wilhelm Wackenroder, Friedrich Schlegel, K. F. von Rumohr and the Nazarenes in Germany, and of A. N. Didron and Alexis-François Rio in France, all of whom were drawn to a reconsideration of Christian art before the High Renaissance.[16] This art, called archaic or primitive, was seen as a purer and more direct expression of Christianity. In art, then, the grand ideal of spiritual expression was to be valued higher than the progressive development of illusionistic skill. Lindsay's treatment of Byzantine art had far more seriousness than was common in Britain, and more flexibility than the doctrinaire Roman Catholicism of, say, the influential Rio, who damned Byzantine art simply on the basis that it was not produced by Catholic artists. Lindsay believed that art did not develop in one long ascending arc, but in a series of almost discrete developments. Of these, Lindsay argued that Byzantine was supreme in architecture, sculpture and painting until the thirteenth century.[17]

Lindsay's Byzantium combined Greek rationality and oriental despotism, and was a place of significant racial interest:

> Byzantium … represents the Contemplative, as Rome does the
> Practical element of the original European character – of the Hindoo
> or Classic branch of the nations of Christendom, – elements worn out,

indeed, and insufficient, considered by themselves detachedly, but which were destined, after the amalgamation of the Hindoo with the Teutonic or Medo-Persian race, of the conquered with the conquerors, to spring up again in renewed youth and vigorous opposition, in the veins of the progeny of that amalgamation, and thus to become the germ of all that is great and glorious in modern history. Pursuing this idea, we shall at once recognise in Byzantine no less than in Roman Art the reflection of the element from which it emanated.[18]

Lindsay's explanation for the accepted stasis of Byzantine history and culture was that at the time of the division of the Roman Empire, Byzantium had somehow extracted and gathered together the contemplative aspects of an original European character. Furthermore, he suggested that in doing this Byzantium split Aryan European culture into its original Teutonic and Hindu parts. These would only be recombined in the art of Giotto, Cimabue and other early Italian masters. Byzantium belonged more to the East than the West. Accordingly, Lindsay could argue that in the East 'Byzantine Architecture has flourished to the present day ... coextensively with the Oriental Churches and with Islamism'.[19] The architectural form that exemplified the eastern character was the dome, 'the peculiar expression of the Contemplative East'.[20]

The historian E. A. Freeman, whose views on Islam were discussed in the previous chapter, shared Lindsay's sense of Byzantium as oriental in its stasis as well as his use of the new formulations of comparative philology. Freeman also combined these with an approach derived from the German idealist historians and their attempt to construct historical systems ruled by unifying laws. At Oxford in the early 1840s Freeman had learnt from Thomas Arnold that 'language was the most trustworthy evidence of nationality'. Through Oxford historians like Arnold and A. P. Stanley, Freeman must have been introduced not only to Barthold Niebuhr's method of textual analysis, but also to his influential ethnic principle of history.[21] Niebuhr's approach was itself a particular systemization of the interest in national artistic characteristics that had been typical of the Romantic movement – Herder and Hegel most notably – and that was crucial to the revived interest in medieval art. Ever since Sir William Jones in the late eighteenth century had employed the term 'Aryan' to postulate a family of languages, many philologists and ethnologists had transferred Jones's Indo-European linguistic axis into a racial unit, separating central and western European peoples from those of the eastern Mediterranean. Such racial groups – based, however, on physical aspects rather than language – and similar organic metaphors, were the primary matter of Niebuhr's historical approach. Freeman's attitude was a mixture of Niebuhr and the philologists. He believed that there were Aryan nations unified by language, habits and institutions, and furthermore, that they were in a continual struggle against the nations of the Orient.[22]

In his *History of Architecture* (1849) Freeman's interest in the underlying causes of styles was clearly motivated by this metaphysical programme. Architectural history was

> concerned with the philosophy of a most noble art, and with the effects produced on that art by the events of history, as exemplifying the character and position of nations, and the working of political and ecclesiastical circumstances.[23]

It was this emphasis on peoples or 'nations', rather than individuals or other forms of social group, as the generator of history, that had supported the central role of race in early nineteenth-century historiography. In this scheme of things Byzantium was to occupy a curious position. It was Christian in religion, its peoples polyglot, its culture rich in Graeco-Roman forms and skills, yet by the very fact of its relative geographical position it had to be oriental and non-Aryan and, consequently, without historical change:

> [The East] is a character not marking a single race or creed, but all who chance to fix their abode within a certain extensive portion of the globe. In these lands nations seem to desert their own character and assume that of the soil. In Europe a more marked distinction exists between the Teuton, the Celt, the Slav ... than can be found in the East between the primary divisions of the human race. It is a character fixed, staid, and immutable; it is not Persian or Arabian, not even Caucasian or Mongolian: it is not ancient, modern, or mediaeval; but, a term of all ages and races, it is Oriental ... Such an Oriental character the Byzantine empire had from its very beginning; and it became gradually stronger, as its connection with Western Christendom was constantly weakened ... the fixed unmoveable character of literature, science, and art, the utter moral and political vacancy of the thousand years of the Byzantine empire, mark it as Roman, as European, in name only.[24]

It followed from this that Byzantine architecture, early established in its characteristic forms, would then remain static:

> On an art so liable to mutations as architecture, fourteen centuries must produce many diversities, even in the East; but the structures

reared to this day by the Mahometans in India exhibit far less deviation from the type of St Sophia, than exists between the Basilica of St. Clement and the Cathedral of Sarum.[25]

Because this architecture was moribund, because it did not seem to be part of or contribute to a dynamic development, then it lacked the 'principle of life', and was not the 'expression of an idea'.[26]

Freeman and Lindsay were not alone amongst architectural writers in employing the new historical schemes borrowed from German idealist thought in order to explain Byzantine history.[27] The eighteenth-century dislike of Early Christianity and the historical pattern of decadence and decline most memorably found in the work of Edward Gibbon, now apparently had to contend with the new German *Altertumswissenschaft* approach, with its accompanying racial and political concerns. James Fergusson was one who clung to the older view of Byzantium, arguing that the buildings of Justinian marked the high point of the style and that after them 'the history of this art is a history of decline, like that of the Eastern Empire itself'.[28] Although this Gibbonian decline or the stasis of Lindsay and Freeman are similar as over-generalized historical judgements, the crucial tendency in the new view was to place Byzantium outside western filiations. Given this placement, it could then become subject to either negative (Freeman) or positive (Lindsay) judgements.

There were partial attempts to apply organic historical schema to Byzantine history when it was regarded as an essentially European phenomenon. This can be seen in the work of George Finlay (1799–1875), the leading Byzantine historian in Britain at this time. Between 1844 and 1861, Finlay published a series of books detailing the modern history of Greece from 146 BC to AD 1864. Having studied at the University of Göttingen (the most influential centre for the new ordering of academic knowledge on the basis of racial theory),[29] met Byron in Greece, and fought in the Greek War of Independence, Finlay's early career had provided him with the imperative to fuse Philhellenism and German method into a more vigorous, if less vivid, outline of Byzantine history than Gibbon's. Finlay's active life also spanned the two contemporary episodes that most affected views of the post-Byzantine present, the Greek and Crimean Wars. If Byzantine history could be more sympathetically excavated after the first, for some its value was made more pressing by the second.

In Finlay's first history, *Greece under the Romans* (1844) (significantly subtitled 'A Historical View of the Condition of the Greek Nation'), the continuity of Greek society and politics, whatever their rulers, was stressed to the detriment of the old notion of continuous decline under the Byzantines.[30]

Finlay had little liking for Byzantine architecture, but its faults were blamed on non-Greek impositions.[31] The next part of his project, the *History of the Byzantine Empire from 716 to 1453* (1853), continued this view of Greek purity 'intruded upon' by immigrants,[32] and was even more avowedly a recuperative history in the face of writers like Voltaire and Gibbon. In order to do this, Finlay devised a new tripartite historical pattern whereby Byzantium resuscitated the Empire, reached its apogee, and only then, after 1057, declined.

Byzantium had acquired a longer active life. Where Freeman had judged it static and lifeless in relation to dynamism elsewhere, Finlay had injected the German organic metaphor to revive its pure earlier history. One had deemed it oriental, the other had brought it back within the Greek fold.

RUSKIN

By the 1850s the atmosphere of British Byzantine studies was slowly warming to Byzantine art, but while scholars were becoming apparently more sophisticated in understanding Byzantine history, Byzantine architecture was regarded as stilled in a moment of crudeness, transitional between more sophisticated styles, or, at best, an expression of purely liturgical needs. It was into this scene, contemporary with Finlay's second major work, that John Ruskin's *The Stones of Venice* appeared between 1851 and 1853. The Byzantine sections in Ruskin's three-volume work, especially the chapters on St Mark's and the Byzantine palaces of Venice, carved out a rich new understanding that bypassed ecclesiology and was quite independent of the various rationalist theories of the French and Germans. Ruskin challenged religious suspicions and notions of crudeness, and instead based his case on a long and close observation of the style's subtle visual and constructional qualities.

There was little to prepare his readers for these revelations in Ruskin's previous writing. He seems to have been unaware of or, at least, to have ignored Finlay's earlier work, and when he wrote a lengthy review of Lord Lindsay's book for the *Quarterly Review* (1847), he made no reference to its treatment of Byzantine architecture. Furthermore, although he appreciated Lindsay's desire to re-evaluate Byzantine art, Ruskin rejected his 'metaphysical analogies', his sense of a dialectical struggle between traditions within Byzantine culture (he would return to this in *The Stones of Venice*), preferring the individualism of great artists as an explanation of change. Ruskin had already read Rio's *De la poésie chrétienne* (1836), and had used it as a guide during his Italian journey of 1845.[33] But although Ruskin was influenced by Rio's theory of art as an expression of religious feeling, there was little in the

French writer's dogmatic Roman Catholicism, in which church history was central to his account of art, that could allow for more than an illustrative appreciation of Byzantium. Ruskin's approach would apply aspects of Rio's expressive theory, a closely observed empiricism, and a different matrix of social and religious judgements, to Byzantine culture.

When Ruskin came to write *The Stones of Venice*, one of his most valued if idiosyncratic sources on Byzantine architecture was Robert Curzon's *Visits to Monasteries in the Levant* (1849). This was less an architectural sourcebook than a travelogue. Here, Ruskin said, 'the reader will find the weak points of Byzantine architecture shrewdly seized, and exquisitely sketched'.[34] Curzon regarded Byzantine as the earliest Christian architecture, and St Mark's as its best western representative. Its affiliations were manifold:

> It is not Romanesque, it is not Lombardic, or Saracenic, though it resembles and is inferior to those styles of building: it took its origin in the decay of science in the latter days of the Christian Empire of Constantinople, when the architects were no longer able to produce any better imitations of Roman architecture. What we call Byzantine they call Roman; and their clumsy buildings were copied by their blundering architects from the examples which they had before their eyes.[35]

In Curzon's view Byzantine architecture was derivative in form but free and *ad hoc* in its construction and organization: it cannibalized Greek fragments and *spolia*, without regard for their original principles; it placed arches on columns where good Roman architecture had always placed arches on piers; in decoration, instead of the 'proportion, symmetry, and grace' of the Romans and Greeks, the Byzantines depended on richness of colour.

Ruskin presented a lengthy analysis of Byzantine architecture in *The Stones of Venice*. He admitted that he had only seen Byzantine in Venice; nevertheless, he believed that Venetian examples could exhibit the typical features of the style. High in importance were the 'singular and minute harmonies of proportion' that Ruskin found in all Byzantine architecture (Plate 15).[36] But his most compelling argument came in the chapter on St Mark's. There Ruskin summarized and then set aside antiquarian discrimination on matters of dating, and launched his reader instead into a vivid comparison of an English cathedral and the Venetian basilica. Everywhere in the English town the cathedral or its influence are visible: the 'small formalisms' of the town watched over by the 'serene sublimity' of the cathedral.[37] In Venice progress towards St Mark's is maze-like and dangerous, passing a mix of the ruined and the modern, with everywhere the signs of a commercialized and idolatrous

PLATE 15 John Ruskin. Fondaco dei Turchi, Venice, 1851–3. Watercolour. (*Works*, 10, Frontispiece)

religion. Out of this the Byzantine cathedral emerges as a revelation of

> lovely order . . . a multitude of pillars and white domes . . . a long low
> pyramid of coloured light . . . the crests of [whose] arches break into
> a marble foam, and toss themselves far into the blue sky in flashes and
> wreathes of sculptured spray.[38]

Despite this image of order and briny abandon, Ruskin was worried by the implications of his comparison. If the English cathedral still influenced its town, why was St Mark's so neglected, why was there so much corruption around it, indeed why had it even 'ceased to be comprehended by its votaries'? Was this neglect due to the decline of the Venetian character, or was it because the church itself, as a 'relic of a barbarous age', was incapable of good influence?[39] In posing these questions Ruskin set up his exposition of St Mark's as a defence of Byzantine against the view of it as a crude and unlovely style, or as a product of oriental superstition and decline – precisely the reservations held by its previous critics.

In Ruskin's view Byzantine's first characteristic was its 'confessed incrustation'.[40] The combination of cheap structural materials such as brick and rare precious stone often saved from older buildings or transported from far away, had led to a system of architecture based upon a declared and positive *duplicity*. It had led the Venetians to build in large cavernous masses faced with marbles and mosaics, and thus to have perfected a method of chromatic decoration sympathetic to 'the great instinct of the Eastern races'.[41] Incrustation had also allowed Venetians to express both their exilic affection for old ruins and their new empire's celebration of the trophies of victory. If, as Ruskin had implied in his opening chapters, Venice was a historical type for nineteenth-century England, then by extension Byzantine might be a model for the architecture of a Christian imperial nation built by men who were 'wise, happy, and holy'.[42]

It was fitting, then, that the dazzling effects of this architecture should inspire an inventory of laws useful to an architect working in a similar incrusted method. Plinths and cornices must be light and delicate. Refinements of structure were irrelevant. Shafts should be solid and of one block, their variable size must be respected and they might sometimes be independent of construction. To suit the materials, decoration should be shallow in its cutting, delicate in form, and inspired by plants and lower animals. Its colour could be free, based on harmony rather than crude naturalism. Finally, because its delicacy required intimate observation, the impression of this architecture must not be dependent on size.

However, if Byzantine was a rich and subtle architectural style, was it also suitable for a Christian society? Ruskin's answer to this question was calculated to address the particular Protestant distrust of ornamental richness with which he himself had been imbued during his childhood. He argued that beautifully adorned buildings were found throughout medieval towns and that ornament was not limited to churches. Thus the qualities of Byzantine were not exclusively ecclesiastical; they were just as suitable for dwellings as for churches. The pictorial quality of this style was brought about because its constructional system created large flat surfaces that required expression. And this expression was to take a religious form so that the church became a place in which common people could read the Bible on its walls. Offering a more orderly version of Victor Hugo's idea of Notre Dame as a great exemplary public book, Ruskin thus saw St Mark's as a codex, a 'Book-Temple': 'at once a type of the Redeemed Church of God, and a scroll for the written word of God'.[43] Its mosaics were the most effective form of religious expression, midway between Romanists' lack of interest in art – at least in comparison with their preference for idols – and the aesthetes' neglect of religion in pursuit of artistic form.[44] The answer, then, to Ruskin's original conundrum, was not that the form of architecture itself had cast a bad influence, but that modern Venice had itself declined, the rigour and purity of its medieval religion had departed; and its inhabitants no longer had the time or the ability to address themselves to the forms of this testimony. This was a significantly different view of Byzantium from those of the other writers considered here, and one that actively presented Byzantine Venice as an exemplary counterweight to the present, especially to rigid practices of professionalism, modern organization of labour, and the decline of faith.

GOTHS AND BYZANTINE

For Ruskin, Byzantine was an architecture rooted in the independence of the crafts, and a style whose undoubted oriental character, far from sullying its interest, was one of the chief ingredients of its success. It was also a style that could, on occasion, be employed in the present. Ruskin himself advocated and, with George Gilbert Scott (who had visited Venice's Byzantine palaces in 1851), helped to design a new Romano-Byzantine chancel for Camden Chapel, Camberwell (1854).[45] Even for Ecclesiologists, a Byzantine-derived Italian medieval style became popular in the 1850s, as demonstrated in the success of Burges's entry for the Crimean Memorial Church. The rich incrustation of William Butterfield's All Saints', Margaret Street (1849–59), was seen by many as Byzantine in its character.[46] Deane and Woodward's Trinity College Museum, Dublin (1852–7), was a Ruskin-inspired essay in a late Byzantine style. It was a logical extension of the mid-century interest in Byzantine to go further east to trace the roots of this style, but only one or two Gothic Revivalists, such as R. P. Pullan and William Burges, seemed to have done it.[47] Finally, in 1864 Charles Texier and R. P. Pullan published *Byzantine Architecture*, the first book in English specifically devoted to the subject.[48] But Byzantine was not completely examined as a revivalist style until the end of the century, when Arts and Crafts architects tried to take up the full implications of Ruskin's work.

In most examples of Byzantine-inspired architecture any oriental under-tones – references to a culture said to be in opposition to that of the West – seem to be barely if at all present. If marble revetment, wall colour or round arches signified a place, it was no further east than Venice. Furthermore, by 1858 the architect George Edmund Street was quite prepared to acknowledge that Byzantine could be a mine of useful suggestions, but he, like other Gothic Revivalists, took another, notably un-Ruskinian lesson from it: 'It indicates', Street wrote, 'a mode of obtaining rich decoration without being dependent on a horde of slovenly carvers'.[49] As will be shown in Chapter 5, Street wanted in his Crimean Memorial Church to give the architect absolute paramountcy, and his vision of Byzantine was of a mechanical means to ornamental richness according to the precise and all-encompassing diktat of the designer.

Thus the growing architectural awareness of Byzantine, as well as the Gothic Revival and the occasional Byzantine Revival approaches, sometimes shared what could be called a disorientated vision of Byzantium – in other words, seeing it as something ostensibly not linked to racial categories – that should be distinguished from the attitudes of Lindsay, Freeman and Ruskin. The disorientation was, however, only a surface effect, a kind of momentary neglect of the oriental Byzantium while its western affiliations were more fully tried out. The most obvious example of this was the Gothic Revivalists' approach and their adoption of John Henry Newman's notion of historical development as the gradual building upon and adapting of religious doctrine.[50] In architecture, the theory of development argued that the most important styles arose out of a confluence of diverse precedents. Thus for Gothicists it seemed as if the structure of history itself would offer a way out of the copyists' dead end. According to this theory Byzantine was a half-developed style essential to the main channel of architectural history that, in George Gilbert Scott's words, 'represents the central mass of civilisation'.[51] This main channel was similar to the philologists' Aryan language group – although without its Indian link – brought together by a selective interpretation of history passing now through one country now through another: in Scott's sequence, from Egypt/Assyria to Persia to Greece to Rome to Byzantium and finally to northern Europe. Byzantium could fit as an interim stage within an increasingly western sequence.

The very complex and often unresolved attitudes towards Byzantium in the 1850s are exemplified in their focus on Istanbul, rather than in the somewhat more familiar confines of Venice. In the Crimean Memorial Church competition, as we shall see in Chapter 5, certain tensions in the disorientated vision were made apparent. Here, in their rules for the competition and in their judging of entries, the Ecclesiologists outlawed any intimations of Byzantine because of its potential for summoning up a confusing oriental affiliation in Istanbul. Any such Byzantine undertaking as George Gilbert Scott's interest in making a domed, centrally planned design, or the several domed designs submitted to the competition, would be more explicitly orientalizing in this context than the architecture solely inspired by Ruskin's work or as a reaction against Gothicism.[52] But at the same time a more reorientated image of Byzantium was being forced on some commentators by the Crimean War, and that event, with the greater public interest in Istanbul fuelled by the reports of soldiers, businessmen, illustrators and correspondents, may have helped to encourage the evident growth of Byzantine studies in the 1850s. Whether it did or not is indeterminable, since concurrently with it appeared the surveys of Salzenberg and Fossati, products of less overt alliances with eastern power. The war had split public opinion between those who felt that any alliance was acceptable if it curtailed the Russian threat, and those who opposed an alliance with an Islamic power against a Christian one on religious principle. In this fraught ideological arena either the Russians or the Ottomans might be seen as the inheritors of the Byzantine tradition.

The Crimean Memorial competition was an attempt to resolve or gloss over such differences, but the grounds for these reactions can be seen in other fields. For instance, when E. A. Freeman reviewed Finlay's histories of Greece in 1855 for *The North British Review*, he saw the relevance of these works to the current Crimean War and made several comparisons between Byzantine history and contemporary events. 'All eyes are at this moment turned to the East', Freeman wrote, 'from contemplating its present aspect, every reflecting mind will naturally turn to contemplate its past history'.[53] For Freeman, Finlay's anti-Gibbonian project would help to correct the predilection of 'the popular mind [which] has suddenly leapt to a strange abstract love of Turks and hatred of Greeks'.[54] Despite his previously orientalist views of Byzantine culture and his initial support for the war,[55] Freeman was now clearly siding with Russia's new Byzantium rather than with the Ottoman conquerors of the old Byzantium.

VIOLLET-LE-DUC

Again, these British attitudes and approaches need to be related to continental work. While Byzantium had acquired symbolic power, no British writer in this period offered the kind of sophisticated rationalist interpretation of Byzantine architecture that was proposed by the great French architect and theorist Eugène-Emmanuel Viollet-le-Duc. Viollet showed that, rather than seeking to revive its methods of work or details, Byzantine could be the source of architectural principles: just as much as Greek, Roman or, even, High Gothic.

In his *Entretiens sur l'architecture* (1863–72) Viollet, following the *Néo-Grec* view of history, saw Byzantine as a synthesis of Roman, Greek and eastern influences. Its arches borne on columns, and its abandonment of Corinthian and composite capitals for more solid yet disguised forms, exemplified the structural logic of its evolution out of preceding styles, although it was not able to develop them fully.[56] For Viollet, Byzantine architecture, infused with Greek spirit if not Greek in form, was vital to the preservation and transmission of Greek rationality to both Islamic and western medieval architecture. For example, it was through Byzantine, and specifically the Nestorian heretics, that Islam had derived the underlying geometrical principles of its ornament.[57] Viollet accepted the view of Byzantine as inert and hieratic, but explained this as characteristic of Greek, not oriental mentality: the Greek mind was a mix of incessant intellectual movement and a fixed attachment to material form.[58] It could present an occidental face to Asians and an oriental face to Romans; it was moving when it came against stasis, preserving when it came against disorder. Where, then, had Byzantines found the elements that had revitalized Graeco-Roman architecture?

To answer this Viollet, who had never travelled in the Islamic world, turned to the recent research of Félicien de Saulcy on Judaic and Phoenician remains. From the early 1850s and particularly in his *Histoire de l'art judaïque* (1858), de Saulcy had claimed an important Jewish role in the development of ancient Near Eastern architecture through reattributing some Greek and Roman monuments to the ancient Judean period. De Saulcy's work was supported by that of his friend, the painter and photographer Auguste Salzmann. Sponsored by the Ministry of Public Instruction, Salzmann travelled to Jerusalem in 1854 and published his *Jérusalem* in 1856, illustrated with 174 calotypes.[59] The extraordinary inky textures of these illustrations – and their flattened scalelessness – documented for the first time the city's stone-carved ornament and patterns of construction (Plate 16). Salzmann's photographs attested with a 'conclusive brutality' to the racial formation of Jerusalem's architecture, whether Judaic, Greek, Roman, Christian, or Arab.

The controversial nature of de Saulcy's beliefs can be measured by the immediate mobilization of forces to dispel them. Viollet's close friend, the leading Semitist Ernest Renan, whose study of linguistics led him to uphold the notion of Semitic inferiority, went out in 1860 to research the remains of Phoenician civilization in the Near East.[60] Unsurprisingly, Renan, in contrast to de Saulcy and Salzmann, could find no distinct Jewish or Phoenician culture. Renan's interests were taken up by the Comte Melchior de Vogüé, whose mission to Syria and the Lebanon in 1861 was partly intended to further the study of Early Christian monuments and partly to show that Jewish culture was essentially derived from Egyptian, thus eastern not western: out

PLATE 16 Auguste Salzmann, 'Fragment of the Stone Entrance', 1856. Photograph. (*Jérusalem*)

of this de Vogüé published *Le Temple de Jérusalem* (1864–5), and *Syrie centrale* (1865–77). Similarly, the dissociation of ancient Greece from Near Eastern influences was crucial to what Martin Bernal has recently called the rising 'Aryan Model' of Greek history: that is, the theory that Greek culture was an entirely Indo-European phenomenon.[61]

Viollet held a modified view of this Aryan Model of Greece. Following leading theory at the time, he believed that an Aryan migration was the key to Greek culture, but that Greek art only sprang into life because of an added influx of Semitic blood.[62] Hence, following de Saulcy, Viollet argued that it was in the monuments of Jewish civilization that the Byzantines had found regenerative forms for their architecture.[63] This was an extraordinary conclusion given the widely held belief that Semites were unscientific and uncreative, and given also that such a formative influence on Viollet as Jules Michelet (from whom Viollet had derived his particular vision of progress and French nationhood) believed that Aryans and Semites had always been engaged in a racial struggle for supremacy.[64]

It seems that the relatively new interest in Byzantine could also be involved in this debate. Viollet's position on the vaunted Greek heritage was to view it as less of a pure Aryan product than many of his contemporaries believed. He argued that just as ancient Greece needed a Semitic element so Greek Byzantium required Jewish ingredients: in architectural terms these were a vigorous treatment of stone and a lively handling of mouldings and ornament in Roman forms. Here Viollet was revising the generally accepted oriental character of Byzantium by adjoining it to a tradition of rational western architecture able to synthesize non-western elements. By turning to supposedly Jewish sources in and around Jerusalem to help to explain Byzantine architecture, Viollet also found a religious logic: it was natural that Greeks 'should seek the elements of a new art in those places which had witnessed the birth of the new religion'.[65] Rationality was still harboured as a western characteristic; the Orient was still inert plunder. In the process, Byzantium could also affix itself to the roots of Christian history.

THE HOLY SEPULCHRE CONTROVERSY

It is perhaps significant, certainly revealing, that the only comparably focused British debate involving Byzantine architecture in this period was that concerning the true site of the original Holy Sepulchre in Jerusalem. Here there was no government-aided archaeology, although there was some co-operation with the military.

It had been quite common practice, even in the 1840s, to attribute a

Christian foundation to an Islamic building because it seemed to possess such familiar elements as a nave, transept or classical capitals. In 1846 one Ecclesiologist had done this with the mosque of Damascus, and the Aqsa Mosque in Jerusalem was often the subject of similar attribution.[66] But the most controversial and long-running of these reattributions centred around James Fergusson's theory that the Dome of the Rock was actually a Constantinian martyrium on the site of the Holy Sepulchre, which, like Hagia Sophia, had been taken over by Muslims. Fergusson first advanced this theory in 1847 and repeated it in books published in 1861, 1865 and 1878.[67] His theory was based primarily on the stylistic evidence provided by the drawings that Catherwood, Bonomi and Arundale had made of the Dome of the Rock in 1833 (Plate 17), although he also reinterpreted the documentary evidence. He was vigorously opposed, in particular by George Williams, Ermete Pierotti, Robert Willis, the Comte de Vogüé and Charles Warren.[68] Part of what was at stake in this debate was the nature and quality of historical evidence, although there was little attempt to integrate this material into an overt and overarching theory of historical development, as had been done in the controversy involving Viollet-le-Duc.

Although Fergusson seems to have won few significant converts to his

PLATE 17 Francis Arundale and Frederick Catherwood. Dome of the Rock, Jerusalem. Engraving from original drawing of *c.* 1833. Section. (J. Fergusson, *An Essay on the Ancient Topography of Jerusalem*, 1847)

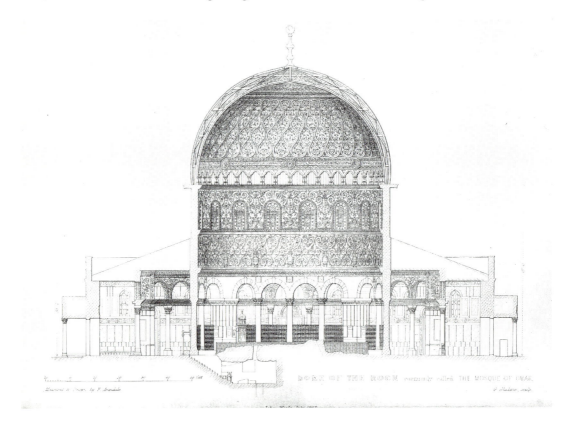

cause, it was not until the Haram al-Sharif was surveyed by Pierotti and later by Warren, that his theory could be materially disproved. As will be shown in the examination of the Anglican church in Jerusalem (Chapter 7), local Ottoman power was still sufficiently strong and independent to forestall this particular alliance of colonial and scholarly interests and Pierotti's evidence was only made possible by his appointment as 'Architect-Engineer' to the Ottoman governor.[69] The controversy stirred up by Fergusson's theory stimulated a new spate of surveys of Jerusalem, but it was not until at least the mid-1860s that the British government even covertly began to involve itself in the cultural conflict over the Holy Land.

Yet the Holy Sepulchre controversy did involve some of the same ingredients as Viollet-le-Duc's theory. For instance, Pierotti helped Renan during his 1860 visit, and Fergusson consulted de Saulcy.[70] Furthermore, Fergusson's conclusions, as we saw in the previous chapter, derived from limited notions of what could and could not be done in a Muslim culture, just as much as on an overgeneralized grasp of what constituted Byzantine architecture.

The affair was also spiked by a very particular combination of religious and political elements, several of which will recur later in this book. George Williams, who defended the traditional site, was a High Churchman who had been appointed chaplain to the Bishop of Jerusalem in an attempt to balance evangelical influence in the city. His vision of Anglican presence in the Near East depended upon the traditional site of the Holy Sepulchre as the symbol of an ancient unity between the Anglican and Orthodox Churches: a unity that could be revived in the present. Fergusson, and such supporters of his as George Grove, seem to have envisaged a much more active ordering of power in the form of the reattribution of land and monuments, making connections between Jewish monuments and the earliest Christian monuments, and purifying them of later Muslim, Catholic or Orthodox associations. Fergusson's work thus shares much of the ideology of the Jews Society's aggressive statement of separate evangelical presence through their new 'Hebrew' church in Jerusalem (Chapter 7). By contrast, Williams's position is linked to the rhetoric of alliance that informed the earlier history of the Crimean Memorial Church in Istanbul (Chapter 5), and the conjuring up of Byzantine associations in Burges's first design for that project. It is not surprising, then, that Burges supported Williams's position and even proposed erecting a copy of the Holy Sepulchre in England.[71]

———————

The British interpretation of Byzantine architecture was characteristic of Victorian attitudes to comprehending the Near East. Viollet's theory exemplifies a convergence of interests that was usually less explicit, less structured and more fragmentary, in Britain. After the *Description de l'Égypte* the French government continued to fund major scholarly missions in the Near East, and their work was often aided by the French army. Hence the weighty tomes of Abel Blouet's *Expédition scientifique de la Morée* (1831–8), Charles Texier's publications on Asia Minor, Salzmann's *Jérusalem* (1856) and de Vogüé's *Syrie centrale* (1865–77). (Meanwhile the Prussian government had financed the research and publication of Salzenberg's work on Byzantine Istanbul.) Such French works did not just pioneer the study of Byzantine remains; like the *Description*, they were also ways of understanding and ordering the intended colonial field. Thus, through a network of ideas about the structure of history, the uses of the architectural past, and racial affiliation, they were linked to the institutions that might wield colonial power.

British interest in Byzantine architecture was generally a much more second-hand (with the notable exception of Ruskin's studies in Venice), unofficial, even amateurish affair. It was not until William Lethaby and Henry Swainson's work on Hagia Sophia (1894) that a painstaking, sympathetic and first-hand analysis of Byzantine architecture (based, in this case, on both expressive and rationalist theories) appeared from the pen of British writers. The more speculative nature of mid-century British work – directed also by the specific interests of revivalism, religion or antiquarianism – was to some extent necessitated by the lack of a tradition of government support for archaeological work. Unlike France, Britain did not have the 'Gallo-Byzantine' churches of the Périgord, nor did it have a coastline that could evoke the pan-Mediterranean vision of Léon Vaudoyer's Byzantine-style Marseilles Cathedral (1856–93). Byzantine architecture seemed to have no similar links to notions of British nationality; moreover, its ties to Orthodox Christianity and its eastern location polarized and confused the responses of the leading archi-tectural commentators in Britain. The hints of an appreciation of Byzantine because of its stasis or as an exemplary synthesis had to compete with the view of it as evidence of an eclipsed historical style and therefore as another expression of that about-to-be-eclipsed world, the Orient.

Part II

ARCHITECTURE AND THE ORIENT

PREFACE

•

In the second part of this book the focus of attention shifts from Britain to the Near East whilst the weight of interest is adjusted from texts to buildings. This is by no means a movement from theory to practice nor is it a chronological development; indeed, many of the events analysed in this section happened contemporaneously with those discussed in Part I. There is certainly more discussion of physical environments and material resources in this section but just as Part I was concerned to place a proliferating orientalist discourse within specific debates and against specific political needs, to see it not just as something written but as something actively practised, so Part II is concerned with exploring whether orientalism could continue to circulate productively in the face of its ostensible subject and under very particular conditions. The real movement, then, is from a multifaceted discourse to a group of differently inflected colonial projects, bearing in mind that a project is 'neither a strictly discursive entity nor an exclusively practical one'.[1] Such projects may be realized, they may remain as projections, or they may be a combination of both.

Each chapter in this part of the book is concerned with the role played by architecture in articulating a colonial project within one of three Ottoman-ruled cities: Alexandria, Istanbul and Jerusalem. By 1840 a number of British architects had gained first-hand experience of Islamic architecture and had begun to assimilate that knowledge into their buildings, but they were not to be the only architects asked to design in the Near East, nor was orientalist-influenced architecture to be the only response to this location, though orientalism always remained a point of reference. The 1840s was the moment when the ground was first properly broken for British architecture in the Near East. The need for new architecture seems to have grown principally out of a rising European economic influence over the area, with the concomitant establishment of influential British communities and missionary groups, a liberalization of laws about religion and property, and an overt and constant rivalry between European powers. But at least for the next four decades, while British economic influence increased, direct British power in the Near East fluctuated despite interventions in the Second Syrian War (1840) and the Crimean War (1854–6), and was by no means always available to or exerted in the interests of local British communities in Ottoman cities. Architecture, and the colonial projects of which it was a part, might be a product of domestic British-based needs, the requirements of a British group based in the Near East, or some alliance of both. With these opportunities came the threat of great disorientation as architectural practice was put in the crucible of very different social and economic conditions. This moment witnesses the birth of something similar to the monster that is now called globalization. That it was a difficult birth is also part of the story.

4

ARCHITECTURE IN CAPTIVITY

JAMES WILD AND ST MARK'S, ALEXANDRIA

•

It might be said that the erection of a new and stately Christian church in a Mohammedan city was so striking an event, that it ought to be commemorated in an especial manner, and that the most appropriate manner was the leading as it were into captivity of the architecture of its already humbled and soon to be vanquished foe.

(Ecclesiologist, *1846)*

In Chapter 1 it was argued that a rigorous and specifically architectural discourse on Islamic culture – the 'new orientalism' – emerged in the 1830s and that one of its principal places of inspiration was Egypt. This chapter describes how this approach was made architecturally manifest in that same country, and so its concern is with the point or moment of contact between an orientalist discourse and its source. It discusses the problems of British identity, Britain's role in modernizing an oriental country, and the material problems of designing and building in a place of growing economic but no formal control by the British. Out of this conjunction of elements emerged a colonial project that was particular to the British in Egypt and to the city of Alexandria. To explore this we need an agent and a building.

James Wild was one of the most important members of this first generation of architects interested in the Islamic Near East. Closely involved with the circle around Owen Jones, described in Chapter 1, Wild also attempted a new orientalist style born out of an eclectic amalgam of largely Islamic and Byzantine elements, which could conjure up an image of exotic newness, even perhaps modernity. He travelled widely in the Near East studying Islamic architecture, and designed buildings for the British community in Egypt during the 1840s. Yet within architectural history this period in his career has been almost entirely neglected. Between his extraordinary announcement of his eclectic orientalist approach in his church at Streatham (1839–41), and his highly influential Northern District School, Soho (1849–50), both in London, it has seemed as if Wild simply disappeared offstage, vanished from the centres of power that architectural history usually sees as its areas of primary interest. But Wild's work at the 'periphery' is not only worth recovering as a marginal contribution to a particular view of history; more importantly, he was, through his articulation of the form and imagery of British presence, involved in the dynamic of conflict and assimilation that radically changed the region's character. It is for these reasons that Wild's design of St Mark's Church, Alexandria, as well as being startlingly unusual, can also be seen to exemplify important aspects of the relationship between informal imperialism, orientalism and architecture.

JAMES WILD

James Wild (1814–92) has long been an intriguing figure for architectural historians. The son of Charles Wild, a painter of architectural scenes and Gothic subjects, Wild was articled to George Basevi, and attended lectures at the Royal Academy.[1] By the age of twenty-six he had built several churches in either a Norman or an Early English Gothic mode but, more importantly, Wild had also established a close friendship with Owen Jones. By 1841 they were sharing the same residential address, and in September 1842 Jones married Wild's sister.[2]

It was almost certainly through Jones that Wild developed an interest in Islamic architecture that was to stay with him throughout his career. The first building to demonstrate this interest was Christ Church, Streatham (1839–41) (Plate 18), but the Islamic element in the church was only one amongst the many ingredients of its rich eclecticism. It was Early Christian in plan, Italian Romanesque in composition, Ottoman in its bay elevations, and Alhambresque, Mamluk, Sevillean, and ancient Egyptian in its ornament.[3] This synthetic eclecticism may have owed something to Thomas Hope's *An Essay on Historical Architecture* (1835) or the example of German *Rundbogenstil* architects, especially in the way that the combination was disciplined by the clear volumes of its Romanesque outline. By the late 1830s there were also several serious and well-detailed sources for the oriental aspects of the design: Lewis Vulliamy's and Owen Jones's drawings of Ottoman architecture, Jones's *Alhambra* (to which Wild had been a subscriber), Hay's or Jones's publications showing Cairene architecture, Pascal Coste's *Architecture arabe* (1839), and Charles Texier's *Description de l'Asie Mineure* (1839), with its copious illustrations of Ottoman buildings.

The Streatham design tempered all these eclectic elements into a 'quiet

PLATE 18 James Wild. Christ Church, Streatham, 1839–41.

severity'.[4] This was accomplished partly by the innovatory brick and terracotta polychromy in which all the exterior details were carried out, and partly by the coherent massing of volumes set off by the commanding site on Brixton Hill. This use of eclecticism within an overall volumetric simplicity set Wild's work apart from that of his contemporaries. It is also worth saying that it was this formal resolution and decorative abstraction that led later writers to call Wild an 'early modernist'. In this respect modernist historians like Sir John Summerson and Sir Nikolaus Pevsner implicitly shared Owen Jones's view that eastern forms were ahistorical and that to use them was, somehow, to avoid historicism, to design without dependence on styles of the past, even to design without style.[5]

Wild was no theorist, and surviving writings by him are scarce. But there are passages in a letter of 1841, shortly after the completion of the Streatham church, which are worth quoting at length. Wild was clearly immersed in contemporary debates on the nature of historicism and the role of copyism:

> I object in the first place to the adopting [of] any style – this word style as the meaning attached to it seems to me to be the chief source of all our architectural failures. It seems that it is supposed in spite of everyday experience that the beauty of antiquity, and the associations connected with the last, can be transferred to new imitations of old buildings. Those who can really appreciate what is beautiful in ancient architecture – apart from the mouldings and

decay – know why it is in vain to imitate the more prominent features as a sort of decoration to new buildings without all the circumstances which created the architecture it is wished to imitate. We must study from all sources and adapt and apply our knowledge with invention, as our forefathers did, or we can but produce caricatures of their works.

His attention had been drawn to the claims put forward for the use of Romanesque and Byzantine structure and ornament:

I should recommend the study of Romanesque architecture not the adoption of the style . . . [In Romanesque] there is much that is only half developed, and interesting only as a transition style. For this reason, I prefer the Oriental type to the German – it is more massive in its character, and the grand feature of architecture the dome more especially belongs to it. To know how to use the Byzantine or Romanesque styles requires a considerable knowledge of the principles of other and purer times of architecture, as although these buildings present the most valuable hints and studies, their details are generally to my taste at least, very trifling, being a transition between a barbarous tradition of classic architecture, and the commencement of the pointed styles. These feelings led me to study very carefully the details of the Church at Streatham. I found the greatest difficulty in determining why certain forms were fit and beautiful, apart from illustrations or the associations of style.[6]

Wild was caught in several dilemmas which are manifested in this passage's inconsistent reasoning. He seems to have thought that the adoption of any one historical style would be an inadequate response to a contemporary situation involving different social and technical practices. He wanted to avoid using style for associational purposes (as Chambers had used Islamic architecture) and yet he was sceptical of a formulated system of aesthetic judgement. Paraphrasing Thomas Hope, he called for an inventive use of eclectic sources. But, unlike Hope, Wild regarded the various Romanesque styles as transitional, part of the way along a development from Classic to Gothic architecture and therefore impure and unexemplary. And yet of these transitional styles he did advocate 'the Oriental type' (presumably Byzantine and perhaps some Islamic architecture) as the best model. The Byzantine inspiration of the Streatham church could be seen in the form of its internal arcades, and its Islamicism was mostly to be found in matters of detail such as the 'Cufic' ornament around its western rose window or its cusped entrance

arch with patterned voussoirs. But in his statement Wild recommended oriental architecture for its use of domes and its 'massiveness'.

Some of the views expressed in this letter were to point the way for Wild's work in Egypt. One was simply the need for a sustained study of these transitional styles. Another was that Wild seemed to be hinting that the use of elements of Byzantine and Islamic architecture could be seen as the dominant part of his aesthetic, around which other eclectic options were grouped.

By the summer of 1842 Wild's new interest in the East had led him and his friend Joseph Bonomi to join Carl Richard Lepsius's great Prussian expedition to Egypt and Nubia. Lepsius, the leader of the expedition, had become interested in Egyptology under the influence of Alexander von Humboldt and Christian von Bunsen, both well known in England. Funded by the Prussian government and backed by Bunsen in his capacity as Prussian ambassador in London, Lepsius's expedition was far more systematic than any of Robert Hay's. It recorded, excavated and sent back over 15,000 artifacts and casts to Berlin, and its findings were the subject of Lepsius's twelve-volume *Denkmäler aus Aegypten und Aethiopien* (1849–59). Bonomi, a generation older than Wild, had already spent eighteen years in Egypt with Robert Hay. Wild, who would surely have felt a novice in Jones's company until he had lived in Egypt, was hired as an architectural draughtsman and a promising orientalist: in Lepsius's words 'a young architect, full of genius, [who] seeks with enthusiasm in the East a new field for the exercise of the rich and various gifts with which he is endowed'.[7]

Early in the expedition Wild worked assiduously on Egyptology, but when he reached Cairo he threw himself into studying and sketching Islamic medieval architecture. He drew stained glass, mosaics, tombs, *muqarnas* vaults and any Cairene domestic buildings to which he could gain access.[8] He also joined the group of orientalists gathered around Edward Lane, who was then living in Cairo and was already well known as the author of *The Manners and Customs of the Modern Egyptians*.[9] It is important to emphasize that this was a network of Europeans many of whom were developing specialist interests in a particular 'medieval' part of an expanding city; not, as is often assumed, individual pioneers isolated in a thoroughly alien and backward society.

Through this network Wild was able to visit many Islamic residences including those of Dr Abbott, an English physician, and John Frederick Lewis, the English painter who lived 'like a languid lotus-eater' in a house in the Islamic part of the city.[10] Wild was not so self-indulgent. Here, following Lane's interests in the patterns and spaces of everyday life to the letter, he drew ground plans, made studies of the *mashrabiyyah* screens and door panelling, and drew measured sections, plans and ceiling studies of the small bath (Plate 19). Lane's influence, and possibly that of French Saint-Simonists via Owen Jones, must be seen as paramount in this painstaking study of Islamic domestic architecture (which he also drew later in Damascus), and as a result Wild developed an expertise of his own as one of the first western architects to devote himself to this subject.[11]

After a short hiatus, Wild left Lepsius's expedition and returned to Cairo in April 1844. This time, often dressing in local costume to gain access to buildings, he was particularly concerned with mosques and baths, vault construction and fountains (Plate 20).[12] Although Wild never published the notebooks which he filled during his stays in Cairo, they were to become a reliable source for later writers.[13] These tireless studies, typical of the new breed of orientalist in the circles surrounding Jones, Hay and Lane, were the work of an architect committed to an ideal of precise, factual recording; going beyond the Picturesque impressions and associational meanings valued by an older generation.

PLATE 19 James Wild. The bath in J. F. Lewis's house, Cairo, 1842. Plan and section. (V&A, E3764–1938)

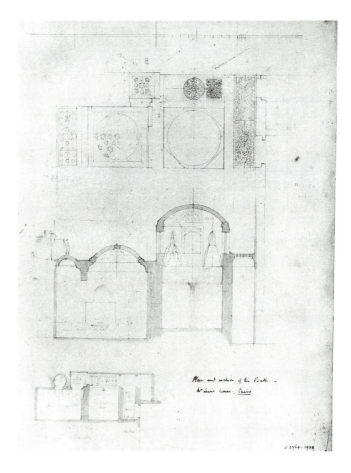

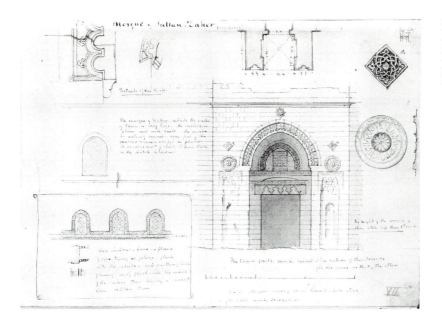

PLATE 20 James Wild. 'Mosque of Sultan Daher', Cairo, 1844. Elevation, details and plan of entrance. (V&A, E3880–1938)

But Wild's early work in Egypt was not limited to recording monuments; indeed, his precocious attempt to establish a new theory of pyramid construction (the short-lived 'accretion' theory) indicates that, like Lane and Jones, he also wanted to elaborate new conceptual frameworks.[14] In Wild this was not a written, scholarly exercise but one based on the making of visual hypotheses. It will be discussed here in three minor projects first before looking at the way it took on built form.

During this second stay in Cairo, Wild was commissioned to design a gate for the English burial ground (Plate 21).[15] He designed a simple entrance through the wall on the street side, framed it with inscriptions and grilled its double doors with *mashrabiyyah*. On the cemetery side the entrance was crowned by a cavetto cornice and flanked by twin pylon-like lodges, containing rooms for the keeper. The gate thus drew upon both the conventional association of ancient Egyptian architecture with death, on the inside of the cemetery wall, and Wild's new-found interest in the architecture of the streets of medieval Cairo on the outside.

If the cemetery gate was perhaps overly simplistic in its two-sided eclecticism, there is another of Wild's designs, probably from this period of his stay in Egypt, that can only be described as an eclectic fantasy (Plate 22).[16] This was an imaginary restoration or invention of a slightly battered two-storied tower or pylon. It seems improbable that the drawing was related to any commission; at least there is no surviving documentation, and the allusions of the fantasy seem unlikely to have been designed for any specific brief. The tower itself is a strictly two-dimensional facade composition,

PLATE 21 James Wild. Design for a British cemetery gate, Cairo, 1844. Elevations, section and plan. (FO 78/583)

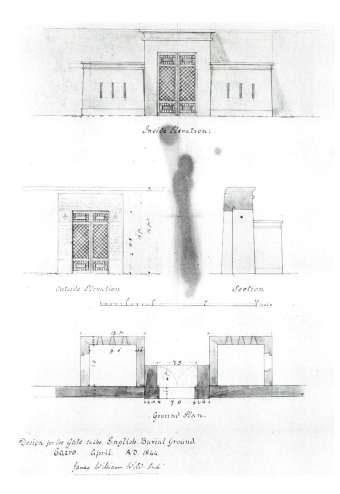

divided into rectangular panels beneath and to either side of a single, *mashrabiyyah*-filled window on each story. Whilst these panels contained animals and figures in a quasi-Egyptian style, the top-most panels had two European-looking seated monarchs, and above these were heraldic devices of shields and crowns. The rest of the facade was filled with inscriptions in an indecipherable Arabicizing script and a variety of ornamental courses, the whole crested with crenellations. The theme of this fantasy was clearly Egyptian history itself, played out on those aspects of its architecture – Ptolomaic, Mamluk and Ottoman – that Wild had studied during his trip.

The third project was not architectural at all but instead some proportional studies of male nudes in standing and sitting poses. Wild identified each of these nudes as a contemporary Egyptian: 'Eunus – a Fellah' (Plate 23), 'Mahomet – a Berber', and 'Behal – Mixed Fellah and Berber'.[17] Evidently, Wild intended a comparison of Berber and fellah physiognomy, because in each drawing the models were posed in the same positions and the

PLATE 22 James Wild.
Tower design, *c.* 1844.
Elevation. (GI ID 27)

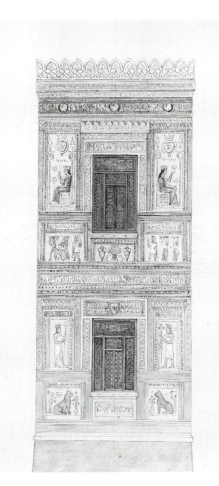

same parts of their anatomy were carefully measured. Within Wild's own
circles the drawings are most closely related to Edward Lane's and J. F. Lewis's
attempts to represent Egyptian ethnography: Lewis's art had been identified
by Ruskin as a 'perception of [human] nature and race which laughs to scorn
all the generic study of the scientific schools', his mission being to surpass
natural history in portraying 'the comparatively animal life of the southern
and eastern families of mankind'.[18] It is also likely that Wild's drawings were
an incomplete attempt to compare the proportions of modern and ancient
Egyptians, for the figures were posed in a kind of ancient Egyptian manner
and the next drawings in the series were of figures in Theban tombs.[19] Here
too Wild's work is similar to that of other orientalists, for David Roberts had
also used this comparative mode in several paintings at this time.[20]

More generally, Wild's proportional studies are a relatively early example
of that characteristic nineteenth-century attempt to identify social and racial
difference through measuring the outer features of the body. A close parallel

PLATE 23 James Wild.
'Eunus – a Fellah', c.
1844. (GI IC 13)

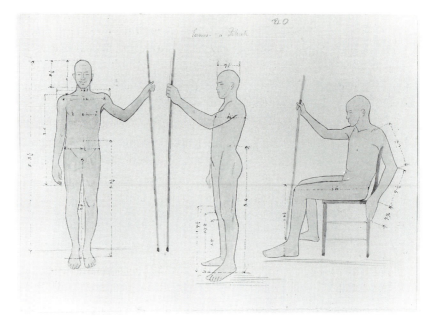

to Wild's approach is the work of Alphonse Quételet, the statistician and
'architect of sociology', who sought in the 1830s to define human types
through examining physical stature, taking as his comparative types the chest
sizes of Greek sculptures and those of Belgian army recruits.[21] It is now well
established that the detection of degeneration and abnormality had an
important role both in justifying the imperial birthright of a normative
western body and in controlling that body's social pathologies – a moral
anatomy. If this seems to inflate the interest of Wild's drawings, we need only
note how his companion Joseph Bonomi later tried to develop a similar
anthropometry into an instrument for recording and identifying police
suspects, and also how, by 1881, the anthropologist E. B. Tylor used
comparisons of ancient Egyptian kings and modern fellahin as a standard way
of introducing students to the notion of the persistence of racial types.[22]

What these three examples of Wild's early work in Egypt reveal is an
architect and scholar who regarded the range of interests that made up the new
orientalism as the continuation of a scientific materialist tradition, the search
for 'man in general' (or anthropology, when it concerned other men). This
tradition, driven by Bentham, Saint-Simon and Fourier, not only aimed to
re-examine western institutions under the radically secularized logic of the
emerging social sciences, but also saw in the East a field of clarifying models
and the chance for exemplary new projects. As we have seen, Owen Jones
found such evidence in the colour and geometry of Islamic design, while Wild
was a relatively early experimenter in the Near Eastern projects that, as
Edward Said has shown, reached their summation in the Suez Canal. It should

be added that something of this vision of an industrially reformed society was shared by many in Egypt, including its ruler Muhammad Ali, and that such technological triumphs were not necessarily seen as impositions; indeed, such conquests of nature might even be regarded as the products of alliance and modern equivalents to the monuments of more ancient cultures.

For most of the next three years, from the spring of 1844 until the spring of 1847, Wild was based at Cairo,[23] although his major work was the Anglican church of St Mark in Alexandria, built for the British residents in that city. The specific nature of this British community and of this reinvigorated Egyptian city, both need to be established if Wild's design is to be properly understood.

THE BRITISH, MUHAMMAD ALI AND ALEXANDRIA

A hint of the complexity of Anglo-Egyptian relations at this time can be detected in a print by David Roberts showing Muhammad Ali receiving the British consul-general Colonel Campbell and the artist himself in 1839 (Plate 24).[24] Roberts seems to have wanted his print to indicate the civilizing benefits of European guidance and alliance. The Pasha sits crosslegged on a divan with a waterpipe in front of him, receiving the stiff diplomacies of the British, who are served with coffee. Beyond this group the Egyptian fleet lies anchored in the harbour at Alexandria, and to the left Roberts has wrapped the classical columns of Muhammad Ali's arsenal, where the meeting takes place, with a huge swag of drapery. Yet while ostensibly showing the consul negotiating the Overland Route to India under various signs of Egyptian power and pleasure, the print, which appeared as a frontispiece to the last, modern volume in Roberts's *The Holy Land* (1855–6), actually encapsulates the mood of ordered, slightly triumphant, alliance *following* Muhammad Ali's defeat in 1841 rather than the more uncertain political situation of 1839. In the accompanying text we are told how magnanimously the Pasha behaved when his ships were replaced by a British fleet: sheltering the British residents ('consider me your Consul') and then gladly accepting concessions 'obtained' by the victorious British from the Porte. This is the politics of the 1840s: coercion, the overlaid pretences of alliance, and the gentling of a cunning despot through the civil decorum of the British.

When Wild arrived in 1842 Britain's commercial priorities in Egypt had been newly established. Egypt would supply cotton and other raw materials, Britain would utilize them in manufacture, and Egypt would provide the market for the finished goods. As Edward Lane had argued, Egypt was to be returned to 'what nature designed it to be, almost exclusively an agricultural

PLATE 24 David Roberts. 'Interview with Mehemet Ali in his Palace, Alexandria', 1856. (Roberts, *The Holy Land*)

country'.[25] Lane's words were written in 1836 at a time when Egypt's internal policies threatened these commercial interests. In the first three decades of his rule, Muhammad Ali had imported foreign specialists to aid his campaign of Europeanization: to build new engineering works and factories, to establish a new educational system and modern manufacturing processes, and to renovate the army on Prussian principles. By the 1830s Egypt's industrial capacity was second only to Britain's,[26] and by 1840 an Egyptian empire bestrode the eastern Mediterranean from Greece to the Lebanon and from there to Sudan: a more potent presence than the Ottoman Empire of which it was still ostensibly a vassal. The modernization of Egypt's cotton industry, and its increasing domination over Levantine economies in the 1830s, was a particular threat to the British need for new markets.

1840 was the turning-point. In that year Britain helped the Turks defeat their powerful vassals in the Second Syrian War and after this date Muhammad Ali's power was limited to the hereditary governorship of Egypt, and the British had succeeded in their policy of preserving the Ottoman Empire as a bulwark against Russian expansion whilst limiting France's influence on Egypt. In the 1840s Europeans gained virtual control of the Egyptian market as local industrialization slowed and factories were closed. European capital flooded in and Egypt, like India, became geared to supplying raw materials to Europe. Lane's wishes had been realized: the scene was set for new representations of Britain's relation to Egypt.

Such a brief and panoramic view of Anglo-Egyptian relations in the 1830s is bound to obscure some of the lesser but paradoxical events of the period. For instance, when the British consul-general withdrew from Egypt during the Second Syrian War, British merchants refused to leave Cairo and Alexandria and were given protection there by Muhammad Ali.[27] As one commentator in the Benthamite *Westminster Review* wrote in 1841: 'In spite of every attempt to awaken his jealousies and his fears, he has allowed us to erect hotels in the desert, and ... to use his territory for every purpose which could facilitate communication'.[28] Even more appositely, in the summer of 1839, in a gesture that seems paradoxical only in the light of the larger political view of the period, Muhammad Ali granted the British community in Alexandria a generous plot on the major square of the city for the construction of a Protestant church, eventually to be designed by James Wild. Wild's church was to become a focus for the elaboration of a colonial project that was local to the British in Alexandria, that was not to be subsumed under larger British interests but to be seen as a particular inflection of broader discourses about Egypt.

Alexandria was the setting for many of the apparent contradictions of Muhammad Ali's reign and for the differing interests of the foreign nationals living there. Before the nineteenth century the originally classical city had endured many centuries of neglect, due partly to the silting up of access to the Nile, and partly to the growth of Cairo and the reorientation of Egypt's trade following the Arab conquest of AD 640. By the time of Napoleon's invasion in 1798 the city had a meagre population of 8,000. Its revival can be dated from the Treaty of Amiens in 1803, which confirmed the establishment in Egypt of foreign trading privileges. When Muhammad Ali became Pasha of Egypt in 1805 he decided to re-establish Alexandria as a major city and built there his own summer residence, the Ras al-Tin Palace (1817). By his abolition of some restrictions on Christian worship he encouraged foreigners, particularly Greeks, to settle in the city. And within a few decades the Italian population had became second only to that of the Greeks, playing a significant role in developing Egyptian postal, medical and sanitary services. Italian engineers and architects were also instrumental in many of the large building projects initiated under Muhammad Ali.[29]

The public and institutional focus for European life was the area around the Maydan al-Tahrir (or Place des Consuls), along the main arteries bordering the most southerly point of the eastern harbour (labelled 'Frank quarter' in Plate 25). The square had only achieved definite shape in the late 1830s when

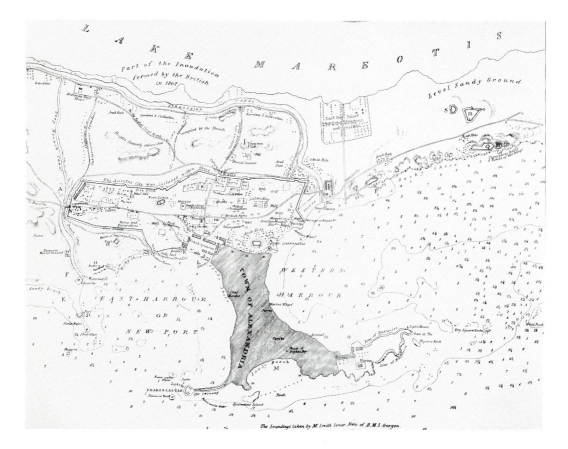

PLATE 25 Colonel E. Napier. Map of Alexandria, 1841. (G. Jondet, *Atlas historique... d'Alexandrie,* 1921)

several Europeans erected houses on the edge of a long rectangular site that had been formally laid out in 1834. However, most travellers were disappointed by this new Italianate town, seeing it as a sham imitation, a dim double, of western life in the midst of the Orient:

> You feel somewhat at a loss, when you look out from your window upon the flaring hot, white walls of that naked square, which mark the Frank's quarter at Scandria. You grow even melancholy over your disappointment; compelled to regret the vanishing fabric of those dreams of oriental glories which had been the fond offspring of your leisure hours ... You grow pale with wrath at this stultification of your sweet fantasies, and almost choke with vexation, dust and perspiration, as you cast your eyes round that hollow square, where you see nothing but flag-poles and consulates; listen to a strange jargon of Lingo Franco, and read involuntarily those flaming signs and mammoth posters, publishing, forsooth, nothing but – 'Overland Route to India' – 'Opera, to-night, Ernani', or 'English Circulating Library'.[30]

By the early 1840s most of the plots around the square had been filled by consulates and large European residences (Plate 26). The town had expanded from 12,500 residents in the 1820s to some 164,000 in the 1840s, and the number of European merchant houses had increased from sixteen in 1822 to over fifty in 1838. Most of the new businesses were British, and there were about 150 Britons living in the city, compared with a third of that number in Cairo.[31] The importance of the British community therefore was more a factor of its strategic position than of its size. In addition, by 1842 more than 3,000 British sailors visited the city annually and over 800 British travellers passed through the city either *en route* to India or as tourists.[32]

ST MARK'S, ALEXANDRIA

The discrepancy between local relations and wider geopolitical concerns marked the project to build a British church in Alexandria, and thus to focus British presence in that city, from its initiation.[33] At the same time as Muhammad Ali granted a site for the church in 1839, Colonel Campbell, backed by British merchants in Alexandria, was in correspondence with Palmerston arguing Muhammad Ali's case against that of the Ottoman Porte

PLATE 26 Plan of the Maydan al-Tahrir, Alexandria, *c.* 1842. (FO 925/3013)

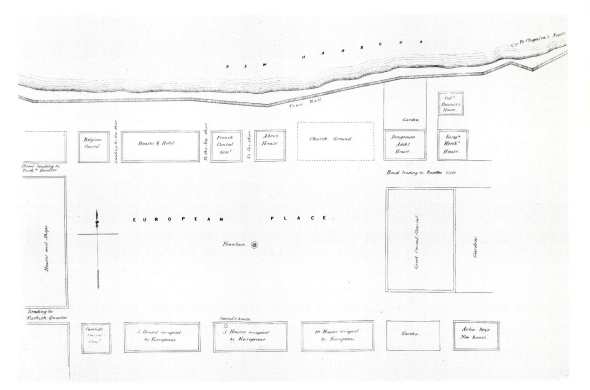

in the Syrian crisis.[34] Possibly the Pasha's gift of the church site, granted specifically to Campbell, was intended as a tribute to his support. It was at least a mark of the good relations between the Egyptian government and the British in Alexandria.[35] The *hodget* or title deed granted by Muhammad Ali contained no conditions about the purpose for which the land should be used. Instead it expressed only rather broad notions of what the Pasha expected: as the *Builder* reported, 'the Pasha . . . expressed a wish that the structure should harmonize with the neighbouring buildings, and be worthy of the English people'.[36] Probably this was nothing more than an unenforced suggestion, but sharply differing notions of harmony and worthiness became a feature of the church's critical reception. The building campaign itself was to drag on, with long periods of inactivity, until 1855.

The problem of funding was partially solved by applying to the Foreign Office for financial aid under the Consular Advances Act of 1825.[37] This legislation was relevant to foreign towns where a British consul was resident and British subjects contributed towards erecting a church, hospital or burial ground. In this situation the consul was authorized to provide a sum equal to the amount raised, providing the plans and estimates had received the prior approval of the Secretary of State. Importantly, the Act did not allow government funds to be granted to missionary societies who were working where there was an insignificant number of British residents:[38] the evangelicals in Jerusalem, for instance, were unable to use this Act to gain funds for their church in 1839.

The first architect selected to design the church was Anthony Salvin, who was something of a pet architect for the Cambridge Camden Society in the early 1840s. Salvin's design was typical of the imitative form of Gothic Revival for which these High Church Ecclesiologists were then campaigning:[39] with a nave and aisles of five bays with round piers, a deep chancel separated by steps and fitted with the appropriate high church furniture, a northern porch, and either a tower with a spire or another porch on the south side. Each vessel was vaulted and each had a separate gabled roof, and the west front was modelled on that of Lanercost Priory, Cumberland.

It should not be surprising, then, that two years later, in a paper read before the Cambridge Camden Society in 1845, Salvin's design was criticized by Benjamin Webb for its unsuitability to a tropical climate. The one climatic adaptation, 'the screening off *inside the church* [by] some great vestibules, in order to get several doors between the outside and the inside', creating a walled-off baptistry and vestry in the western bays of each aisle, was reprehensible to Webb precisely because it did not also accord with the morally argued exterior expression of function that was the cornerstone of the Society's thinking.[40] Elsewhere in his design Salvin had been able to apply this principle, but a vestibule system adapted to the climate could not be reconciled with the still doctrinaire policy of the Cambridge Camden Society. Here he had very similar problems to those faced contemporaneously by J. M. Derick, who in 1844 had provided an Early English design for the Afghan Memorial Church at Colaba, near Bombay (Plate 27). For Webb, both Salvin and Derick's designs had misstated the problem: 'They read the problem thus. Given, an English church, to fit it for the tropics. Instead of, Given, the tropics, and such and such *principles* of architecture, to build by the latter a church to suit the former'.[41] It was not to be for over a decade, and then for a church in Istanbul (see Chapter 5), that a British architect restated the problem in a manner that might have suited Webb's terms.

PLATE 27 J. M. Derick. Design for Afghan Memorial Church, Colaba, 1844. (*ILN*, 1845)

WILD'S DESIGN

PLATE 28 James Wild.
St Mark's, Alexandria,
1846. Engraving of side
elevation and plan.
(*Builder*)

In the same year as Webb's paper, James Wild replaced Salvin as architect of
the church. Wild produced a design based on a simple Early Christian round-
apsed configuration, whose most notable features were a dominating western
portal and a campanile (never built) forming part of a precinct wall distinctly
set off from the main body of the building (Plate 28). Each vessel was well

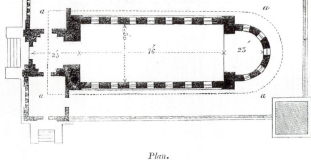

Plan.

proportioned and clearly contrasted by framing devices. Greeted by a deep gateway-like vestibule, visitors would pass under another arch into a relatively narrow nave without aisles. This was separated from the apse by a third remarkable arch, again pointed and horseshoe-shaped. The whole building, campanile and all, was lifted up onto a walled platform articulated by steps and projecting plinths.

Early in its construction, however, the church's design was changed in several external features. The first scheme was recorded in the engraving published by the *Builder* in 1846 and the altered scheme in a perspective drawing (Plate 29) and an engraving (Plate 30). The most apparent difference between the two versions lies in their free-standing bell-towers, which used Islamic and Italian prototypes. The first showed something more like a minaret than a campanile. It was divided into several levels, one half-screened by *mashrabiyyah*, and another with a balcony supported by a *muqarnas* cornice, and topped by a polygonal pavilion or *mabkhara*, itself surmounted by a scalloped cupola. By contrast, the second version had a tapering Venetian

PLATE 29 James Wild. St Mark's, Alexandria, *c.* 1846. Perspective. (V&A, E3660–1938)

PLATE 30 James Wild.
St Mark's, Alexandria, *c.*
1846. Engraving of
sections. (V&A
E4084–1938 R.5.b.)

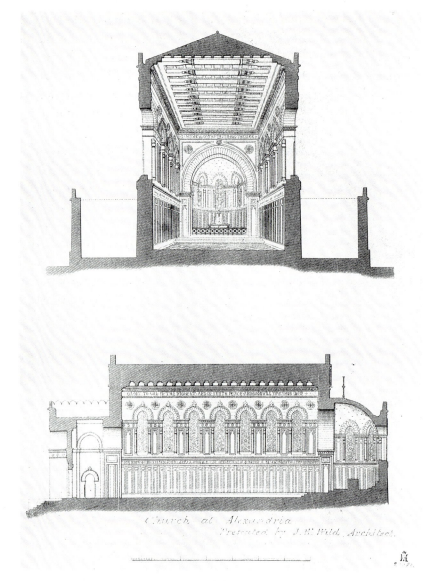

campanile with a pyramidal spire and exhortatory inscriptions in English. There were other differences in the ornament of the two main elevations. The precinct wall in the first scheme continued the recessed panel motif of the bell-tower, while that of the second was blank like its campanile. The spandrels of the nave were decorated with inscribed crosses in the first elevation and with medallions in the second. Finally, the nave windows of the later scheme had cusped archivolts, which were absent in the earlier scheme.

Wild had shifted the focus for his allusions. The first elevation, published in the *Builder*, showed the design then being built and indicated the height of the construction in September 1846. Before the upper parts of the building were completed, Wild had adopted the decorative scheme indicated in the perspective and the signed engraving. During this process he applied more of the Islamic ornament he was then studying in Cairo, transferring the Islamic aspects of the design from the tower to the church's external ornament. Yet although the design became more Islamic in its details, by losing its minaret-like tower it also lost its major orientalist feature.

Wild's church was provocatively eclectic yet largely non-specific in its references. This was especially true of its many Islamic motifs. The *mabkhara* of the first version, and the elaboration of the carved crenellations, medallions and archivolts, might all be based on the ornament that Wild had studied in Islamic Cairo (see Plate 20).[42] Similarly, the *muqarnas*-decorated beams of the wooden roof, visible in the engraved transverse section, were close to those that Wild drew in several Cairene houses.[43] However, the large horseshoe-shaped arches of the portal and interior could have come from a multitude of Islamic sources. But there was one specific borrowing, seen in the bulbous capitals of the window surrounds found in the engravings, similar to those in the Mosque of Ibn Tulun, Cairo.

What was the intention behind this eclecticism and what could it have meant to contemporaries? Wild's design was published with a statement justifying its style as an attempt

> to conciliate the opinion of the Arab inhabitants, and to meet the comprehension of the native artificers ... while [the church] agrees in plan and mass with the style of art used by the early church architects, [it] carries out a general sentiment of Arabian detail.[44]

According to this statement, then, Wild's design successfully referred to the Early Christian history of Alexandria through its use of the earliest Christian architecture, matching the consul-general's invocation of Alexandria as 'the nursery perhaps of our Early Christian discipline'.[45] At the same time its style was also seen as a concession to the present-day Arab inhabitants of the city. Wild had, in effect, added Islamic resonances to those Early Christian associations that the consul-general, consul and residents had increasingly favoured over a Gothic Revival style.

An interesting theoretical parallel to Wild's approach was presented by James Millard in a paper read to the Oxford Society for Promoting the Study of Gothic Architecture, in April 1845. Taking the unsuitability of J. M. Derick's design for the Afghan Memorial Church at Colaba as his starting-point, Millard proposed that in colonies already possessing a national style British architects should adopt that style rather than import a climatically inappropriate European style. Crucial distinctions of identity would be established through 'symbols of creed in form and ornaments'.[46] For Millard an oriental style – presumably Islamic – was not 'essentially opposed to the main principles of Christian architecture', and a church built in this style would also gain from the skill of local craftsmen.[47]

However, the very uniqueness both of Millard's proposition and of Wild's church, and the subtlety with which different forms of reference in the church were balanced and articulated, meant that such eclecticism was inevitably open to differing interpretations. In one of the longest reviews *The Ecclesiologist*'s critic recognized that Wild was attempting a new idea of a Christian church, but argued that a simple symbolism was more important than aesthetics or a 'mistaken spirit of eclecticism' in this setting. There could only be two apparent reasons for Wild's transgressive design:

> The first is deference to the prejudices of the Pasha, who gave the site, and expressed a wish that the building might be handsome; but this we can hardly admit ... The other is that it might be deemed the prelude of the future triumph of Christianity. It might be said that the erection of a new and stately Christian church in a Mohammedan city was so striking an event, that it ought to be commemorated in an especial manner, and that the most appropriate manner was the leading as it were into captivity of the architecture of its already humbled and soon to be vanquished foe. We trust that the Christian Church in Egypt will in her good time spoil the enemy; but the time is not yet come; as yet she must wear her own well-known peculiar garb in things external as well as internal.[48]

For *The Ecclesiologist*, the architectural periodical of the High Church movement, style was a matter of religious identification and national prestige, and Wild's church was a failure – indeed a betrayal – in these terms. In a place of intense rivalry on these fronts only English Gothic or, at least, some form of northern Gothic would do. Only with dominance attained might concessions be made.

The clearest statement on this issue from the residents and their architect is found in a leaflet advertising for subscriptions that they had published earlier in 1846. The leaflet explained how, due to Muhammad Ali's request for some sense of local style, it had been decided

> to adopt a style of architecture creditable to the national taste and not repugnant to the feelings of the local population ... The establishment of the Protestant Church at Alexandria may also, by its

simplicity and spiritual worship, be the means, under Divine favour, of ELEVATING CHRISTIANITY IN THE EYES OF THE NATIVE POPULATION, who have only known the Christian religion through the medium of the Greek and Roman Churches of the East, in which Images and Pictures form their chief ornament, but to which all Mahommedans have a strong repugnance.[49]

The leaflet argued that a missionary role was part of the function of the church and that this could work best by appealing to the Muslim population. Instead of conciliation, the idea of a persuasive proselytism was advanced as a way, at least, of attracting funds. Instead of 'Images and Pictures' the church was to use the same range of resources as Islamic architecture: inscriptions (in English – Plate 31), decoration derived from architectonic forms, geometrical and flattened plant ornament, and elemental symbols of faith (the cross and the six-pointed star).

These texts agreed that the primary issue with Wild's design was about what it stood for rather than purely how it looked. Their divergences centred on how what the church represented would be understood by those meant to receive its meanings. Ostensibly, in both texts, the ideal public was a Muslim Egyptian one: defined as the 'supercilious' followers of a false prophet, with

PLATE 31 James Wild. St Mark's, Alexandria, 1845–54.

an aversion to figurative forms and a tendency to be impressed by spectacle. But the actual audiences to whom these statements were addressed were British architectural groups and potential sponsors of the building. Such audiences might well have been aware of the aggressive competition between France and England in Egypt, but they would have been unused to the employment of an Islamic style for anything but the decoration of ornamental leisure buildings where national prestige was not usually an issue.

Millard's argument for the use of an oriental style and the disagreement over the meaning of Wild's design essayed the terms of a debate that were only fully to be explored thirty years later over the question of a 'Hindu–Saracenic' style for British architecture in India. As Thomas Metcalf has argued, that style attempted to subsume elements of Hindu and Mughal architecture as a metaphor for the conciliation of those cultures under the benevolence of the British Raj.[50] Similarly, Wild's church joined Christian and Islamic forms as a way of epitomizing the bridging tolerance of British presence. Seen from this perspective, Wild's design was nothing less than a trial run for a new form of imperial architecture. In fact, I would suggest that Wild was not merely aiming at an image of tolerant control, rather that there was a genuine appeal for him in the early, 'primitive', forms of monotheistic religions. Taking this further, Wild seems to have been reaching towards an architectural statement that would say something like this: the culture of Anglicanism is not, or should not be, as distinct from the artistic and religious values that have, seemingly, held sway in the Near East since the first few centuries after Christ; Anglican and British culture can be renewed by taking up those forms and this does not imply an indifference to meanings but the possibility of coexistence. Thus a form of ideology was being cast from the very surfaces and spaces of this building.

Without its tower, which was never built, and with most of its ample plot unoccupied, Wild's church must always have made less impact in the square than was originally intended. When the surrounding buildings were replaced with higher structures after their fiery destruction during the British bombardment and the Urabi riots of 1882, even the scale of the church was diminished.

—————

Building a church in Egypt had been a very different experience from building one in England. It was an unprecedented event: the first public statement of Anglican presence in the Near East that was also recognized, or rather propagandized, as a statement of religious toleration. The Protestant chapel at Izmir had been built within the walls of the British consulate (probably during the 1820s); the chapel at Istanbul (destroyed in 1831, rebuilt and destroyed again in 1847, and rebuilt in 1856 – see Chapter 5) was within the compound of the British embassy; and the church at Jerusalem (1839–49 – see Chapter 7), contemporary with St Mark's, could only be built with the proviso that it be attached to a consular residence. With the completion of St Mark's in 1854 there were therefore at least four Anglican churches in the Near East, but only St Mark's might be called a public building and recognized, or rather propagandized, as a statement of religious toleration. Although the purchase of ground by foreigners and the erection of new churches was forbidden in the Ottoman Empire at this time, St Mark's had circumvented these restrictions through the support of Muhammad Ali: first, obliquely, because his aggressive policies had created some ambivalence about Egypt's official subordination to the Porte and to Ottoman laws;[51] and, second, because he had given the site to the British consul-general without any stipulations for its use.

One of the major problems in building the church, as its long construction history shows, was the acquisition of knowledge about local resources and their mobilization.[52] In England, although practices might change, skills decay, quarries become exhausted and taste demand different means, there were nonetheless vernacular traditions of building expertise and institutions through which knowledge could be gathered, preserved and disseminated: institutions such as the architectural press, the Royal Academy and its library, the pupillage system, and the Royal Institute of British Architects. When Wild was building Christ Church, Streatham, he could draw upon inherited knowledge of the properties of stock London brick and its suitability to the climate. He and his contractors knew the skills available amongst masons and bricklayers, and his designs, although innovatory, took cognizance of these locally available resources.[53] He could also prepare estimates (and stay within them) based on reliable experience of the market, of the costs of labour and transportation. By contrast, Wild had been in Egypt barely four months when he first provided a design for St Mark's, and he almost certainly did not speak Arabic at this time, if ever. What knowledge he had gained of architecture in Egypt when he was awarded the commission in June 1845 seems to have been limited to ancient and medieval buildings. His only building commission there had been for a British cemetery gate in Cairo: small, simple in its allusions, and probably unbuilt. Furthermore, Alexandria presented special conditions in Egypt, and apart from passing a couple of weeks in the city after his arrival in September 1842, it seems unlikely that Wild had spent any other time there. One of these special conditions was the boom in Alexandria's building industry, a recent phenomenon brought about by Muhammad Ali's development of the city and the influx of foreign populations. The British community, without specialists in this area, had not yet been involved in this construction boom. When they came to build a church they had to employ European foremen living in Alexandria, Egyptian labour, and a British architect fortuitously travelling in the country.

The most workaday practices in England became exceptional in this situation. Bayle St John, who lived in Alexandria during the mid-1840s, observed some of the work on the church:

> We . . . stopped on the Great Square, to see the keystone put into the great arch of the English church. The working architect, a German, of the name of Weit, seemed actuated by considerable enthusiasm; his hand absolutely trembled with anxiety as he directed the operation. When the stone was let down into its place, and he found it fit to a hair's breadth, he could not contain his delight, and turned to shake hands with me, though I was a perfect stranger. I was surprised to observe that the Arab workmen were not, as in most cases, indifferent and awkward assistants. They had been well trained, and, being adequately paid, felt something of natural pride on the occasion.[54]

This passage also draws attention to the labour employed on the church. It was difficult to retain trained labour, not only because of the construction stoppages but also because the best workmen were often diverted by the Egyptian authorities to work on their own buildings.[55] Since there is no mention of British craftsmen being brought in to do the church's stone carving, such details as the carving of the crenellations, the medallions, window surrounds, cornices and even inscriptions were presumably carried out by local craftsmen. If this is so it would also fit the prescriptions of Millard and others for an indigenous style suited to local skills.

The act of building in a foreign country often indicates permanent intent. The building might be the authentication of real colonial power or the symbolic vessel of intended power. In Wild's church the question of how to embody the nature of British intentions was acutely problematic. The style of St Mark's can be seen as another development of that attempt to find a new style which was local to Wild and the circle around Owen Jones and which involved both rationalist ways of viewing the East and also a clinging to standard themes about it, including a Romantic longing for an unspoiled fusion of art, society and religion. The style could thus question associationist, revivalist and ecclesiological orthodoxies. If there were problems in under- standing the meaning and implications of Wild's design it did at least realize what Islam was popularly meant to be: outwardly showy, non-figurative, intricately decorative, and even ceremonious. It could be accepted that this was no attempt to be Islamic, but to represent Islam.

But the style was local in another way: local to the needs of the British residents, the interests that they shared with Muhammad Ali, and the circumstances of Alexandria in the early 1840s. And it was this aspect of the project, lying between the twin poles of Islam and England, which was ignored in Britain. Simply, the church was built in the midst of a Near Eastern imitation of a European city; built amidst a familiar yet estranging 'jargon of Lingo Franco'. Around it were neither Islamic mosques nor English town halls, but neoclassical consulates and hotels built by Italian architects.[56] Although largely dependent on outside funds, the church was not supervised at a distance but guided by members of a building committee who actually lived in the rapidly changing city and who, as diplomats and businessmen, were continuously aware of the rivalry of other European powers.

If I am right in hypothesizing Wild's intentions, they may be seen as different from, yet complementary to, those of the majority of British residents. For the latter, the mildly transgressive character of the church, the sense that it was vesting itself in the adornments of another culture, could therefore be understood as a deliberate attempt to make it stand out from its immediate European-styled context. While satisfying the religious needs of the Anglican community, it could make affiliations with certain passages in Egypt's history. And by joining Early Christian forms to Islamic details it could be seen to reify a desired harmony between the British community and Egypt's present. It thus attempted to create a myth in which British presence was depoliticized – losing its contingent, fabricated quality – and made to seem a natural result of knowledge and understanding. This message was, of course, more acceptable than the one I have imputed to Wild, but it fits the appearance of the church just as well as his.

5

THE SPECTACLE OF ALLIANCE

BRITISH ARCHITECTURE IN ISTANBUL

•

*Beyoglu is an isthmus between Europe and the Islamic world. From there you
see Istanbul through a telescope.*

(*Cevdet Pasa,* c. *1870*)

On a beautiful day in October 1858, a stone-laying ceremony was held for a
new Anglican church in Beyoglu, Istanbul (Plate 32). Sited on steeply sloping
ground, the church looked southwards across the Golden Horn to the Topkapi
Sarayi and eastwards over the Bosphorus to Uskudar. Journalists reported that,
during the ceremony, an *imam* could be observed inspecting the scene from the

minaret of a neighbouring mosque. After prayers and the singing of a hymn, accompanied by a harmonium, a speech was given by the British ambassador, Lord Stratford de Redcliffe. Stratford drew attention to the new church's function as a memorial to the Crimean War, to its visibility from the sea, and to its proximity both for British residents in nearby Galata and for British merchants in Beyoglu. To explain the church's closeness to the mosque, Stratford referred to 'the increased demand and high value of ground for building [which had] brought the Turkish quarters into requisition'.[1] This should be seen, he argued, as 'at once a proof of the difficulty, and a sign of progress in the advancement of liberal ideas'. Furthermore, it was hoped that the new church would embody the sense of alliance and the continuing 'sympathy and union between rival Powers and repulsive populations'. 'It is not beyond hope', Stratford continued, 'that the same causes may continue to operate, and that the religion of Christ, the religion of peace, may spread far and wide its civilising influence'. After more speeches and prayers the ceremony was concluded by three cheers for the Sultan, who had granted the land, and as many for the Queen.

From at least the moment of this ritual inauguration, the Crimean Memorial Church was implicated in the shifting political, religious, military and economic relationship between Britain and the Ottoman Empire. Stratford regarded it as a monument both to the successful alliance that had fought the Crimean War and to the post-war reform programme that he had helped to impose on the Porte. The church was to symbolize the wider proselytizing role of Anglicanism in the Ottoman Empire. Specifically, its design had to assimilate such local elements as to make it effective while clearly signalling its Britishness: a distorted image of that imperial 'central building' whose model Ruskin had found in the Ducal Palace. The new church had to be used by the British community in the city, yet it was almost entirely the result of the sometimes contradictory wishes of the British at home, particularly of their official representatives in church and state. Finally, it had to satisfy the notion that British presence in Istanbul was somehow benevolent, while simultaneously being the result of European expansion into Muslim quarters.[2] These are the parameters of the colonial project that Stratford saw articulated by the Crimean church, a project with both a particular political job and a multitude of audiences. In these and other respects the resonances and meanings of the Crimean church, both as an ideal project at the time of its competition, and as a completed building, were more intricate than any previous British building in Istanbul and, arguably, more richly layered and overdetermined than much contemporary architecture in Britain.

This chapter describes a constant movement to and fro of resources and discourses between Britain and Istanbul. Those discourses drew heavily on the ideas about Islamic and Byzantine architecture and their settings that were described by the chapters in Part I of this book. These ideas were brought to bear upon the representational burden that the Crimean church, unlike other British architecture in Istanbul, had to carry: that of discreetly placing tokens of orientalism into a structure that was identifiably British and religiously appropriate, meanwhile organizing a site, materials and various agents, often from some distance. Orientalism was ultimately to prove inadequate and even irrelevant in the face of this task and the intractabilities of Istanbul. Other British architecture in the city had found its own means of building. This architecture was official but it was also gauged to local conditions, without the same complex aspirations of the Crimean church.

EARLY BRITISH BUILDINGS IN ISTANBUL

Unlike Alexandria at the time that Wild's church was first mooted, Istanbul was already regarded by the British as sufficiently important to erect government-funded buildings there well before the idea of the Crimean Memorial Church. Both the number of British residents and the number of British ships visiting the city had increased rapidly during the 1840s.[3] Furthermore, as the political capital of the Ottoman Empire, it was crucial to European powers that their embassies be located there. The British built a new embassy in 1842–54, and in 1846 a seaman's hospital was started. In 1849 three other buildings were begun: a consulate, a consular prison and a new chapel in the grounds of the embassy. All five of these buildings were the work of William James Smith, a British architect resident in Istanbul who also worked for the Sultan and members of the Porte. Another British architect, William Barlow, had previously been employed in designing the new Turkish arsenal (1834) on the banks of the Golden Horn.[4] A little way up the Bosphorus, at Ortakoy, the British community erected a small church to the designs of George Wood in 1856. Furthermore, during the early years of the campaign for the Crimean Memorial Church, a large part of the British community in Galata and Beyoglu were planning the erection of their own separate church. Thus, for diplomatic, commercial and religious purposes, the British had gone some way by the mid-1850s towards securing an architectural presence in Istanbul, and their architects were also employed by the Ottoman authorities.

The most prolific of these architects, W. J. Smith, is a fascinating but little-known figure. In 1841, Smith was working as assistant surveyor to Sir James Pennethorne in the Office of Woods and Forests when he was sent out to Istanbul to arrange for the building of the new embassy.[5] The old embassy,

PLATE 33 W. J. Smith.
British embassy,
Istanbul, 1842–54.

PLATE 34 W. J. Smith.
British embassy,
Istanbul, 1842–54.
Courtyard.

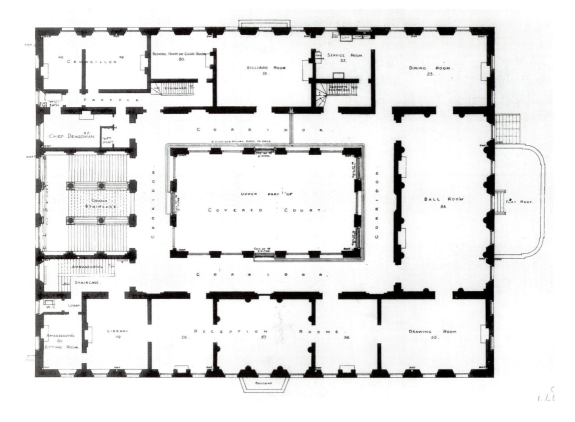

built by Lord Elgin in 1801, had been destroyed in the huge fire of September 1831 that had also devastated most of Beyoglu and almost all the other foreign embassies.[6] The building designed by Smith in 1842 was a grand urban palazzo set incongruously far back within a large walled site on the brow of the hill at Beyoglu (Plate 33). The three-story rectangular block was intended to accommodate all the reception rooms required by the embassy and also residences for most of the embassy staff. The design was based, via Charles Barry's Reform Club (1837–41) in London, on various Roman Renaissance models. Following Barry's building, the embassy sported a glazed inner courtyard, around which were placed all the circulation areas, with the grand staircase on the short northern side of the block (Plates 34 and 35).[7] Like any large London residence, grand public rooms and male and female reception suites – dining-room, drawing-room, a double-height ballroom, sitting-room, card-room, library and billiard room – were located on the first floor.[8]

This quoined, rusticated, urbanely attired building was little different from its fashionable Italianate contemporaries in England. Its familiarity can be explained by the use not only of an English architect, but also an English clerk of works and English foremen, all of whom were sent out to Istanbul.[9] (Building operations were directed from the Office of Woods and Forests in

London, causing lengthy delays in all manner of decisions.) It was also, of course, the representative building of British political presence in Istanbul. No wonder then that one of the most tried and yet most contemporary of styles in England was chosen – it was modern yet steeped in the classical heritage. This was not without its problems. Because the local joiners were unfamiliar with classical detailing, most of the joinery had to be made in England.[10] Smith was disappointed by both the speed and quality of work produced by the local masons.[11] In addition, trained Turkish workmen were forced away by the Sultan's troops to work on the huge Dolmabahce Palace, then being erected down the hill on the banks of the Bosphorus, and good local limestone quarries were taken over by the same project. Such delays meant that, although the ambassador had moved into one floor by 1849, the embassy was not completed until 1854.[12]

PLATE 36 John Murray. Map of Istanbul, *c.* 1871. Arrow indicates location of Crimean Memorial Church. (*A Handbook for Travellers in Constantinople*)

The embassy was built in that part of Istanbul known as Beyoglu (or Pera by the British), located to the north-east of Galata (Plate 36). These two areas, on the other side of the Golden Horn from the old city of Istanbul, were dominated by Europeans and their protégés, and they exemplified the transformation of Istanbul that was noted and regretted (even if they enjoyed its benefits) by many visitors in the 1830s and 1840s.[13] The embassy was just one of many new palatial blocks used by the European ambassadors and placed on either side of the main street through Beyoglu, the Istiklal Caddesi (or Grande Rue de Pera). Most of these embassies were built and rebuilt on ground originally given in the seventeenth century, and had come to form the centre of their 'nations' of officials and merchants. The most imposing of them was the Russian embassy, designed by Gaspare and Giuseppe Fossati in 1837.

Below Beyoglu, rising above the docks and warehouses of the waterside, Galata was the historic town of business and commerce whose role dated at least as far back as the Genoese occupation in the twelfth century. European banks and businesses were situated downhill from the Galata Tower, and it was here in the late 1840s, some two miles from the embassy in Beyoglu yet in the heart of the British community, that the British established many of the elements of what might be termed a consular compound: these included a government-funded seaman's hospital (Plate 37), a prison (Plate 38) and a consulate (Plate 39), all designed by Smith. By 1858 the compound had taken shape (Plate 40), and in 1861 consular shipping offices designed by Henry Pulman, Smith's successor, were added in the same idiom (Plate 41). A British post office, designed by Joseph Nadin (a locally based architect), was built almost opposite the hospital in 1860, and by 1862 houses in this same road

PLATE 37 W. J. Smith. Seaman's hospital, Istanbul, 1846–54. Elevation of 1846 design. (Works 10/42/1)

PLATE 38 W. J. Smith. British prison, Istanbul, 1849–58. Elevation. (Works 10/42/1)

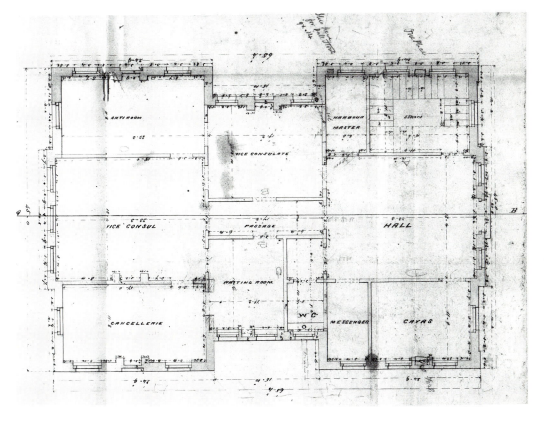

were used as residences by members of the British medical staff.[14] Throughout this period the British were able to invoke local statutes in order to demolish wooden structures that stood close to their stone buildings.[15]

Smith also built a new chapel, St Helena's, within the grounds of the embassy; the last of three chapels that had served embassy staff since 1618.

PLATE 39 W. J. Smith. British consulate, Istanbul, 1849–58. Plan. (Works 10/42/1)

PLATE 40 British
buildings in Galata,
1858. Block plan.
(Works 10/44/5)

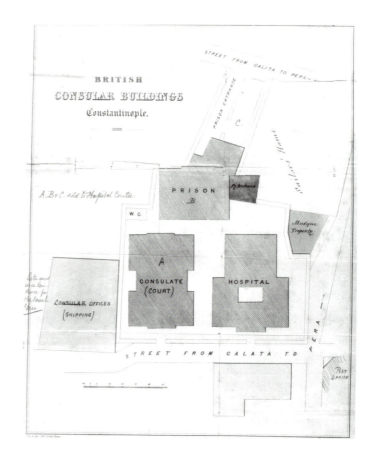

When Smith's building, designed in 1849, finally got under way in 1856,[16] construction was unusually rapid due to the use of British army materials and, inspired by the employment of French soldiers to repair the French embassy, the pressing into service of British sappers and miners stationed in Istanbul because of the Crimean War. Stratford cogently explained this unusual arrangement: 'The case was exceptional; the occasion urgent; the object, economy'.[17] As built, the chapel was simply a preaching box with a shallow apse, a prominent pulpit, and very austere elevations (Plate 42).[18]

Although their restrained classicism is similar to many early nineteenth-century buildings in British India, none of the buildings that W. J. Smith designed for the British government in Istanbul could be said to be recognizably British; certainly European, but not specifically British. In fact, nowhere in the documents relating to these commissions was national identity an articulated issue. Instead, function and institutional decorum were the main concerns. The use of style as an overt agent of affiliation only seems to emerge in British buildings in Istanbul after the Crimean War.

The other interesting aspect of Smith's career in Istanbul came about

PLATE 41 Henry Pulman. Consular shipping offices, Istanbul, 1859–61.

PLATE 42 W. J. Smith. St Helena's Chapel, Istanbul, 1849–56. Side elevation. (Works 10/44/1)

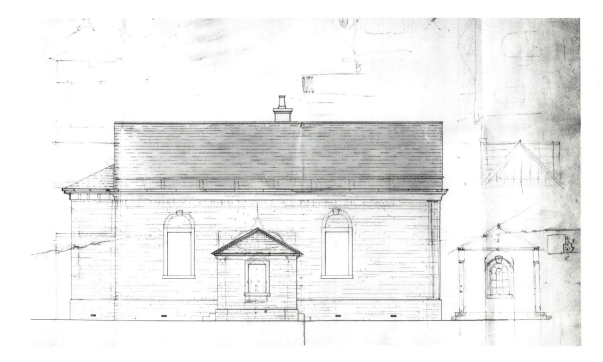

because, while working on the embassy and waiting for his consular buildings to gain approval, Smith began to receive lucrative work on the side. In practice, his career in Istanbul had two faces. He became probably the first foreigner to teach young Muslim architects,[19] and just as remarkably, he acquired a large number of Ottoman commissions for buildings; so much so that he must be counted amongst the most important nineteenth-century architects in Istanbul. Smith designed a variety of buildings: a Turkish military hospital and a naval hospital, a school of medicine (1846–7), the Mecidiye Barracks (c. 1853) and the Selimiye Barracks in Uskudar (c. 1848 – originally started by Kirkor Balian in the 1820s), a winter garden and two kiosks for the Sultan Abdul Mecit I, a building for the Board of Trade, the Naum Theatre in Beyoglu (1851–2), a school for poor Armenians, and houses for Ottoman ministers.[20] When the Board of Works in London enquired about these commissions Smith replied in grandiloquent terms: the work was 'a humble source of aiding … the advancement of civilisation', it was done without payment for 'pure love for my profession and of being useful in a barbarous country struggling to civilise itself … I have done good to British commerce and manufacture'.[21] His self-puffery and sheer effrontery (he had requested an honour from the Porte for his work on one of the hospitals) as well as the knowledge of Turkish that he had learnt on first visiting Istanbul, seemed to have served him well in his intermediary functions.[22] For the Ottomans he was able to supply a European style of architecture and to promulgate modern European building methods as well as a professional model for the architect's role.

One of the most interesting of these buildings was the Imperial kiosk at Tophana, designed for the Sultan in 1853 (Plate 43). The Sultan's decision to build the new Dolmabahce Palace at Tophana (1853, designed by Karabet Balian – Plate 44), on the Bosphorus shore of the European city, was itself a recognition of the new political pre-eminence of that part of Istanbul. Furthermore, while it retained some of the internal arrangements of traditional Ottoman palaces – such as the sequence of *selamlik*, throne room and harem – the new Cinquecento-style palace was outwardly a statement of European architectural ambitions.[23] For British critics, who generally admired it, it represented a fascinating attempt by Turks to speak as modern Europeans. Like the fez that replaced the turban as official Ottoman garb, it was an incomplete attempt since the building displayed a deliberately 'composite' or hybrid appearance. The employment of W. J. Smith to design one of the kiosks or pavilions further down the coast from this palace provided another knowing nod towards modern Europe. Here again a typically Turkish building type, the kiosk, intended for receptions or simply the enjoyment of cool breezes, was dressed in a European architectural style – now a simplified

PLATE 43 W. J. Smith.
Imperial kiosk, Istanbul,
1853. (*Builder*)

PLATE 44 K. Balian.
Dolmabahce Palace,
Istanbul, 1853. (*Builder*)

Venetian Renaissance – and fitted with European furnishings. The facades are notable for their continuous arcades of windows, roof terrace, and covered balcony looking out over the neighbouring artillery parade ground.

Smith's Ottoman commissions, both royal and governmental, are quite exceptional given the near monopoly held by the Balian family of architects.[24] The only comparison is really with the Swiss-born Fossati brothers, who were originally sent from Moscow to Istanbul to build the Russian embassy much as Smith had been sent from England. In Istanbul the Fossatis peddled a similar if more ponderous form of urban classicism, tending more to the forms of the Greek Revival than the Italian Renaissance. After the Russian embassy (1837), they designed the Dutch embassy (1855), and between the two were engaged on new buildings for the Porte (1843) and the massive Istanbul University (1846).[25] The Russian embassy is particularly noteworthy for the massive attached Doric columns of its annexe looming over the Istiklal Caddesi, while the university's Greek portico was raised well above the surrounding streets to look out over the Sea of Marmara.

Smith finally left Istanbul in 1856, having stayed in the city for most of the previous twelve years. He had helped to forge the new European images of the Ottoman establishment and had designed and erected the diplomatic buildings that were to serve the British in their period of greatest influence in Istanbul. He had purveyed the imagery of European culture and the methods of European architects, but not the visual signs of a specifically British architectural politics.

EFFECTS OF THE CRIMEAN WAR

While Smith's work established a continuity of style and practice, the Crimean Memorial Church, the most discussed and the most ambitious British building in Istanbul, has to be seen as a much more one-off affair. This was in part because of the event that it commemorated. Britain's involvement in the Crimean War fundamentally affected both her relationship to the Ottoman Empire and the role of the British in Istanbul. In the short term there was much talk about alliance and the 'sympathy' between nations and, as we saw in Chapter 2, a temporary impetus given to orientalist representations of Turkey. The war also provided a wide conduit for British influence and it seemed to confirm the sequence of reforms, known as the 'capitulations', that Britain had long desired.[26]

There were several obvious effects on British architecture in Istanbul. The war justified the completion of the British consular and hospital facilities already initiated during the late 1840s. Effects of a different kind were brought about by the liberalization of the laws imposed on religious minorities. The British could now purchase ground for the erection of Anglican churches, even if that ground still had to be held by an Ottoman subject or a female foreigner.[27] This they did first in the church designed by George Wood and built for the British middle-class residents at Ortakoy, a few miles up the Bosphorus from Galata, in the spring of 1856. Tiny, cheap and wooden, this first public expression of Anglicanism in Istanbul – the first Anglican church separate from a consulate anywhere in the Ottoman Empire outside Alexandria – was also built in that most reliable of national styles, Early English Gothic.[28]

The rebuilding of the embassy in Beyoglu and the establishment of a consular complex in Galata had defined the immediate areas of British presence within the new city before the Crimean War. After the war the entire European enclave took on a more confident and expansionist attitude. Their quarter of the city, Beyoglu and Galata, was mostly inhabited by members of the non-Muslim commercial mediator class – the 'noncomformists of Turkey'[29] – many with diplomatic protection, and made up of Armenians, Jews and Greeks. One Turk described Beyoglu as

> The creature of the capitulations. The foreign ambassadors reign there. You have the streets in which you cannot walk, houses jammed together without a plan, and a population which is *la crème de la canaille* . . . It shows what is gained by withdrawing people from their natural rulers.[30]

By 1858 half of the suburb's inhabitants were not subject to the indigenous legal institutions.[31] Some Europeans even admitted that the reason that diplomats lived in Beyoglu was 'The desire . . . to domineer – to inhabit a place in which they can insult the Turks'.[32] Muslims were pushed out into the peripheral, less salubrious areas.[33] An overt identification with European institutions took place in the non-Muslim areas: an opera house and various private clubs opened, a philharmonic society was formed, and the city's first public gas lighting was installed.[34]

In this context, the influence of the British community vastly outweighed its still minuscule if increasing size. Its influence was proportionate to its ability to apply diplomatic and commercial pressure. It had its own newspapers, it endowed schools and colleges for the 'redemption' of eastern Christians, its businessmen often dealt in legally prohibited articles, and, by the late 1850s, it had its own consular buildings and several churches planned or already built.

Another element entered this brew in the 1850s when the Society for the

Propagation of the Gospel in Foreign Parts began supplying chaplains to British forces in the Crimea, and took over as their own the idea of erecting a prestigious church in Istanbul.[35] Established in 1701, the SPG was High Church and had missionaries and churches all over the world. Although conversion was against Qu'ranic law, an Ottoman edict of 1856 had bound the Porte not to persecute converts.[36] Thus encouraged, the SPG had installed two chaplains in Beyoglu well before work had started on the Crimean Memorial Church.

During the 12-year period (1856–68) in which the Crimean Memorial Church was discussed, revised and finally erected, the fortunes of the SPG in Istanbul fluctuated wildly. It was the most prominent Anglican religious force in the city, and in the post-war years it emerged as a missionary force aimed at Muslims. By the time that its church was completed, however, the SPG had been forced to limit and moderate its activities just at the same moment as the influence of the British in Istanbul was being eclipsed by that of other powers.

THE COMPETITION – CONDITIONS AND THEORY

The discussion now turns back to England and specifically to those High Church and architectural circles where prevailing notions of church architecture were proposed, debated and adapted as solutions to the very different context of Istanbul. Much of this discussion concerns style, both as it was perceived in the submitted designs and as it was thought it might be understood in Istanbul. Victorians had, as we have already remarked, an openly and avowedly communicational conception of style: it was 'phonetic', or it had 'expressional character'.

An international competition for the new building was announced on 28 April 1856 by a committee made up of vested interests in the state, church and military. They chose five judges and set the rules of the competition.[37] Amongst the judges the dominating force was A. J. B. Beresford Hope: Tory politician, architectural theorist, and wealthy High Church patron. His influence is detectable in the conditions and in the outcome of the competition, and he was the linchpin in all the decisions and manoeuvres made in the frustrating years before George Edmund Street's appointment in 1863.

The terms of the competition demonstrate how architectural style was intended to convey very specific cultural and religious messages. The major problem for the competitors was their ignorance of the size and location of the site, for none had yet been secured. They were given relatively specific instructions on the style, cost and size of the building, though little idea of what kind of church was envisaged. Entrants were restricted to a Gothic style modified to suit the climate, with southern European Gothic indicated as a suggestive source. Any imitation of forms suggesting Islamic or Byzantine architecture was expressly forbidden, thus implicitly prohibiting the use of domes.[38] Nevertheless, in apparent deference to what was perceived as one of the salient characteristics of Islamic culture, the competitors were not allowed to employ representations of the human form, either inside or out. A Byzantine style, which might have been seen as aptly expressive of East–West alliance, was rejected partly to avoid any ambiguous association with Orthodox Christianity or confusion with the converted mosques of the city, and partly because of the idea, still prevalent in British architectural theory – as discussed in Chapter 3 – that Byzantine was a crude, half-developed style.

The conditions of the competition were meant to keep the church free from stylistic and therefore semantic confusion with Greek Orthodox or Islamic buildings. Beresford Hope explained the judges' prohibition of this style, and anything redolent of it, in terms of propriety and national identity:

> I have yet to learn if [Byzantine] types are suitable to our own Church or if they can with any advantage or any success be so adapted as to reappear in the form of what I must for want of a better name style 'English Byzantine' . . . If we build our Church in imitation of a Greek Church is it not much to be feared that the authorities and the members of the Oriental Communion, who have hitherto known us by the light of their prejudices and not of their knowledge, may take umbrage at the proceeding and imagine that it is a liberty rather than a compliment on our part – that in short we wish to sail under false colours, and take borrowed credit from them? To make them like us we must first make them respect us, and this can best be achieved by our honestly taking our stand in our own character.[39]

A similar combination of principle, expediency and predicted response had guided the *The Ecclesiologist*'s response to Wild's Alexandria church. The new church in Istanbul had to be of 'our own character', but for High Victorian theorists, especially for High Churchmen, this was a rapidly evolving concept in the mid-1850s.

The stipulation to adopt a certain form of Gothic, and its use as an image for the SPG, must thus be seen in relation to the relevant debate on style within British architectural discourse. Crucially, two of the five members of the committee, Robert Willis and Beresford Hope, were closely involved with that elite High Church periodical, *The Ecclesiologist*. More than a decade earlier

The Ecclesiologist's architect, Anthony Salvin, had advocated an Early English Gothic model, largely unadapted to the climate, for the new British church in Alexandria. Benjamin Webb had pointed out the inappropriateness of that model and, by the late 1840s, Ecclesiologists had revised their arguments. In 1846 they called for two different kinds of colonial church architecture: a hyperborean style for the north and a speluncar style for the south. The former was to be thin, linear, light and monochrome. The latter was to be a thickly walled, polychromatic tropical style based on the precedents of Gothic architecture in southern Europe.[40]

In the 1850s High Victorian theory had moved quite far from the spare strategy of English Gothic copyism and adaptation of the previous decade. A key new concept in this move, as David Brownlee has shown, was that of 'development', as understood by John Henry Newman and adopted from him to justify elaborating and modernizing a static model of architectural correctness.[41] In addition, Ruskin's *Seven Lamps of Architecture* (1849) and *Stones of Venice* (1851–3) drew critical attention to the virtues of Italian Gothic. Furthermore, in their theory, as well as in their buildings, G. G. Scott and George Edmund Street had justified the use of foreign versions of Gothic and even the adoption of what were regarded as classical principles, such as that of horizontality.[42] Street and William Burges had introduced the High Gothic of thirteenth-century France with their entries for the Lille Cathedral competition of 1855.

This eclecticism, always woven into a Gothic matrix, was also espoused by Beresford Hope.[43] He saw that Gothic could no longer be used simply for its narrowly national associations, but that it could represent a broader notion of Christian civilization suited to an imperial vision:

> That Gothic *must* be the main ingredient appears to us demonstrable from the fact that Gothic was the universal emanation of the mind of Christian Europe, or at least of its active portion, in the days when that polity which is now overspreading the world was cradled. It was European – it was Christian – it was conclimatic with the chief regions of organised civil polity.[44]

He also saw how, in the case of the Crimean Memorial Church, this issue was made acute:

> A single church in the middle of Constantinople built in Northern Gothic would have been in partial, if not offensive, contrast to every other building in that city, and would accordingly have proved an architectural failure, and not improbably the cause of much social

heartburning. On the other side, a church which was not Gothic at all would have erred in the opposite extreme, and been unworthy to have been the monument of a western nation.[45]

The solution was to use a form of southern Gothic. Hope had a large range of examples in mind, from Seville to Crusader churches in Palestine.[46] But Italian Gothic seemed to be the safest option for most entrants. Of course Italian Gothic was not just a transalpine form of northern Gothic, simply made appropriate for a different climate; it was often deeply infused with the Byzantine architecture of Ravenna and Venice and the Islamic architecture of Sicily.[47] Furthermore, for the immediate concerns of the Crimean church and the memorialization of the English dead, Italian Gothic might seem incongruous and connotatively obscure, to say the least. But there were at least two views that could justify it to laymen. First, the adoption might perhaps be seen as an expression of the European alliance that had aided Turkey in the Crimean War. Second, as with Beresford Hope, the style could be regarded as an expression of the co-nationality of Gothic architecture which arose, not on a national basis, but – so the rhetoric went – out of a certain family of nations: Gothic equalled Europe which equalled Christianity.[48] But even if this equation was desirable, it could rarely be expressed so baldly. Instead, the effective theoretical sleight-of-hand was to see Italian Gothic, unlike northern Gothic, without any specifically Italian connotations but as merely instrumental; while any northern elements synthesized into the design were to be actively symbolic, signifying nationality.[49]

COMPETITION ENTRIES

The judging of entries and the responses to the designs reveal much both about the significance accorded to this building and the purposes of its builders. All four prizewinners – the winner William Burges, George Edmund Street, who was placed second, the third-placed George Frederick Bodley, and William Slater, who was awarded a special prize – were members of the Ecclesiological Society and all used Gothic styles. Every submitted design had a review or a description in the contemporary literature, providing a good sense of the range of designs entered. Many of the designs used an extensive amount of internal and external polychromy in an attempt to evoke Italian Gothic. Both 'hyperborean' and 'speluncar' solutions were adopted for the climatic conditions, but most of the rejected designs were far too ambitious for the stated funds and did not take account of the climate or the guidelines concerning materials.[50] Several were simply too homespun, still using an

PLATE 45 G. E. Street.
Competition design,
Crimean Memorial
Church, 1857.
Watercolour of interior
of chancel. (RIBA
V19/89)

PLATE 46 G. E. Street.
Competition design,
Crimean Memorial
Church, 1857.
Watercolour of west
front. (RIBA V19/91)

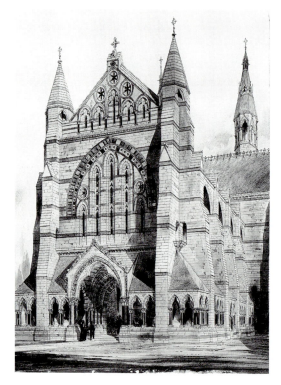

unmodified form of English Gothic. Others were discarded because they ignored the implied veto on domes. And the seven entries by foreign architects all received dismissive reviews.[51]

Several of Street's much-admired competition designs survive and these show a design that was strikingly unusual in at least two respects, both of which seem to be contextually orientated (Plates 45–8).[52] First, an exterior cloister was wrapped around the sides of the nave, linking with the west entrance to form a narthex. This was intended as a barrier to the heat but also served to veil the massiveness of the buttresses and to create an unusual amount of roof area on and around the nave. It may have been inspired by a similar feature in J. M. Derick's much-discussed design for the church in Colaba, Bombay (see Plate 27), which also had a memorial function as a church to the English dead of the First Afghan War of 1840, and certainly this feature continued to appear in British buildings in India.[53] The second unusual feature was the pair of slender polygonal bell-towers that Street placed in the angles between transepts and chancel. Perhaps the minarets of mosques in the background of Street's engraved view were intended to alert people to the source for the shape, and even the number, of these bell-towers, but no such correlation was made by any of the reviewers. Otherwise, the constructional polychromy of the exterior, with its thin parti-coloured bands, had been learnt by Street from Italian Gothic and recommended by him in 1855.[54] Street used

PLATE 47 G. E. Street. Competition design, Crimean Memorial Church, 1857. Perspective. (*Builder*)

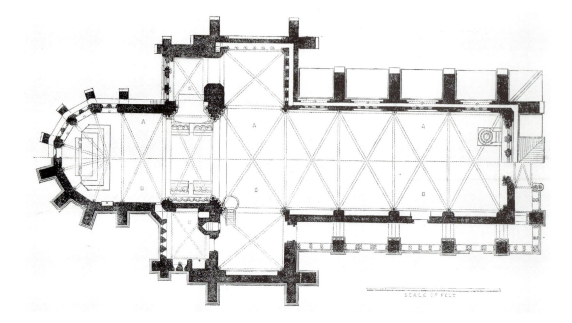

SCALE OF FEET

both inner and outer tracery in order to modulate the light of the slender windows. Below them, in the nave, vast wall spaces were left bare, presumably for commemorative inscriptions as frescos were excluded by the terms of the competition.

Although Street's design was recognized by Beresford Hope as an 'Italianizing translation of Middle Pointed', it was also seen by him and the other judges, despite the two features noted above, as unadapted for Istanbul and insufficiently southern.[55] However, to confuse the issue, *The Ecclesiologist* preferred Street's design for this very reason: no English architect was better qualified 'to engraft Italianising features on Northern Pointed', yet Street had chosen to 'clothe a Northern thought in the expression and detail of the South, rather than to borrow the original idea from the South, and translate it into a Northern dialect'. Thus it was 'rugged', 'austere', and 'unmistakeably English'.[56] Such characteristics meant that his entry was also preferred by more aesthetically conservative periodicals such as *The Gentleman's Magazine*, which opposed the use of Italian Gothic as a 'mongrel' style, 'not indigenous and never fully naturalized'.[57] Certainly the predominant effect of the design was derived from Anglo-French sources, with relatively minor ingredients taken from Italian Gothic. But other factors must also have played a part in denying Street first prize. The prodigious stone groined vault (covering an open aisleless plan that recalled Albi Cathedral or King's College Chapel) would have demanded an expensive structural system. In his memoir, Street had specifically defended the design's chapel-like aspect, but in scale it was more like a cathedral: the breadth and depth of the sanctuary, for instance, which was of the same height as the nave, seemed fitted for a bishop's seat.[58]

BURGES'S COMPETITION DESIGN

Evidently there was some confusion over the type of building that was expected by the judges. Where the third-placed G. F. Bodley supplied a parish church, Street designed a large chapel of cathedral proportions. Burges, on the other hand, submitted a small cathedral, and it was his design – with its tripartite internal elevation, and its aisles, transept and ambulatory – that proved closest to the thinking of Beresford Hope (Plate 49).

The periodical owned by Hope, *The Saturday Review*, had greeted the announcement of the competition with a fulsome call for a major architectural work:

In a monumental church built in such a place, for such an object, and at such a time, there is no room for any compromise between magnificence and economy – no possibility of remaining satisfied

PLATE 49 W. Burges. Competition design, Crimean Memorial Church, 1857. Plan. (RIBA W16 Set no. 1)

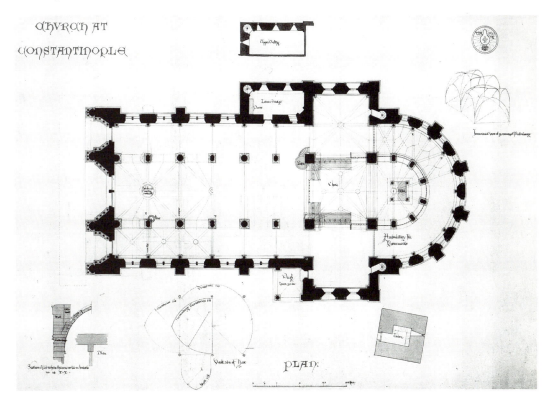

with a cheap and unpretending structure … we must build at
Constantinople what everybody will understand when we call it a
Cathedral.[59]

Beresford Hope was fully to formulate this thinking, using Burges's design as
one of his models, in his 1861 book *The English Cathedral of the Nineteenth
Century*. There he argued that modern cathedrals, and those elements of
architecture that denoted a cathedral, were urgently needed to help evangelize
within the teeming cities.[60] He recognized Burges's design as a miniaturized
form of a continental type, implying that this was important not only because
of the church's role as a flagship of Anglicanism in Istanbul but also for future
evangelizing efforts.[61]

In an astute piece of marketing Burges announced that he had based his
design on the thirteenth-century church of S. Andrea at Vercelli (Plates
49–52). Burges's competition memoir referred to the theory that Vercelli had
been built by English money and English workmen, and therefore in
circumstances apparently close to those of the projected Crimean church – a
similar problem similarly resolved.[62] Arguments about Vercelli's 'Englishness' had hinged on the single feature of the square choir. It is curious then

PLATE 50 W. Burges.
Competition design,
Crimean Memorial
Church, 1857. South
elevation. (RIBA W16
Set no. 1)

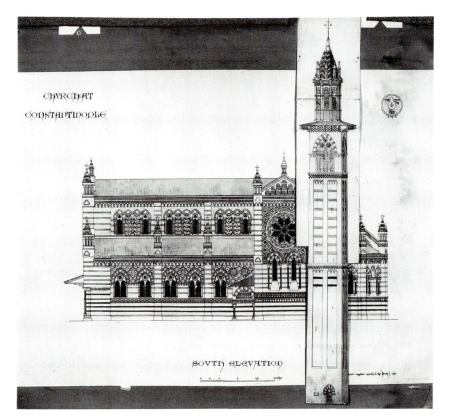

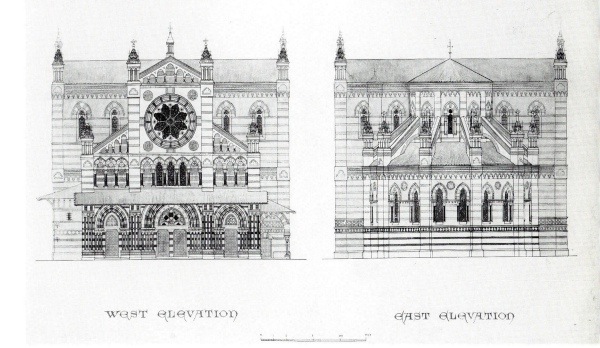

CHVRCH AT
CONSTANTINOPLE:

WEST ELEVATION   EAST ELEVATION

that Burges replaced this with a semi-circular French apse (with an ambulatory intended for monuments) and chose to imitate the most un-English aspects of his model: the arcaded corbelling, the deep portals, the square pinnacles caged in by colonettes, and even the campanile placed at an odd angle to the body of the church; borrowings which were largely unnoticed by the reviewers. By contrast, G. F. Bodley had insisted that the square east end of his design was its most important link with Vercelli.[63]

Burges's drawings, like some other entries, were brilliantly coloured.[64] On the exterior much of this colour took the form of diaper or zigzag patterns in the spandrels and the panels placed between buttresses (Plates 50–51). The deepest red was reserved for the surface revealed behind the blind arcades on the west facade, while yellow marked the upper walls of the transept and apse. Non-figurative ornament was used in roundels, and the design was bound together by chequerboard courses, coloured voussoirs, and columns of different marbles.

The interior was as rich in its applied and constructional colour as the

PLATE 51 W. Burges. Competition design, Crimean Memorial Church, 1857. West and east elevation. (RIBA W16 Set no. 1)

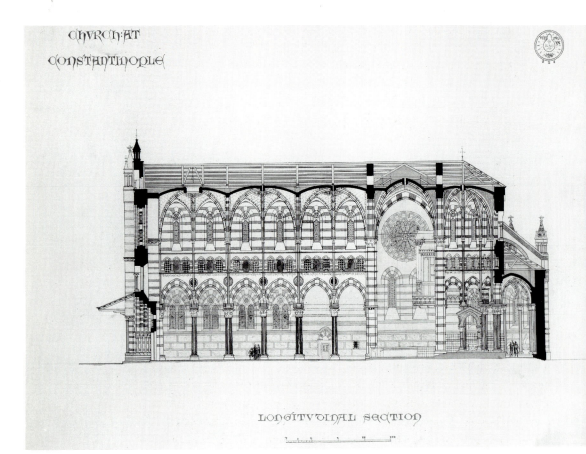

CHVRCH·AT
CONSTANTINOPLE

LONGITVDINAL SECTION

PLATE 52 W. Burges.
Competition design,
Crimean Memorial
Church, 1857.
Longitudinal section.
(RIBA W16 Set no. 1)

exterior, although here Burges more actively plundered from Early French Gothic (Plate 52). The walls of the aisles were to be banded with black limestone above a panelled dado of red and white marble. The nave columns would be of alternately red and black marble with white marble capitals and gilt abaci, and above them the stone filling the triforium would be decorated by incised patterns, with the incisions then filled up by black mortar. Arches everywhere were shown with alternately coloured voussoirs. Ribs would have alternate voussoirs of red terracotta and stone. In the chancel the coloured decoration was richer still: the chancel vaults were painted blue with yellow stars, the pavement was of inlaid marble, the capitals of the columns were coloured, and the triforium had mosaic decoration. There are two particularly interesting features of this interior. One is the subtle allusion to shallow Byzantine domes that Burges made in his nave vaulting by giving the meeting of the sexpartite vaults a broad circular decoration emphasizing the coloured boss stone. The other – a theme that will be more fully developed in due course – is the fact that in his memoir Burges stated his intention to utilize local mosaic and marquetry for some of this decoration, thereby appealing to the Romantic orientalism of many of his viewers and immediately setting himself apart from almost all the other entrants.[65]

BURGES'S DESIGN – INTERPRETATION

Although the judges had little doubt that Burges had made the best synthesis of national and southern elements, other critics demurred, and the debate over the character of Burges's design was extensive. This reveals both the pressing need to clarify the projected meanings in a design of this importance, and also the way in which meaning could change as the design was measured against different interests.

In the judges' opinion northern Gothic had been 'kept in view' and Italy referred to for examples: 'so many of the English characteristics', they said, 'are retained as are not inconsistent with the climate; but those which are so have been boldly changed'.[66] In a lengthy review *The Ecclesiologist* raised its own doubts about the appropriateness of the winning entry, especially on its right to be granted first prize given its 'thoroughly un-English' style compared with the 'unmodified Teutonism' of Street's.[67] *The Builder*, noticing the ambiguity of the competition rules, called the style Byzantine and argued that the extent to which Burges deployed coloured horizontal banding – 'emphatically a Mahometan feature' – must have crossed even the confused interdictions of the rules of the competition.[68] The reviewer linked this banding to the theory of cladding that the architectural theorist Gottfried Semper had traced back to pre-Islamic nomad tribes. Nevertheless, *The Builder*'s reviewer was sympathetic to Burges: the 'excess' of the design's external colour was appropriate since it would fit the building to the climate, the adjacent buildings and even the local costume.[69]

There was clearly good reason for reviewers to detect an orientalizing element in Burges's design. They either pinpointed this as something specific such as the penthouse roof on the west facade, or they detected it more generically in the minaret-like campanile. Elsewhere the hybridism inherent in Gothic meant that the ogee arches of the apse windows, or the vibrant banding of the walls, could be doubly allusive. Any of these things might represent the Orient, and yet they could all be justified with occidental precedents. Paradoxically, one virtue of this was that the allusion could simply be ignored, as Robert Willis did when he saw nothing but the 'decidedly Italian' in Burges's front.[70] By contrast, *The Ecclesiologist* had an insufficient sense of that kind of climatic adaptation 'which could tell its own story of an English monumental church planted in the city of the Sultan'.[71] *The*

Gentleman's Magazine came to similar conclusions by different reasoning. It saw Burges's design as thoroughly Roman Catholic in its plan and arrangements, and Street's as preferable: 'for an English memorial church at Constantinople, let us have a church English in design, English in its character, and one suited to the service of an English church'.[72]

Burges answered this kind of criticism several years later when he described the way medieval builders had adapted their style in Jerusalem and concluded:

> Had we followed their example of sound good sense in the works required in our Colonies and in India, we should never have seen such a monstrosity as Calcutta Cathedral, to say nothing of sundry Lincolnshire churches with their large windows and high roofs transplanted to the burning climate of India.[73]

Presumably if there were English or Teutonic references in his own Crimean design they were never intended to be quite so blatant, nor so blatantly inappropriate. Burges's words indicate the particular value of his own solution to colonial church-building, and recognition of this can be seen in the influence of his Crimean design in India itself. Walter Granville's Kanpur Memorial Church (1862–75), G. G. Scott's Senate Hall for the University of Bombay (*c.* 1876) (Plate 53), and William Emerson's All Saints, Allahabad

PLATE 53 George Gilbert Scott. Senate Hall, University of Bombay, *c.* 1876. (*Builder*)

(1869–93), all adopted many features of his colourful synthesis of Gothic features and climatic adaptation, discreetly open to non-western allusions.

It is significant that there was considerable critical disagreement and confusion about how to designate and how to assess Burges's exterior and yet very little of this in reactions to his interior and plan. Perhaps this interpretative division can be explained in terms of a rift between how the public and private worlds of the British community in Istanbul might be perceived. Whilst the meaning of the private inner space is unquestioned, the exterior, the public realm of exchange with Turkish culture and the object of oriental scrutiny, is stretched in these comments between the allure of exoticism, the need for self-representation, and the seemingly irrelevant Italian factor.

A crucial part was played here by the manner in which Burges had presented his design in his watercolour and engraved views, purposely adopting an assimilative ploy by matching his design with an imagined Turkish environment (Plate 54). On one level this was a deliberately confounding device, as in the case of the campanile drawn on the exterior views but quite impractical given the limited funds available. On another level, Burges's scenographic assimilation was a way of intimately binding or drawing his building within the compass of an exotic East, while retaining its discrete High Anglican meanings.

It is no coincidence that the Turkish crowds represented in the foregrounds of these perspective views have the same clutter and are involved in the same eastern customs that were so closely observed in the literature and paintings of contemporary orientalists.[74] A myth is being created here of a distinct, traditional way of life contained by and in harmony with the proposed church. In the watercolour these activities crowd around the front of the church, where the porch roof, both literally and symbolically, shelters the Turkish brethren. The church is harmonized with the buildings surrounding it. The view is framed on the left by the coved cornice of a wooden house; a form that is echoed by the curves of the pointed arches and rose window in the church. Behind the church is the dome of a mosque, but the exact physical relationship is unclear: a clever, if perhaps underhand method of giving the church scale and grandeur while keeping to the competition rubric excluding Byzantine and Islamic elements. But more importantly, this linkage was also a way of negating differences, assuming equality, and absorbing oriental architecture into the British scheme. The free-standing tower, for instance, is placed in an ambiguous relationship to both buildings. Partially hidden at the bottom by the crowd and a cast shadow, and camouflaged mid-way up by the projection of an eave belonging to a house in the foreground, the tower might easily be mistaken for a minaret. Furthermore, in the *Building News* engraving

the arcaded corbelling on the transept of the church is placed close to the drum arcade of the mosque immediately behind and above it. Indeed, so closely alliterative are these parts, that the mosque might seem to be of the same style as the church. Finally, above the whole scene, the cross of the church and the crescent of the mosque sail in apparent equality. Burges's design might then be seen as a kind of allegory of empire that narrativizes the components of Britain's ideal relationship with its host.

Although this kind of allegorical integration was intended for a home audience, its method of exchanging and apparently merging outward appearances might be understood in parallel to the rhetoric of diplomatic relations. At this time the British indulged in a remarkable amount of ritual and symbolic interaction with the Ottoman establishment. Best remembered, and most unprecedented, was the Sultan's attendance at a British embassy fancy-dress ball in 1856, but there were also inspections of the British fleet, a presentation of the Order of the Garter to the Sultan, and the gift of Hittite antiquities to the British Museum.[75] Such interactions were largely unilateral in their initiation, however, and certain members of the Porte felt that the Sultan and the government lost prestige in the eyes of their own public through their participation.[76] Nevertheless, these kinds of spectacles of alliance could extend also to a gift of land and a stone-laying ceremony, and for a British audience they could find their expression in an architectural competition and the exhibited and published views of the winning design. With all of them the alliance is one between governments, between national representatives, and this is the key to an understanding of the particular colonial project that gathered impetus behind the Crimean Memorial Church and that was dissipated as the political moment departed.

BURGES IN ISTANBUL

Like Wild when he travelled to Egypt, Burges would have been familiar with debates about orientalism in England before he arrived in Istanbul. He knew Owen Jones's work and he knew Ruskin's, but their open conflict in the late 1850s had not yet clearly emerged and it is unlikely that Burges, who was both a Romantic medievalist and a professional and practising architect, would have felt any need to favour one to the exclusion of the other. He reached Istanbul in June 1857 and stayed for four months, having prepared himself with the standard guides and travelogues and made some attempt to learn Turkish.[77] Intelligence gathering was the real purpose of this visit. Burges's practical objectives were to inspect and make a plan of the site, to make enquiries concerning materials and labour, and to investigate local crafts.

PLATE 54 W. Burges. Crimean Memorial Church, 1857. Watercolour. (RIBA N38)

Istanbul was expensive. Burges found that labour was double its cost in England due to the rate of work, the many feast days, and the difficulties of transporting materials.[78] He made contact with British residents who had knowledge of the local building industry, learning from them and his own observation more precise information about local quarries and the relative costs of marble, bricks, rubble and wood.[79] Thus equipped he could then decide which parts of the building it would be feasible to ship out from England, given the price of freight and import duties. It must have been quite clear to Burges from this information and the relative costs of the Russian, British and French embassies – all built within the previous twenty years – that Turkey's spiralling inflation could cripple any lengthy building project.[80]

Although most of his time was spent in negotiations and enquiries concerning the Crimean Memorial Church, Burges was also fascinated by the practical and aesthetic tips that he could glean from Turkish artifacts and architecture. Ottoman mosques held certain lessons: 'how ... an effect of breadth is obtained by restraining the ornament to a very few places'; the importance of massiveness in the use of columns (confirming something that he had learnt from French Gothic); and the constructional and aesthetic use of tie-rods (in this case substantiating hints he had already gleaned from Italian architecture and applied in his competition design). The Suleymaniye was particularly praised, and favourable comparisons were made with St Mark's, Venice, and Hagia Sophia. Most of all he commended the decorative work that he saw: the carvings on the insides of the caiques, the double-glazed stained glass, and the richly decorated furniture.[81] In his notebooks he listed the most typical medieval objects: 'The shops have shutters like in Viollet le Duc's Dictionary ... The door handles ... divans around room ... ceilings ... padlocks ... the chests ... the gratings in front of windows'.[82]

Undoubtedly much of this fascination with Turkish crafts was generated by Burges's desire, expressed in the memoir that accompanied his competition design, to incorporate some of them into the decoration of the Crimean church. But it was also an interest that Burges was specifically instructed to pursue by the SPG. Before leaving England he was directed to look at the 'local art manufactures' of Istanbul, particularly for instance a 'peculiar school of mosaic painters', to see whether such work could be incorporated in the church.[83] The term 'art manufactures' is worthy of note here. It had gained currency in the 1840s with its use by Henry Cole and the Society of Arts to mean artist- or architect-designed decorative work for industrial production, rather than a factory-based system of production where design might be left to specialist functionaries within the system. It was also posited as an alternative to an older and apparently dying tradition of independent craftsmen, designing and making their own products. By the 1850s this emphasis on the artist or architect's ruling authority was common amongst Gothic Revivalists: certainly to Beresford Hope, Burges, and other Ecclesiologists.[84]

In Istanbul, then, it seems that Burges was exploring local crafts in order to find out which were most suitable to the church and to his own role as the design leader. In the SPG's directions, the phrase 'with or without modification' may imply a kind of comprehensive but guiding role on the part of the architect. But there was certainly not to be any possibility that these crafts were to have the kind of freedom that Ruskin had come to envisage at about this time, where the artisan might have a role almost indistinguishable from the architect. In this sense Burges, though he admired Ruskin's work, was clearly closer to that vision of the procedures and effects of oriental design contributing to a modern organization of labour; closer to Owen Jones and James Fergusson and to an idea of empire as springing outward from a rationally and industrially driven centre but building on the appropriate models at its periphery. Fergusson, similarly, marvelled at India as a medieval culture, threatened by the importation of western forms and methods, whilst also being a staunch advocate in Britain of basing architecture on the example of industrial production and the division of labour.[85]

It was thus a necessary paradox that, in common with those travellers to Istanbul who often commented on the westernization of the city, Burges deplored the influence of his own culture, whether it was printed Manchester cottons, English and French carpets, or dull European clothes.[86] He adopted standard opinions about the areas of Istanbul on the northern side of the Golden Horn. Galata and the old city were still, as Burges later wrote, like a kind of Pompeii for the medievalist; whereas, in awful proximity, Beyoglu represented what the medievalist was escaping:[87]

> The population of Pera exactly answers to Gibbon's description of that of the Latin kingdom of Jerusalem. The state of society is utterly bad, avarice is the ruling passion and everyone cheats everybody else.[88]

Again, Burges's reactions were guided by previous literary authorities: here it was Gibbon, but it could also be Viollet or any of several recently written travelogues. This clearly accords with what Edward Said has called the citationary or reiterative element in orientalism, that chain of authorities that was enough in itself to prove its contentions.[89] Yet Burges's orientalist lens was to prove inappropriate and ultimately irrelevant to the task of seeing his designs realized.

THE SITE

Burges's fears about inflation were to be justified, but of more critical immediacy was the question of where the new church was to be built; a question, as with all the other buildings considered here, of wider significance than simply that of finding a place for the church. When Burges travelled to Istanbul a site had still not been acquired. After adapting his design for a site equidistant from both the British embassy and the landing at Tophana (with its British naval offices), a site was finally acquired just off the Kumbaraci Yokusu (Plate 55 and see Plate 36). This had the drawback of proximity to a mosque, but it was twice the size of the granted land at Galatasaray and had excellent visibility.[90] Here the projected church could be a beacon of Anglicanism and, it was hoped, a harbinger of change.

While the location of this site demonstrates the degree of European expansion in the new city during these post-war years, it also shows that change could be both transient and to some extent resisted. Burges predicted that although the site was on the edge of areas of European residence, and some distance from the British living in Galata and the embassy in Beyoglu, it would soon be encompassed:

> The fact is that it *was* the Turkish quarter, but the Europeans are gradually encroaching upon it; and in a few years (even if our Church should not have been built there) it will cease to be inhabited by the Turks.[91]

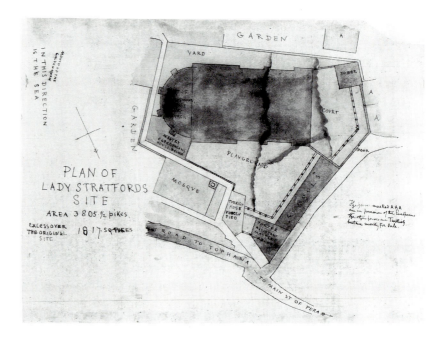

PLATE 55　W. Burges. Plan of the Kumbaraci Yokusu site, Istanbul, 1857. (USPG CLR 90)

In the site plan that accompanied this letter Burges marked houses around the site that were already inhabited by 'Franks' and noted that the others were mostly ready to be sold. From this and from contemporary maps it can be seen that this final site, on one of the steeper slopes to which the Muslim population had by now been pushed, was also located on the expanding fringe of the European enclave.[92] But it is doubtful whether this area was ever completely taken over by the European town, and it certainly never became a British area. The church was always isolated from other churches in Beyoglu and some way from both the British diplomatic centre and from their residential and business district.

FRUSTRATIONS – 1858–63

In the seven years between arriving in Istanbul until G. E. Street's appointment as architect in 1864, Burges remodelled his design at least five times. Like the problems with the site, the reasons for Burges's frustration indicate many of the difficulties of building in foreign conditions, and specifically in an environment of informal economic control. The stone-laying ceremony itself in October 1858 had been no worthy prospectus for the good intentions of the enterprise. In Stratford's speech all mention of the SPG was deliberately excluded and Burges's name was forgetfully omitted. During the ceremony any sight of the nearby mosque, apart from its minaret, was shut out with boards, and soon after the ceremony Muslims in the neighbourhood were threatening to destroy the foundation stone.[93] Each year brought further worries: with finding suitable builders;[94] with the rising prices of labour and materials in Istanbul; and especially with the sudden slump in property prices.[95] The year 1861 was particularly difficult. Continuous financial crisis affected almost every merchant house in Istanbul, and sharply reduced the real value of the funds available for the church.[96]

Burges produced the final modification of his design in July 1861 (Plate 56).[97] By contrast with his original competition design, this last design could make little claim to cathedral status and had none of the oriental allusions that the use of Italian Gothic had originally allowed. It was now a compact chapel with an ambulatory and the remnants of a crossing. Faced with the problem of creating a narthex for what would now be a very short two-bay nave, Burges devised the ingenious solution of supporting the penthouse roof on five freestanding supports, thereby creating an exterior narthex or porch. The tower had long been discarded, the rich polychromatic palette of the original design was washed away, and there was a new ruggedness and simplicity in its details. The design was now nearer the speluncar principle, more cavelike, but it was

PLATE 56 W. Burges.
Crimean Memorial
Church. Final design,
July 1861–May 1862.
West elevation. (RIBA
W16 Set no. 5)

also obviously an impoverished version of a once grand conception. The Early French Gothic elements of the original design had now almost entirely pushed out any Italian features. There was in short a new consistency about the design, but it had become less compelling, less able to visualize the complex conditions of its brief.

BUILDING STREET'S CHURCH, 1863–8

In the summer of 1863 G. E. Street, who had recently joined the SPG, replaced Burges and by December he had produced a new design for the church, attempting to remodel his competition design without making it seem simply impoverished.[98] Street exploited the site's steep slope to lift the chancel above a chamber intended to be used as a schoolroom.

Street chose to use a home-based builder who would go out to Istanbul and install an English foreman in charge of the works. The Gosport firm of

Rogers and Booth, who were at that time building Street's church of St Peter's, Bournemouth, tendered and within a month had signed a contract with the SPG.[99] The SPG agreed to cover any unforeseen customs dues or fees payable to the Turkish authorities, and it was agreed that monies would be adjustable according to the fluctuating exchange rate.[100] The builders had clearly learnt how to draft a contract suitable for the conditions of Istanbul and the slowness of communications. However, the proposed two-year construction period was optimistic even by comparison with the contracts drafted with earlier builders. Furthermore, except perhaps for seeing his specimens of building materials,[101] they seem to have benefited very little from the knowledge of local skills and resources that Burges had gathered.

When construction of the church finally began in June 1864 communication between the two countries had considerably improved. In the 1840s, mail had taken an average of three weeks to travel from London to Istanbul via steamship, and in the 1850s this had been reduced by several days. In addition, by 1858 diplomacy had been transformed by a new telegraph line,[102] and by the early 1860s the line could be exploited for communications concerning the church, especially the more important contractual and building decisions. Another innovation that began to be employed by architects at this time was photography. Street made use of photographs to learn about the site and the state of construction, as well as to check matters such as the carving of ornament.[103] But despite this technology, progress towards completion proved almost as difficult as getting the work started.

One key incident pointedly illustrates the way that Street's apparently more pragmatic, but in fact more dismissive, approach to local building practice actually created problems. Booth, the contractor, reported how the requirement to execute 'the work of the same quality to that done upon Mr. Street's churches in England . . . [had thrown] all the native workmen off their regular habits'. One salient example of this was the facing of the external walls:

[The] specification provides for the work being done 'in the way in which the best random walling in Constantinople is executed' now I fully expected that I could find men in Constantinople able to execute this walling but it proved that no such local work existed as a sample . . . therefore local men could not be employed, great waste of material was necessitated and I was compelled to send a Plymouth mason out to instruct the native men.[104]

Where Burges had at least considered the accommodation of local skills, Street showed little interest in travelling to Istanbul and assumed that there would be the same working procedures available locally that he was used to in England. Street's assumption remained when he built the American church in Rome (1872–6), insisting not only that the church's form and style, but also its methods and materials conform to the practice of the English Gothic Revival.[105] In both instances construction was intended to be carried out through the English system of general contracting in which, to the disgust of Ruskin and, later, Street's own pupils William Morris and Philip Webb, most Gothic Revivalists worked. One consequence of this system, in which buildings were subjected to the division of labour of large-scale manufacturing, was that architects' working drawings dictated the precise form of construction and ornament, and these were carried out to the letter by a workforce devoid of individual initiative. For Street this system reached its apotheosis in his work on the Law Courts in London: there, using one of the biggest general contracting firms, Street prepared a remarkably detailed book of specifications and some 248 contract drawings.[106] For the Crimean church Street presumed that, because oriental craftsmen supposedly worked on simple and repetitive designs, they would naturally be amenable to this tightly controlled form of direction. But it must not be forgotten that Burges's attitude, although initially more enquiring, would certainly have resulted in a similar outcome.

A long sequence of difficulties plagued construction until the church was finally consecrated on 22 October 1868, almost exactly ten years after Lord Stratford de Redcliffe had made his stone-laying speech (Plate 57). Not surprisingly, Rogers and Booth had sustained considerable losses on the enterprise.[107]

Did the church as built satisfy the objectives of the original competition? Certainly there was none of the exterior structural polychromy learnt from Italian Gothic that had been evident in Street's competition design. Also, many of the aggrandizing forms of the earlier design were dropped: there were now no transepts, no polygonal apse, and only one bell-tower. But instead, and perhaps this was a lesson learnt from southern Gothic, there was a greater certainty about the appropriate adaptation of the forms of Early English and Early French Gothic. Illumination was reduced to minimal openings punched into plate tracery in the highest parts of the walls. These windows were shaded from most sunlight by a system of buttresses, eaves and relieving arches. In the chancel the tall angle buttresses joined arched frames projecting over the clerestory roundels. These frames were at the same time eaves (with the roof meeting them flush), relieving arches, and perhaps the outer skin of the walls. If an outer skin, then the level of wall at the roundels was an inset or revealed lower skin. Lower down this opened into another arch over another inset or third skin of wall facing the crypt. The resulting illusion was that of a curious

PLATE 57 G. E. Street. Crimean Memorial Church, 1864–8. Perspective. (*Building News*, 1868)

Ground Plan.

Scale.

CHANCEL   NAVE

VESTRY   CLOISTER

PULPIT

FONT

10 5 0   10   20   30   40 FEET

structural inversion; the walls seemed to be shedding their layers, or getting thinner, from top to bottom.

Street retained the external cloister of his competition design around the nave walls and west front, but he made some adjustments to its articulation. He removed the arched canopy that shaded the clerestory windows in the competition design and instead drew the buttresses to the full length of the wall so that they could support the overhanging eave of the roof. On the north side the contrast between the nave and chancel elevations was now clearly stressed. The loss of the transept was compensated for by making the single remaining bell-tower rise direct from the ground, turning its curved lower wall into the same plane as the outer wall of the cloister and baptistry (now a distinct volume on the north wall), and binding all three units together with a continuous stringcourse and a greater emphasis on the outer treads and risers of the staircase. On its other side, the bell-tower bordered on one of the chancel buttresses, completing a succession of varied shapes and functions convincingly linked together. The result was a compact and rugged design.

On the south elevation, bereft of either bell-tower or baptistry, the effect was less happy (Plate 58). Here the continuous roofline and boxy rectangular volume of the church were plainly seen despite all the variety of fenestration. The west front lost not only all of its decorative colour and its scale (originally based on the premise that the site would be flat), but also its intended sculptural intricacies (Plate 59). Instead, below three simple lancets and roundels, was a cavernous portal. The new muscularity is indicated in one telling detail. Where the competition design had used an elegant trefoil on

PLATE 58 G. E. Street. Crimean Memorial Church, 1864–8. South elevation.

PLATE 59 G. E. Street. Crimean Memorial Church, 1864–8. West front.

the west front to bridge the transition from angle buttresses to spirelet, in the finished building this became an almost primitively simple stepped corbel.

Inside Street replaced his polygonal apse and its illumination deflected through a delicate internal screen, with a flat wall and a plate-traceried rose window (Plate 60). The drawing of the original chancel shows that Street intended this space to be a rich focus of colour centring on a reredos with inlaid Byzantinesque design (see Plate 45). The polychromatic striations on the wall were not used in the built church, but a light blue stone enlivened both the chancel vault and the upper walls of the nave, where it also provided outer voussoirs for the windows. The high windows meant that most of the nave walls were only articulated by relieving arches, presumably left largely blank to provide wall space for commemorative plaques.

The finished church was far more than a simplification of Street's competition design. It represented instead an entirely different and original solution to the structural and climatic problems of a tall, single-vessel Gothic

PLATE 60 G. E. Street.
Crimean Memorial
Church, 1864–8.
Interior looking
eastwards.

church in a Mediterranean setting. With its outer layer pulled back to expose
its tendons and musculature, it was mission Gothic of a new and commanding
ruggedness.

The manifesto of Anglican presence in Istanbul took many more years to be delivered than had been initially hoped. Stratford's stone-laying speech had expressed its original aims: it was to be a sign of a new religious toleration and the spreading of Protestantism, a symbol of alliance, and an index of British presence in the capital of the Ottoman Empire. These aims were to be carried out by a developed Gothic architecture that would be both climatically apt and representative of nationality. But when the toughened and reduced Crimean Memorial Church was eventually finished in 1868, an event largely unnoticed in the British press which had heard far too much of its problems in the previous eleven years, the act was much less a manifesto than an in-house bulletin. Perhaps this can be explained as the result of an irreparable dislocation between the vision of those who promoted the church and the actuality of the interests and conditions implicated in its construction. As Nicholas Thomas, more broadly, has written about colonial projects: 'because of their confrontation with indigenous interests, alternate civilising missions and their internal inconsistencies, colonial intentions are frequently deflected, or re-enacted farcically or incompletely'.[108]

When the Crimean Memorial Church was first proposed in 1856, a different architectural agenda from that of previous British buildings in Istanbul was established. Here was a commission with national and even international prestige backed by prominent public figures, with a well-publicized competition, exhibitions of submitted designs, and great debate in the pages of national periodicals. All of this happened in England and inevitably none of the architects who submitted designs had any experience of building in Istanbul.

The new church was directed at much more diverse and perhaps contradictory audiences than previous British buildings in Istanbul. Unlike those buildings the new church was envisaged with home audiences in mind. Apart from those who provided a vast market for various images and memorials of the war, there were at least three specific groups to whom the church was addressed in England: High Anglicans; the architectural profession; and the British government. Ideally, of course, these groups would be inseparable. Thus it could be felt that Burges's Italian Gothic design reconciled ecclesiological theory, missionary dogma, British foreign policy, and elements of unfocused orientalist discourse. Accordingly, unplaced competition entries could be regarded as unsuccessful at this act of reconciliation, and critical reviews could be seen as directed at different and irrelevant audiences.

But in Istanbul there were other audiences: the British community; European powers in the city; the Turkish authorities; the Orthodox Church; Muslims and other possible converts. There were irreconcilable differences both within these audiences and between them and the audiences in England. Here, in Istanbul, there could be no ideal merging of identities. Instead they were relegated to secondary consideration and given typifying attitudes: Orthodox Greeks would appreciate the building's distinct style as representative of a different kind of Christianity; Muslims would be insulted if figurative imagery were to be used; orientals attached much importance to the dignity of appearances; British expatriates required a religious focus for their community; and so on. Here the supple theory of writers like Beresford Hope was bolstered by a rigid and more simplistic view of other audiences.

This approach was hijacked and then diverted by the conditions that it faced. The enterprise was hampered by lack of money and an inadequate knowledge of the building context of Istanbul. There was an unwillingness if not inability fully to mobilize what knowledge had been acquired of building conditions there by other British builders. Furthermore, the promoters of the vision – whether Street, Burges, the SPG, or Beresford Hope – could only gradually grasp the fact that their practice of architecture would not fit easily into the inconsistent development typical of informal imperialism.

There was some space early on for the idea of a fusion of eastern and western elements in the creation of a new 'central building': a model alliance of hybrid elements, much as Ruskin had found in the Ducal Palace. But this was to be strictly regulated. There was certainly not any space for a dream of setting free the Ruskinian 'savagery' of oriental craftsmen. Indeed, both Burges and Street adhered to a controlling vision of those crafts; a vision that, despite their stylistic adherences to Gothic, was closer to the orientalism of Owen Jones. Ironically, as almost all of the southern Gothic elements in Burges's and Street's designs were abandoned, and with them their more complex historical messages, so a newer, up-to-date British taste prevailed, one that had more limited allusions, and more evident national significance.

While British banks and British trade were dominating the city, the success of British architecture was a haphazard business. It had little continuity, it was unable to establish a working relationship with the city's building industry that would facilitate construction, and at the end, with the Crimean Memorial Church, it was functionally inappropriate to the only one of its audiences that would use it – the British community in Istanbul.

6

DIGNIFIED PROGRESS

LATER BRITISH ARCHITECTURE IN EGYPT

•

{We note} the importance attached by oriental nations to the greater or less degree of dignity, however exhibited, by the Representatives of Foreign Powers.

(*British residents in Alexandria, 1857*)

We cannot stand still, if we wish to maintain our position in the world's estimation. To remain inert is to recede and be left in the lurch.

(*T. L. Donaldson, 1861*)

This chapter returns again to Egypt and especially to Alexandria and to the question of how British officialdom could find its architectural expression there in the third quarter of the century. Since the building of St Mark's Church the city had changed rapidly as international rivalry intensified in the competition for Egypt's Eurocentric favours. But there was a contradiction here, as T. L. Donaldson observed, in that to maintain position Britain had also to be seen as dynamic and modern. As its expatriates perceived, Britain had to project an image of dignity, of consistent authority, and yet it was also engaged in a fierce imperial rivalry. It had to display its values and deal formally with an oriental government increasingly in its debt, while it was also engaged in a scramble for concessions, prime sites, investments and contracts. France's success in Algeria, which it seized control of in 1830, provided warning enough. How could dignity be both distinct and universally recognized? How could an official British architecture, diplomatic building in all senses of that term, be designed for these purposes? Could it choose between resolving or expressing such contradictions?

Other British architecture in Egypt, in this period before the Protectorate, staked out a number of different ways of responding to Egyptian conditions. When, in 1859, it was decided to build a British consulate in Alexandria, the representational and functional needs of the building were more complex and more contradictory than those encountered by these other buildings, as well as by W. J. Smith in Istanbul. The building was to take its place beside Wild's Anglican church in the centre of the European town. There, jostling with the other European consulates, it would provide an expression and a focus of British power. Given that over a period of eleven years during different administrations at least eight designs were submitted by five architects, it is not surprising that a distinctive colonial project is hard to define. It was only, indeed, with the direct intervention of a government minister, that we can begin to see a coherent project coalescing. This, then, is a very different situation from that described in either Chapter 4 or Chapter 5: there was no strong expression of local interests here, nor was there the imposition of a domestic mandate. Against the backdrop of rapid change, especially urbaniza-tion in Egypt, British official architecture seemed deeply uncertain of itself. Although strands of orientalism were undoubtedly present here, most interestingly in the forms of technological and social appropriation, they did not unite to effect any compelling solution. Nothing, at least, that might be equated with the military solution to the incoherence of Britain's position in Egypt.

URBANIZATION IN EGYPT AFTER MUHAMMAD ALI

The building of St Mark's Anglican Church had been part of the creation of a European area in Alexandria centred around the Maydan al-Tahrir (Place des Consuls), and with its villas and gardens to the south along the Mahmudiyyah canal. Many of the Europeans who lived and worked in these areas had been invited to Egypt as part of Muhammad Ali's enterprise of modernization. With the success of that enterprise and its foreign takeover in the 1840s, increasing numbers of European businessmen and diplomatic personnel had come into the country. Egypt's relative openness encouraged tourism, and this itself required the coexistence of economic and technological development on the one hand, and archaeological and perhaps social preservation on the other. Just as tourism relied on maintaining an image of the Orient while providing many of the accoutrements of western life, so the city depended on a visual and social separation of its 'Arab quarter' or 'native town' from its 'Modern' or 'European' area, while in fact the two were structurally and economically linked.[1] The European city's modernity was testified by what was seen as a stereotypically chaotic and bedazzling town lying outside it, much as the West's progress was often seen as inversely related to the East's stasis.

An outline of the physical changes that took place after Muhammad Ali's death in 1849 can be seen in successive maps of the city, though these maps are as much purposive interpretations of the regulation of space as they are records of it.[2] In the early 1840s most of the plots around the Maydan al-Tahrir were filled with European consulates and residences. In Napier's 1841 map this 'Frank quarter' was coalescing not as the centre of a separate new town but at the southern edge of a large shaded area almost filling the peninsula between the two ports (see Plate 25). This shaded area, ungraspable and undifferentiated to European eyes and repeated in many other maps, was usually known as the 'native' town. Between the square and the canal to the south there was no significant development and the area within the old city walls was deserted.

By the time of Charles Müller's 1855 map, two diagonal axes, emanating from the square, had thrust their way southwards and eastwards towards the city walls, and the new town was beginning to suggest the organizational rhetoric of its European cousins (Plate 61), its rectilinearity and apparent autonomy in contrast to the incoherent appearance of the native area. To the

PLATE 61 Charles Müller. Map of Alexandria, 1855. (G. Jondet, *Atlas historique . . . d'Alexandrie*, 1921.)

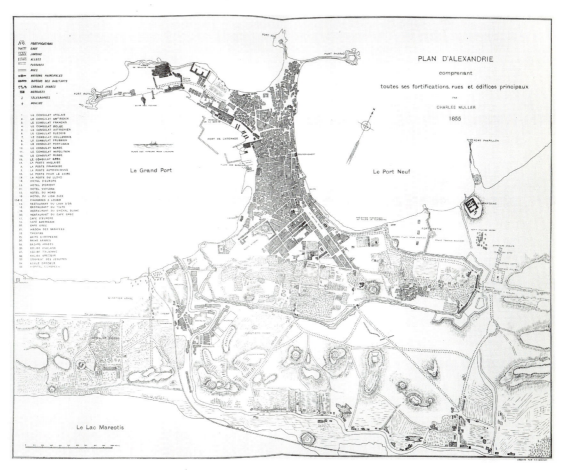

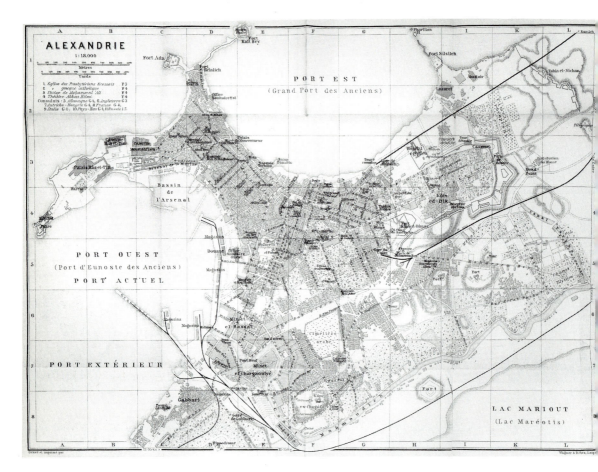

PLATE 62 Karl
Baedeker. Map of
Alexandria, 1877.
(K. Baedeker, ed.,
Egypt, 1898)

north of the square land had been reclaimed from the eastern harbour. At the western port end of the canal, a complex of warehouses and factories was clearly taking shape, and military establishments were scattered over the whole area. In the square itself Müller indicated a variety of European institutions: as well as consulates and residences there were now cafés, banks, hotels and post offices.

Most development in this period was involved in extending the main axes centred on the square and filling their interstices with a grid plan. The city thus spread mainly south-westwards and eastwards. By 1877, the date of Baedeker's map, those still unbuilt areas within the old city walls had been organized by streets and gardens (Plate 62). Also, inside these walls, a railway terminus for Robert Stephenson's new Alexandria to Cairo line was completed in 1856 and a station, the Gare du Caire, was built in 'Anglo-Italian character' by Edward Baines (Plate 63).[3] This was a low building with an arcaded centrepiece, whose scanty palatial allusions hardly vied with its utilitarian form. In part another manifestation of Anglo-French rivalry, the railway

station also became the hub of a new development. Baedeker's map emphasizes these nodes of communication and shows that a coherent grouping of hotels and houses was established around this station. Meanwhile a goods railway serving the western port had augmented the canal and brought extensive industrial development; so extensive in fact that it was beginning to border the villas and estates along the canal. The 'native' town had filled the peninsula by 1855, and it can be assumed that most of the development south and west of the city walls after this date was to accommodate its population.[4] Beyond the city to the east was the dormitory suburb of Ramleh, where many of the diplomats and bankers who worked in the city lived on land given by the Khedive Ismail (who had taken the new title after becoming ruler in 1863).

Even this brief cartographic survey demonstrates that the European penetration of Alexandria had taken definite physical and visual form by the time of the imposition of the British Protectorate in 1882. Fiorillo's photograph of the square (Plate 64), taken just before the 1882 bombardment, pictures it as both the very model of European urban improvement and of certain tame, contained and clarified notions of the Orient.[5] The square is trimly paved and gas-lit. A circular pond and fountain are framed by railings. In the middle of the square, within its tree-lined promenades, are a

PLATE 63 Edward Baines. Alexandria railway station, 1856. (*ILN*, 23 January 1858)

PLATE 64 L. Fiorillo.
The Maidan al-Tahrir,
Alexandria, c. 1880.
Photograph. (Royal
Commonwealth Society
Library, Cambridge
University)

neo-Islamic bandstand and a bronze equestrian statue of Muhammad Ali. The square is bordered and defined by an array of three-storied neoclassical edifices. (And, hidden behind trees in the far left-hand corner of the square, is that other representation of Islam-in-captivity, the Anglican church of St Mark's.) The labyrinthine and monadic otherness of the native town is indicated by what this square represents. It is a place of citizenship and civic decorum, or at least of their rhetoric; a place of collective and institutional life whose commercial elements are hidden in Fiorillo's image.

Most of what had been built in the square, as well as most of what replaced those buildings after 1882 (only the Bourse and St Mark's Church survived), were designed by Italian architects. Many of the structures were multifunctional *okelles*, a French rendition of the Arabic *wikalah*, meaning a combination of urban warehouse and hostel for merchants. The word itself typifies the manner in which colonizing cultures adopted terms originating in the indigenous culture to describe architecture and small-scale urban forms. Better known examples in India are words like bungalow, godown, verandah and compound, all developed in this ethno-semantic manner.[6] Unlike these words, however, *okelle* seems not to have entered the common usage of the colonizing cultures, always retaining a specifically Alexandrian application.

In 1868 the Maydan al-Tahrir had the Okelle Anglaise, the Okelle Française, the Okelle Nuevo, the Okelle Anastasi, and the Okelle Abro.[7] These *okelles* might have a café, a theatre, a hotel, shops and a European post office, with the ground floor devoted to commercial activities, while the upper floors were given over for hotel and residential uses. They were usually pierced by two public passages at right angles to each other, dividing the building into four parts and providing ventilation and lighting through the middle of the structure.[8] As I will show, this building type – in which an indigenous building form was amalgamated with the particular needs of colonial leisure and commerce – was also considered by the British for their new consulate in Alexandria.

Under Said Pasha (1854–63) and Ismail (1863–79), Egypt's governmental policy became deliberately, indeed excessively, pro-European. The collapse of Muhammad Ali's attempt to generate autonomous economic change had led to Egypt's subordination to a global system of economic dependence, centred on the European powers.[9] Eventually the threat of local revolt amidst the induced conditions of national debt led to the imposition of a British Protectorate in 1882.

One effect of such economic and political changes was that by 1870 Alexandria had lost its pre-eminence to Cairo, which now truly emerged as a modern city. Favoured by Ismail, Cairo was reshaped using the methods of, and with something of the same intent as, Baron Haussmann's replanning of Paris. But again, as with Muhammad Ali, modernization was not simply imported from without. Ismail Pasha and Ali Mubarak, his Minister of Public Works, had travelled to see the Exposition Universelle of 1867 and were guided around Paris by Haussmann himself. A Frank quarter had existed in Cairo since at least the late sixteenth century, then, initially under Muhammad Ali and more spectacularly under his successors, this was extended into and took over the area around the Azbakiyyah pond.[10] Around the gardens that replaced the pond European hotels, consulates, churches and schools were built, and the Egyptian authorities encouraged European styles of architecture.[11] The Ismailiyah area towards the Nile was replanned and the city expanded over to the west side of the river. During the 1860s and 1870s Mubarak attempted to link this European enclave to the Islamic city and the rapidly developing areas to the west by a series of grand boulevards cutting through old quarters and meeting at Haussmann-like *étoiles*. The scale of this aggressive development and Egypt's subsequent collapse into debt and foreclosure transformed Cairo and set up the conditions for what Janet Abu-Lughod has called a 'physical mitosis':[12] on the one hand preserving a town equivalent to the unmarked areas we observed in maps of Alexandria, a 'traditional' town of narrow alleys, inward-looking houses and craft-based production; and on the other hand a European city of boulevards and administration, even larger than those that had already been formed in Alexandria, Izmir, Beirut and Istanbul.

BRITISH ARCHITECTURE IN EGYPT

In Cairo, as in Alexandria, building materials were often imported, most building work was in the hands of Italian architects and contractors, and British involvement was unusual. But there were a few exceptions. In 1865 the Oriental Hotel Company employed Christopher Wray, recently civil architect to the British government of Bengal, to build their New Hotel on a site facing the Azbakiyyah gardens.[13] The building was intended for British tourists as well as travellers passing through the city on the overland route to India. Wray designed a three-storey structure with arcades shading verandahs wrapped around the building (Plate 65). The appearance was closer in external effect to an exhibition building than to a royal palace and quite in keeping with the imported styles of its environs. Pavilions on the wings were surmounted by pyramidal roofs, while the central pavilion had a portico projecting in front of a massively arched and gabled facade which in turn was capped with a convex mansard roof. On the ground floor of one of these pavilions was housed a 'public bazaar', a safe venue for some of the oriental

PLATE 65 Christopher Wray. New Hotel, Cairo, 1865. (*Builder*, 1869)

sensations otherwise excluded from the building.

Apart from Wray's hotel, a post office designed by T. L. Donaldson at Suez (1862), and a hospital built by Colonel Collyer also at Suez (1867), the only recorded works by named British architects in Egypt at this time were for Egyptian clients.[14] Pascal Coste's pavilion at Shubra (1826–36) for Muhammad Ali was not the only royal commission for a European architect; indeed, under Said and Ismail they multiplied into debt-inducing extravagances. In 1860 Robert Stephenson, well known in Egypt following his successful work on the Cairo to Alexandria railway, designed an iron kiosk for Said Pasha (Plate 66). This was fabricated in London and intended to stand at the end of a pier projecting from the banks of the Nile at Kafrellais. The kiosk was erected on a platform supported by cylindrical pilings. On top of the platform was a cruciform structure with its internal angles filled by minor domes harbouring low seats around the central space. Over the crossing was a large ogee-shaped double dome surmounted by a crescent. Glass windows with louvres took up most of the space on the sides of the structure and arabesque patterns were woven over all the domes. Inside, the kiosk was 'fitted for all the comforts and luxuries peculiar to Imperial Ottoman life': a bath was suspended from the centre of the dome and enclosed under the water level by plate glass jalousies, while chandeliers illuminated the plaster-lined interior at night.[15] Similarly, when the German architects Frantz and De Curel built the neo-Islamic

PLATE 66 Robert Stephenson. Kiosk on the Nile, 1860. (*Builder*)

Gazirah Palace (1863) in Cairo (Plate 67), they used cast-iron elements which were made in Germany and assembled in Cairo by imported labour.[16] The kiosk, like the palace, represents a curious coming together of interests. On the one hand they both demonstrate and confirm a western fascination with notions of oriental luxuriance. On the other hand they show a certain hard-headed ability to employ western technical know-how in order to supply, with the kiosk at least, what must have been a relatively cheap and quickly constructed frippery.

Another beneficiary of royal patronage was Owen Jones, who, in 1861, was employed by Said Pasha to design a domed pavilion as part of the palatial complex at Gazirah (Plate 68). The location of this palace complex is worth mentioning because, like the Dolmabahce Palace in Istanbul, it seems to have been deliberately placed on the European side of the city, so that some form of identification with change and Europeanization was intended. The Moorish fantasy produced by Jones must have accorded well with what Said Pasha and his advisors intended when they employed Jones, for he was still best-known for his scholarly work on the Alhambra. The designs show a domed structure centred on a series of pools and water channels, its interior decorated with complex *muqarnas* vaults, coupled columns, tiling and stained-glass windows. But the pavilion was not built according to the drawings that survive and has since been demolished.[17] Another Egyptian commission came to Jones in 1863 when he designed carpets, as well as wall and ceiling decorations for fifteen major rooms in the main palace building at Gazirah, which had also

PLATE 67 Frantz and De Curel. Gazirah Palace, Cairo, 1865. (G. Ebers, *Egypt: Descriptive, Historical and Picturesque*, 1879)

PLATE 68 Owen Jones. Pavilion at Gazirah, 1861. Longitudinal section. (V&A, 8277 C, A.204)

been inspired by the Alhambra. These decorations were prepared and completed in London in a style 'as perfect and exact as is exemplified in the tombs of the Caliph in Old Cairo'.[18]

It is clear that Said and Ismail's pro-European policies were matched by a willingness to employ European architects on their own building schemes. (Said spoke French and replaced the traditional kaftan with the frock-coat.) Yet, paradoxically, these architects did not design western-style buildings (as W. J. Smith had done for the exterior of his Imperial Kiosk at Tophana, Istanbul) but instead presented their clients with a variety of western images of the Orient. This was quite different from the mixed oriental and European styles typical of Muhammad Ali's patronage and quite different again from the 'collective reappropriation' of Arabic motifs in architecture of the turn of the century that consciously paralleled the Egyptian political renaissance.[19] It was, rather, a western expertise in the imagining of the Orient that Jones's and Stephenson's work provided through Alhambran, Mamluk and Ottoman sources. It is likely that the dominance of Europeans, particularly Italians, over the architectural profession, as well as the popularity of European architectural styles, probably implies that there were few, if any, Egyptian or Ottoman architects capable of providing Egyptian rulers with both the technological comforts and the desired oriental images of their rule.

This absence of indigenous architects in Egypt was recognized by Islamic specialists and consular officials and by some it was seen as another aspect of that oriental decadence which had created a vacuum that should properly be filled by British skill and capital. One of these Islamic specialists was Thomas Hayter Lewis (1818–98), a respected historian of Islamic architecture and also a Biblical archaeologist. As already discussed in Chapter 2, Lewis had designed the 'Egyptian Saracenic' Panopticon (a popular scientific centre) in Leicester Square (1852–4), and later he was to make designs for a similar building for the Khedive Ismail.[20] In 1859 Lewis gave a lecture to the Architectural Photographic Society in London in which he argued that Islamic impotence could allow the full flowering of a British imperial style. Expanding on comments about the Islamic monuments of Cairo, Lewis launched into a sermon on the role of architecture within imperialism:

> The Englishman has put his foot upon the holy soil, and Cairo is now the stepping-stone between Malta and Aden. That long black line of rail that marks our path to India will do more than shorten, by some few days, our path to it; and we can almost see the beginning of the end foretold in the brilliant *Eothen*: – 'Islam shall wither away, and the Englishman, straining for ever to hold his loved India, will plant a firm foot on the banks of the Nile and sit on the seat of the faithful' . . . Even now, the race of cunning architects who planned these works has gone and left no heritors behind them; and for the new temple in the citadel, the new palace in the capital, the Moslem summons the Englishman or the Greek; and remember that our nation is the only one now spreading itself on the earth . . . Shall not, then, the temples that we worship in, our rulers' palaces, the homes we love, speak to the future of our proud race? And if we hesitate in this; if we leave the print of the Italian or the Greek upon the land where the power of the Englishman only has been, let us think of the traces that the Greek and the Roman left of their own nation's art in the countries that they peopled, – that the Moslem has left marks in India and Persia, in Egypt, and in Spain, and in their nationality, though in our own style, let us learn something even from the Arab.[21]

The passage displays a fear of rivalry and of the passing opportunity, but it also hints at that operative conjunction of imperial ambition with the claimed objectivity of scholarly knowledge about Islam which, following Edward Said, is at the heart of orientalist discourse. In connection with Egypt this has been seen before, most notably in the work of *Description de l'Égypt*,

Edward Lane and James Wild. Lewis is unusual, however, in suggesting a direct connection between this vision of Egypt and a doctrine of imperial representation through architecture. The 'prints', 'traces' and 'marks' of previous empires indicated to Lewis that the means used must be a national style; or at least identifiable as British work. What that style was to be is not so apparent, and Lewis himself was silent about it at this time. Like other architectural theorists, he could call for a modern national style – a truly imperial style – without categorizing its form. Rather than the substance of a solution, his words indicate a hope that the problematics of style at home could be resolved by taking the model of other imperial nations, not just the Greeks and Romans but, more unusually, Arabic civilization as well.

Speaking in 1859 of a future British imperial architecture, Lewis may well have known of contemporary plans to build a British consulate in Alexandria. Whether he knew of the consulate or not is unimportant, for what he advocated was crucial also to the men who would make decisions about and produce blueprints for this first official British building in Egypt. How could they show that they were responsive to the past, that they could 'learn something even from the Arab' in Lewis's words, and still be the 'proud race' that would shape the future?

THE BRITISH CONSULATE IN ALEXANDRIA

In 1857 British residents in Alexandria offered their government a vacant space on the large site used for St Mark's Church.[22] Two years later it was decided that the consul-general would obtain plans for a consulate from local architects, but that the final designs would be prepared in England under government direction.[23] The envisaged building would house a dwelling for the consul and a British post office, as well as offices for the consular courts and public archives; later, residences for various consular officials were also stipulated. It would uphold British dignity in the face of French rivalry and oriental scrutiny.[24]

In the first design, possibly by the consul-general Robert Colquhoun, all the consular functions were grouped around a central courtyard with consular residences above (Plate 69). The building would tailor itself to the local monumental form, for, as a structure having several functions with a wide passage through it to a courtyard, Colquhoun's design had a generic resemblance to the *okelles* that filled most of the plots around the square. Thus his initial and influential ideas on the subject were established.

Colquhoun also acquired designs from local architects, the first of whom was a 'Mr. Sofio', a Greek who had studied architecture in Italy (Plate 70).[25]

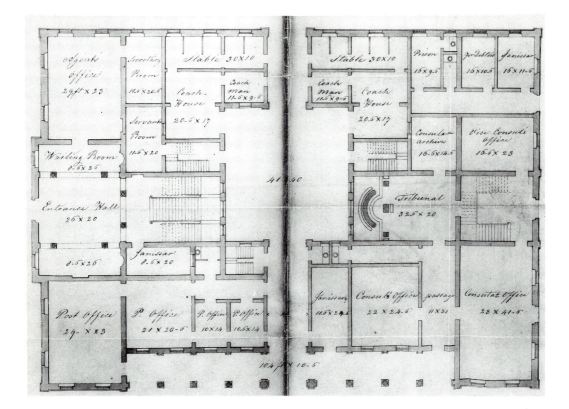

PLATE 69 Robert
Colquhoun. Alexandria
consulate, 1859. Plan.
(FO 78/1714)

PLATE 70 Sofio.
Alexandria consulate,
1860. Elevation. (FO
925/3017)

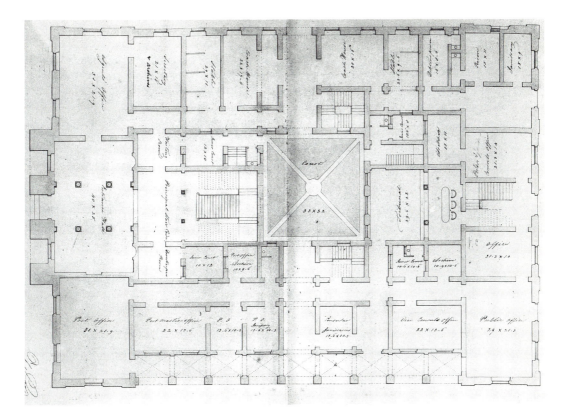

PLATE 71 Sofio.
Alexandria consulate,
1860. Plan. (FO
925/3017)

Sofio explained the style of his design as partly conditioned by the need for regularity and simplicity so that local labourers could execute it.[26] In appearance it was like many of the buildings that stood around the square at this time, with its rusticated and pedimented facades designed in a light if unconvincing Palladian style.

The most interesting aspect of Sofio's design was its internal arrangement (Plate 71). The ground-floor plan was similar to Colquhoun's plan of 1859, although now the courtyard was made smaller to accommodate an enlarged stairhall and four tiny 'inner courts'. These were designed not as light wells but to aid ventilation and temperature control within the building. Colquhoun pointed out that these inner courts were 'of Arab origin' and led to outlets on the roof that could be adjusted to face the prevailing wind.[27] Captured on the roof where the air was cleaner, the wind would pass downwards through the rooms and into the courtyard where it would push the warm air upwards. The use of such windcatchers, or *malqaf*, was a common, indeed essential feature in Egyptian domestic architecture and one which was still apparent in the houses of Cairo and Alexandria in the mid-nineteenth century. Accordingly, a local architect of any experience would have had first-hand knowledge of them. It is instructive to compare this kind of expertise,

PLATE 72 Carl Heinze. Alexandria consulate, 1860. Elevation. (FO 925/3011)

learnt from indigenous practice, with the imported expertise that is represented by Stephenson's kiosk or Wray's hotel. Sofio drew upon the locally tested and proved techniques of environmental control. Stephenson seems to have been r .ore concerned about the display of recent western science; what can be called a technologism. Wray imported a ventilation system from British building experience in the *maidans* of India, hoping that it would be appropriate to Cairo. Of course Sofio's design made no Islamic references in its facades. Its borrowings were internal and practical.

A month after sending Sofio's designs Colquhoun had acquired and dispatched another set of designs by Carl Heinze, a locally based architect who had recently arrived from Berlin where he had been a pupil of F. A. Stüler, the director of the Berlin Academy. Heinze's design displayed the Schinkelesque eclecticism of his master: a discordant combination of neoclassicism and *Rundbogenstil*, intended to be carried out in brick and terracotta (Plate 72). Again, its classical palazzo form, articulated by an unlikely system of canopies, would not have been out of place in the square.

One of the most interesting aspects of both Heinze's and Sofio's plans were the 'divans' provided as part of the consul-general's suite of rooms on the first floor (Plate 73). Presumably these were intended not so much as council-chambers, but as part of the agent's set of reception rooms; they were probably imagined as comfortable smoking-rooms, although a specific function need not have been required. In English usage the word had several senses that were related to each other like the different senses of the word 'cabinet'. The divan was an Ottoman council of state, a council-chamber, and a long seat in the form of a bench or a raised part of the floor. Since the seventeenth century, the last of these definitions had been used to describe low couches. But in the nineteenth century there was a new inflection of the word extending the topos of the leisured East. Just as the topos could be associated with garden buildings, so it could also cover certain interior rooms. Thus, for instance, early in the century 'divan' had come to mean a smoking-room furnished with couches, often as part of a cigar shop.[28] Later, in the 1880s, the 'Arab Room' or divan became a more fashionable, upper-class smoking-room.[29] In the process divans had both become associated with a masculine domain and lost any class specificity that might have been attached to them.

PLATE 73 Carl Heinze. Alexandria consulate, 1860. First-floor plan. (FO 925/3011)

Sofio and Heinze's idea of the divan seems to encompass all of these usages: council of state, low seat, and smoking-room. The word itself presupposes such a familiarity and ease with exotic leisure that a token of this leisure could even be integrated within the official British residence. These meanings are particularly apparent in Heinze's design. Where Sofio's divan was a simple square chamber, Heinze envisaged it as the last and most richly modelled in a sequence of reception rooms. Along the main front there

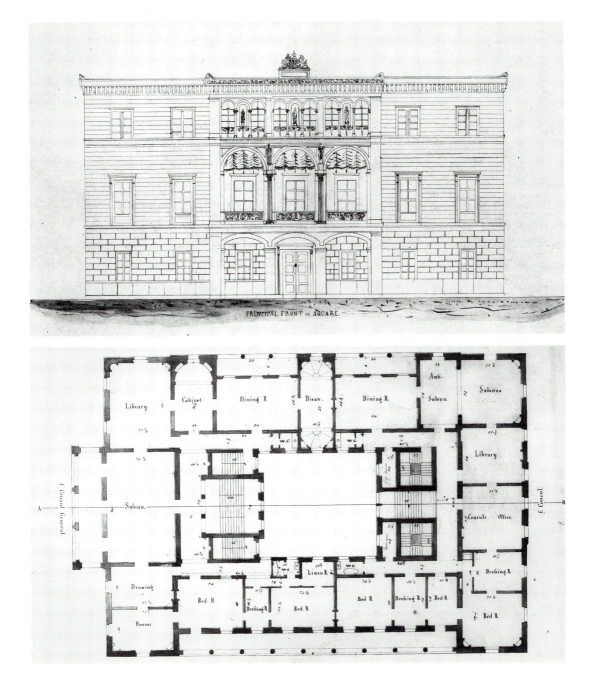

would be drawing-rooms, a saloon, and a library with corner niches. This sequence would be extended along the west side with an apse-ended cabinet, a dining-room with a balcony, and finally – the widest of the three rooms – a divan with niches in its corners and a fan-shaped ceiling. Its functional redundancy and aura of semi-concealment was implied by its appended position within the sequence, yet its symbolic fitness was inherent in its distinctive spatial articulation. Space was envisaged as an arm of diplomacy, the locale of persuasion.

It is clear, then, that designs produced in Alexandria for the British consulate drew upon a specialized and locally effective knowledge of Near Eastern forms – the *okelle*, the windcatcher and the divan – to provide an appropriate setting for officials engaged in the immediate rivalries of informal colonialism. In no sense, however, were either these elements or the designs' external treatment directed at a British public's conception of national dignity. In any event, sensing the growing significance of the project, the authorities turned to a British-based architect instead.

T. L. DONALDSON'S DESIGNS

On the face of it, T. L. Donaldson (1795–1885), an academic and member of the professional establishment, seems an unlikely candidate. Then in his sixty-fifth year, he had lived and toured abroad but had never been to Egypt. Yet Donaldson clearly wanted the commission and probably used his influence with Lord Palmerston, the Prime Minister, and all his relevant experience to gain it.[30]

When Donaldson arrived in Alexandria early in 1861 he quickly established contact with influential intermediaries such as Linant de Belle-fonds, the chief of the Egyptian Board of Works, and Yusuf Hekekyan Bey, who had been a technical advisor to the Egyptian government on engineering projects between 1840 and 1850. Both of them had close relations with British orientalists. The first was typical of the European specialists whom Muhammad Ali had invited into the country; the second was one of the European-educated technocrats who mediated Egypt's modernization.[31] These men supplied Donaldson with useful information on materials, labour and transport, and Hekekyan Bey was also to become a personal friend. Donaldson supplemented these contacts with assiduous preparation: he visited the quarries of Torah, as well as brickfields and lime kilns; he inspected recently erected buildings in Cairo; he met Sofio and Heinze, took plans of the French consulate in Alexandria, and visited the residences of consuls, merchants and postmasters.[32]

On the basis of these preparations in Egypt Donaldson designed a classical urban palazzo in a Florentine Quattrocento style (Plate 74). Its most distinguishing feature was probably the greater height and size given to the consul-general's apartment than equivalent European residences. This was explained as a ploy to rival the local merchants' way of life in order to gain

their respect.[33] But Donaldson's estimates were rejected and he was asked to produce a reduced scheme.[34]

The radical change in the appearance of Donaldson's new design was not the result of economic restrictions alone. By September 1861 Austen Henry Layard (1817–94), the Radical MP and new Under Secretary of State for Foreign Affairs, had taken a personal interest in the project. Layard was an art critic, politician and orientalist. He had achieved considerable fame during the 1840s when he explored Assyrian remains in Persia and published *Nineveh and Its Remains* (1849) (actually a study of Nimrud). He was also known as an expert on the Ottoman Empire because of his extensive travels in the area, a posting at the embassy in Istanbul, and his work as a co-founder and chairman of the Ottoman Bank. In 1853 he had even been offered the post of consul-general in Egypt.[35]

Layard's views on architecture and imperialism at this time are difficult to untangle. During his frequent travels in the East he had occasionally expressed admiration for its architecture, both ancient and medieval varieties.[36] Quickly on the scene after the Indian Mutiny of 1857, Layard had called for greater assimilation and a more active British presence in India. He was against the treatment of Indians as a separate race and advocated greater Indian participation in government (policies that were eventually implemented and were manifested in the Hindu–Saracenic style in Raj architecture) and he remained close to his radical utilitarian roots in castigating the neglect of education and public works, as well as the half-hearted diffusion of English language and Christianity.[37] Yet Layard also disliked the 'formal types of ornament' that were disseminated by Cole and the utilitarian design reformers at the South Kensington Museum.[38] In 1861 he supported George Gilbert Scott's Gothic design for the Foreign Office and later, when he was made Chief Commissioner of Works under Gladstone in 1868, Layard tried to Gothicize London's new public buildings, but without the despotic power of Haussmann's impact on Paris.[39] One of the objects of these ambitions was G. E. Street's Gothic Law Courts.

This evidence suggests that Layard had a strong sense of the political impact of architecture, and that both his private and his official interests in the Near East extended into a lively concern with the kind of architecture that Britain built there. The Alexandria consulate project shows that Layard also believed that a solution could be found in an overtly Islamicizing style.

When Donaldson was requested to produce a new design, Layard suggested that he should also change the style of the building.[40] By the end of 1861 Donaldson had delivered to the Foreign Office – 'intended only for Layard's eye' – a sketch 'conceived in the Eastern style', together with 'sketches taken from Buildings at Cairo ... containing like features ... from which I derived the details'.[41]

The alacrity with which Donaldson adapted his design to an Islamic style should not be surprising. Although he was recognized as an expert on classical architecture and occasionally took up a strong anti-Gothic stance, he held flexible, eclectic views on modern architecture which he had promoted in his *Preliminary Discourse* (1842). Here an appropriate selection from the admirable qualities of all styles was tentatively suggested as a solution to the problem of finding a nineteenth-century style. For Donaldson an architect could choose to apply any style 'with peculiar propriety on some emergency'. In these emergencies – the word seems like a cover for the old theory of associationism used for minor or unusual projects – the best architect was one who could at need command any style: Classic, Gothic and even 'the brilliant fancies of Arabic'.[42]

Donaldson's new consulate design, shown in the International Exhibition of 1862,[43] demonstrates a startling shift towards an overtly orientalist exterior (Plate 75). There had been previous borrowings from Islamic architecture in Sofio and Heinze's consulate designs, for purposes of practicality, custom and the symbolic power of certain rooms. But by their nature these ideas were only apparent in the plan and the interior of those designs. By contrast, the new design was dressed externally in Arab garb, but it excluded most of these internal borrowings, perhaps with the exception of the remodelled cruciform court that was now even more suggestive of the Alexandrian *okelle* (Plate 76). On the ground floor the main entrance hall was to have a coffered barrel vault with sculptured busts lining the walls.[44] The decoration of the consul-

PLATE 75 T. L. Donaldson. Alexandria consulate, 1862. Second design – elevation. (FO 925/3012 Part 2)

general's reception rooms on the first floor would consist of light rococo flourishes contained in a geometric scheme of mirrors and panels.

But if the interior was consolingly European, the exterior of the consulate was mostly dressed in the colours of Islamic Cairo. Islamic elements such as paired pointed horse-shoe arches, *muqarnas* capitals, and shaped crenellations were distributed across the design and harmonized with the other elements through the consistent use of coloured voussoirs over every opening.[45] Armorial shields and an English royal coat-of-arms completed the set of allusions. The design might be seen as both Gothic and Islamic, although the weight given these allusions had been reversed by comparison with William Burges's Crimean design. Like Burges, Donaldson had orientalized his exterior but the difference between this and the 'English' interior was now much greater.

Although its intended neighbour, St Mark's, was monochrome, in both buildings it could be said that Islam was not merely an attribute but the veritable subject of the design. By seizing on essentialized qualities through stereotyped or abstracted forms, Islam could be represented without the need for a convincing similarity to any particular Islamic building. The link between the church and the consulate design was one more of sharing certain

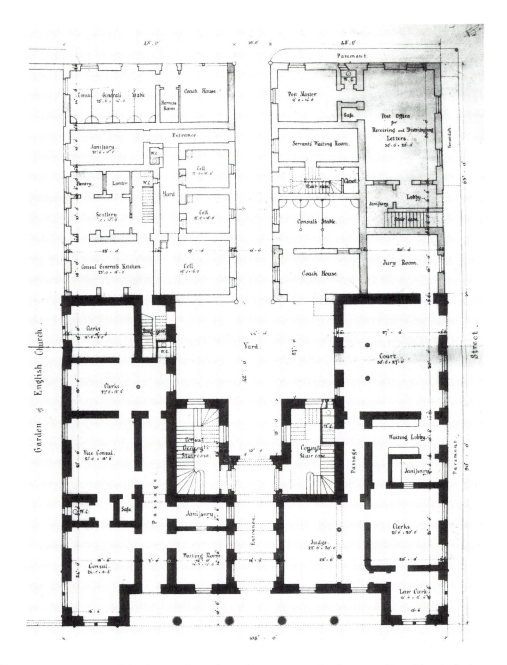

PLATE 76 T. L.
Donaldson. Alexandria
consulate, 1862. Second
design – plan. (FO
925/3012 Part 2)

signs of the Orient than of visual consonance. In this sense Donaldson's design
and Wild's church can be compared with the oriental costume worn by
orientalists like Edward Lane, J. F. Lewis, or Linant de Bellefonds. As Timothy
Mitchell has described it, visitors could thereby 'immerse [themselves] and yet
stand apart':[46] the wearer of such disguises could penetrate into the Orient,
take on something of its romance, gain acceptance, and gather privileged
knowledge about the subject, that could then be turned into improving

matter for an English audience using the testimony of detailed descriptive effects.

Broadly, Donaldson's design could be taken to imply continuity, harmony and control. In this sense, his solution to the problem of a colonial building style might be related to the development of the so-called 'Hindu–Saracenic' style by the British Raj from the 1870s until the end of the century. As Thomas Metcalf has argued, that style was intended by the all-knowing imperial power to blend and resolve what were seen as discrete cultural traditions in India,[47] much as Wild experimentally attempted to blend Early Christian and Islamic components in St Mark's Church. This shaped harmony was in the hands of the successors, those westerners who saw themselves as in command of history and the historicist sensibility, and therefore the rightful inheritors of the land.

But neither Donaldson's 'eastern' design for the Alexandria consulate nor Wild's prototypical design was entirely identical to this later approach in British India. There were good reasons for this. Egypt was not a formal colony and an Islamic empire, however Europeanized, still controlled it. Furthermore, despite Lane's work, the understanding of ethnography still awaited its ramification into colonial institutions, unlike in India. There was therefore little to underpin a particular reading of this design. Yet, if not identical with the 'Hindu–Saracenic' style, Donaldson's design was close to its earlier manifestation, the 'Saracenic' style called for by some participants in the debate over the post-Mutiny style of British architecture in India, and especially to the initial position of William Emerson (a pupil of William Burges) and Lord Napier in the early 1870s.[48] These men advocated a 'Saracenic' style in India partly because of its association with Early Christianity, partly as a model for the adaptive use of indigenous architecture by an imperial culture, and partly because the British would thereby take on the mantle of a previous empire. Their arguments were at least eight or ten years later than Donaldson's work, but his work might be taken to be an embryonic version of similar thinking. Not only had Layard been politically involved in readjusting Britain's policy towards India after 1857, but also the links between Early Christian and Islamic architecture had been made concrete in Wild's St Mark's Church. Furthermore the lessons of Islamic architecture as an imperial model had been suggested by James Millard and T. H. Lewis, and debated in the critical reaction to Wild's church. Donaldson and Layard – the architectural liberal and the orientalist Radical – would surely have been sensitive to the repercussions of their design and to have desired an understanding of it in these terms.

However, the propriety and style of Donaldson's design were criticized, most crucially by Colquhoun. It lacked propriety in many respects: the main staircase was too narrow; according to local custom, the bedrooms should have been on the same level as reception rooms; and the servant accommodation was wrong since Arab servants 'can from their habits, *never* be allowed to sleep on the same floor as the Masters'.[49] Donaldson could make little adequate defence of his design in these terms. Instead he argued largely about style: how, for instance, did Heinze's classical facade harmonize with the 'Moorish' style of the church? Significantly Donaldson did not explain his own design as an attempt at matching, but as a similiar exercise in creating an 'Eastern aspect'.[50] In the event, however, both his and Colquhoun's local designs were frozen and then apparently forgotten as the government reconsidered its provision of judicial services in Egypt.[51] Two sets of designs were produced in 1867 by Martin MacDermott, an engineer, but these were quickly rejected.[52]

JAMES WILD'S DESIGNS

The last architect involved in this saga was James Wild. It had been nearly twenty years since he had set foot in the Near East, and the intervening period had been disappointingly unproductive for him, probably due to failing health. On returning to England in 1848 he had obtained little substantial architectural work. His knowledge of Islamic architecture helped gain his appointment as decorative architect to the Great Exhibition (1851) and in 1853 he was appointed as an expert on Islamic art for Henry Cole's new South Kensington Museum, where he also designed the decoration for the Indian Court (1863).[53] Wild thus became the first of those great gatekeepers of orientalist knowledge at the museum, who later included Sir Caspar Purdon Clarke and Sir George Birdwood.

The design submitted by Wild in July 1869 drew upon his knowledge of Alexandria's building conditions, but it was by no means simply a secular version of St Mark's Church, nor was the main inspiration oriental (Plate 77).[54] Like much of Wild's small output, it was a carefully proportioned composition of distinctly articulated volumes, decorated with integrated surface ornament. It was unlike those previous works, however, in the style of this composition.

When Wild exhibited his delicately drawn perspective at the Royal Academy in 1870, admiring reviewers described it as 'a highly wrought-out Classic work', a 'refined classic type of architecture', and 'Italian architecture, adapted to a certain extent to another climate and country'.[55] Wild's originality was also praised: it was a work such 'as no architect in England in the present day is producing'.[56] These comments indicate recognition of Wild's ability to mould elements taken from different sources into a

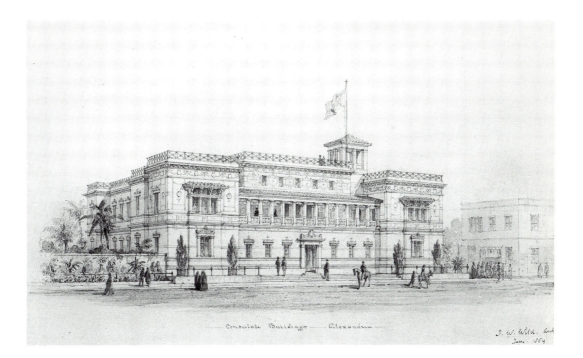

Consulate Buildings — Alexandria

J. W. Wild. Arch
June 1864

PLATE 77 James Wild.
Alexandria consulate,
1869. Perspective. (FO
925/3010)

composition of 'quiet severity', like those of his Streatham and Alexandria churches. The main inspiration came from the Italianate villa form, fused with the rigorous tectonic logic of the Greek Revival, as had happened in the contemporary work of Alexander 'Greek' Thomson in Glasgow. It is very likely that Wild knew Thomson's entry for the South Kensington Museum competition (1864), with its stepped-back storeys held between projecting outer units, and its superimposed ranges of fenestrated podium, trabeated colonnade and recessed attic.[57] Such elements were also common to the buildings of Schinkel and Klenze, and Wild's Streatham church had already evinced an interest in the work of these German architects.

However, the wall ornament used by Wild on his consulate design could not have been seen in any of these sources. Since no colour was indicated on the designs, and given Wild's knowledge of the humid and salty Alexandrian air, this decoration was probably intended to be inscribed into the stucco of the wall. It was most striking on the second floor, where a rectangular grid between the windows contained delicate cross and snake-like forms, as well as ribbons, festoons and flourishes. Such framing devices, and the linear and isolated objects within them, were taken from the Second Style interior wall paintings of Pompeii and Herculaneum that Wild had sketched during his return journey from Egypt in 1847.[58] There was an interest in the Pompeian style in Second Empire France, but Wild's notebook sketches predate this. The Government Schools of Design had been teaching Pompeian ornament since

1843, and Owen Jones included examples of it in his *Grammar of Ornament* (1856). Furthermore Jones and J. G. Crace had used Pompeian-inspired decoration in the 1860s. But as used by Wild in Alexandria, what might this Pompeian style have meant? Was it more than simply an appropriate surface articulation of a Mediterranean building?

If the meaning of the exterior style must remain ambiguous, in its spatial articulation the design was far more legible (Plate 78). The plan provided fewer facilities than any previous scheme, and a great amount of this space (half of the site) at the centre of the plan was used for an arcaded courtyard and circulation. A large hall, corridors and a vestibule (all of which were barrel-vaulted) took precedence over a central staircase, which was relegated to one side. The same arrangement was utilized on the second floor, which provided a barrel-vaulted tribunal and court offices, the consul-general's reception areas, and the rest of the post master's accommodation. Each corner of the building projected, casting some shade across the fronts and creating greater variety of room shapes within while expressing their functional articulation on the exterior.

The reason for Wild's planning is immediately apparent. By moving all the rooms to the outside of the building and serving them through single-loaded passages around the courtyard, he created an alternative solution to the problems of ventilation and access. Wild's planning also enabled him to loosen the palazzo block found in all the previous designs. Instead, his principal facade was plastically related to every other facade. The front facing the square

PLATE 78 James Wild. Alexandria consulate, 1869. Plans. (FO 925/3010)

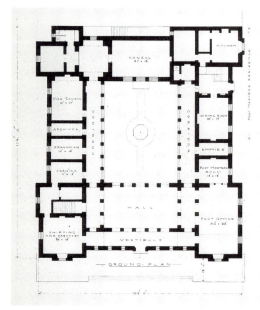

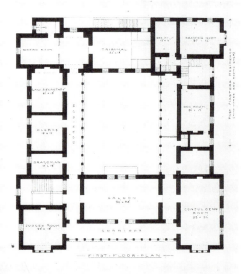

was a symmetrical grouping of four rectangular units with a fifth smaller one adding asymmetry to the ensemble. Two of these units were the two-storeyed projecting 'wings' with mullioned windows shaded by stone-bracketed pent-roofs for the judge's and consul-general's rooms on the upper floor. Recessed between these wings on the first floor was the main range of the front: the seven bays of the vestibule including the main entrance. Above and set back from this was the double-height block of the saloon, and linking all four units together was a square-piered loggia directly above the vestibule and providing a corridor between the upper rooms. All of these blocks were given flat roofs that could be used as roof gardens. The fifth and highest unit was an open belvedere placed at one side of the saloon block.

The sculptural quality of Wild's design also indicated his concern about its relationship to the city. He seems to have understood the nature of the site and its relation to the square and the church far better than any of the other architects involved in the project, all of whom had been to Alexandria. He understood, for example, that the building would be free-standing, visible from some distance on two sides and facing onto narrow streets on the other two. Moreover, the site was near the corner of a long square. Hence his design's partial asymmetry to address the centre of the square, its elevation onto a plinth, and the regulation of space in front of it through projecting platforms, steps and railings. With these means Wild would have established an honorific presence on the square, not by the use of symbols of authority and heavily articulated cyphers of power and wealth like most of the other designs, nor by the mildly transgressive and allusive effect of his own church or Donaldson's 'eastern' design, but instead through the visual, physical and, one must presume, ultimately psychological control of space. This continued within the design. The cocooned peristyle courtyard, the arcaded hall, and, above, the coffered saloon lit by attic windows; here were some of the major elements of Pompeian houses now made into the processional spaces of a colonial public building. The visitor would pass through carefully staged areas from public to notionally private domains; from the exterior Levantine space of the square (which, as has been shown, itself signified ethnic and cultural distinction from the 'native' town) to the interior English space of the square within, the enclosed courtyard with its octagonal pool. The required sense of social or national distancing would thus be achieved by an ordered spatial sequence, rather than a change of style from exterior to interior in the manner of Burges or Donaldson. It would continue that marshalled and edited sequence of urban spaces that we saw manifested in contemporary maps of the city. Wild's design might be understood as an attempt to emphasize and extend the institutional civility and graded physical distances of the modern city in contrast to the private and organic chaos deemed typical of the native town.

It is worth briefly comparing this design to an apparently similar building designed by Wild, and one that was actually built soon after this. An official British building was required in Tehran, the capital of Persia, for similar reasons as the Alexandria consulate. Tehran was at this time modernizing itself with a new *Ringstrasse* redefining its limits,[59] and Persia was undergoing the same economic domination by European powers as the Ottoman Empire. A new embassy building was required, first, because of international rivalry (in this case with Russia, which had started building a new embassy in 1866); and, second, because of trade and communication routes with India. Wild's building (Plate 79), designed in 1869 and finished in 1874,[60] forms three sides of a quadrangle. In contrast to the temple-fronted neo-Palladian Mission House (with mud-built annexes) that it replaced,[61] it deliberately gathered its various functions into a unified compound, and articulated them through a controlled oriental eclecticism: with a Byzantine chapel at the end of one wing, an Early Christian tower on the other, a polychrome entrance portal harking back to Wild's Cairene sketchbooks, and a wide-eaved pavilion above the central suite of reception rooms. This pavilion is particularly interesting (Plate 80). Mughal architecture in Persia and India had used such *talars* (stylar porches) on the second floor as viewing or reception platforms and also as signs of imperial presence: apart from Isfahan they can be found most notably in the Kasr-i-Qajar, the Shah's summer palace outside Tehran, illustrated by Pascal Coste in his *Monuments modernes de la Perse* (1867). And indeed Wild's building, set back within a grove of trees in a new suburb of the city, has a more evident relationship to this rural building type than it does to the kind of western urban palace with which Wild's Alexandria consulate, for all its carefully articulated parts, still aptly belongs.

PLATE 79 James Wild. Tehran legation, 1869. (RIBA 143A Z1/67)

By comparison, Wild's design for Alexandria might be regarded as a fantasy. He was not working according to any agreed set of provisions for the

consulate, and the rationality of his planning was enabled by a very simplified brief.[62] Such were the confusions and cross-purposes concerning the project that, when the Foreign Office received the design, far from considering its merits, they were baffled as to how Wild had even been employed.[63] Furthermore, by the time that Wild submitted his complete design in July 1869, the Foreign Office had lost all interest in the project, preferring to locate its consul-general in the newly expanding Cairo. By 1872 a British company, run by many of the leading members of the community, had taken over the site and begun building an edifice with offices and shops on the ground floor and residences above.[64]

The main reason why the consulate could not be built, at least not in any way acceptable to the government, was that in Egypt the British had neither the colonial administrative apparatus nor the logistical capacity to manage building work. British engineers did work in Egypt, particularly on schemes connected with the overland route to India, but they were employed either by British companies or by the Egyptian government. British architects practising in Egypt were an even rarer breed, and for good reasons: they were unlikely to be supported for long by British government or commercial commissions, and, even if they wanted, they were unable to penetrate the Italian-controlled building industry. Britain's relation to Egypt in the mid-century was that of the informal colonialist, and colonialism by proxy entailed a minimal official presence. Only after 1882 could the British set about remodelling the government, as well as the educational, penal and legal systems, and other elements of the state.[65] The imperial enterprise in this informal state was more a matter of establishing and controlling communications, tying commercial bonds, hiding inefficiency and doubt. The long-term financial and representational investments of architecture were poorly fitted to these needs.

Nevertheless, under these circumstances some British architecture was built in the Near East during this period. Despite the difficulties, these buildings were seen through to completion by organized interest groups backed by financial resources largely based in England. In Alexandria itself the Anglican church had been erected by the local British residents with funds from the Consular Advances Act and donations from companies with transit interests through Alexandria. In Jerusalem, as we shall see, and Istanbul, missionary societies possessed relatively reliable conduits for funds and expertise to enable them to build their churches despite official and local vagaries. The exception to these examples was of course the British consular architecture in Istanbul. But there, where it had substantial diplomatic interests to justify the expense, the British government had installed its own Office of Works architect who was able to oversee building work and to acquire a knowledge of local practices. With neither a committed client community in Alexandria – the British residents never organized themselves in support – nor a controlled means installed in Egypt of seeing the building through, the abandonment of the consulate project always seemed inevitable to many of the participants in the episode.

The subsequent amnesia regarding the consulate project has occurred because of its virtual containment within the memoranda and dispatches of government ministries. The only times that evidence of the project became public in England were in 1862 when Donaldson exhibited his second consulate design at the International Exhibition, and in 1870 when Wild showed his design at the Royal Academy. Wild's design was displayed when it had been practically abandoned, while Donaldson's design, lost amongst the welter of exhibits, seems to have gone unnoticed by the critics. Without exposure, the division of interests within government ministries and between

London and Alexandria, and their continually changing relation to Egypt – expressed and sustained by the various designs – was never forced into a fixed, built form.

The consulate project has to be seen therefore as a dramatic but strictly limited narrative about official architecture in Egypt; a drama that was rehearsed amongst a few actors who also had leading parts in the creation of policy towards that country, backed by supporting actors responsible for cultural mediation. The leading *dramatis personae* were Colquhoun, Layard, Palmerston, Donaldson, Wild, and perhaps Hekekyan Bey: the colonial administrator, the orientalist politician, the aloof pragmatist, the professional liberal, the Islamic expert, and the Ottoman technocrat. The scenario was compounded out of accurate knowledge of the setting and inherited prejudices about the subject. But its script was continually redrafted, never acted out.

7

NEW JERUSALEMS

EVANGELICAL ARCHITECTURE IN JERUSALEM

•

May this prove the beginning of the restoration of a pure Christian Church
and worship in this city ... a distant but genuine shoot from the primitive
stock, preserved for these many centuries in the distant isle of Britain, and now
in these last days transplanted back again to its original native soil!

(*John Nicolayson, 1838*)

The 'distant but genuine shoot' of the above passage first grew into a church
and compound of buildings within the walls of the old city of Jerusalem then,
fifty years later, produced offspring in the form of a hospital sited in the
expanding suburbs of the city. These buildings form the twin focuses of this
chapter, and both of them, as we found in previous chapters, are products of
a dynamic but uneven interplay between home and foreign locations. Both
were built in the Ottoman-ruled city by the Low Church, evangelical London
Society for the Promotion of Christianity Amongst the Jews (also known as the
Jews Society). An essential part of the society's colonial project in the city was
to represent a militant evangelical view of religious history, a view consonant
with the revived intensity of seventeenth-century Protestantism. Inherent to
this were the doctrine of conversion and a pious yet not necessarily prudent
imperialism, either of which might collide or collude with changing British
political interests in the Levant as this evangelicalism strove to reach the same
prominence in British policy that it had achieved in British India. Furthermore, unlike Alexandria where Wild's eclectic, orientalist church represented an ideal alliance between the local British community and a notional
Muslim host, or Istanbul where Burges's design was to embody an alliance
between governments, in Jerusalem there was no British community and the
overt proselytizing efforts of the Jews Society were aimed only at the still small
Jewish population. Conversion was to be achieved by exemplary difference
rather than orientalist persuasion.

John Nicolayson, an evangelical missionary in Jerusalem, regarded the building of an Anglican church there as an opportunity to return a pure form of Christianity to the city of its origination. For Nicolayson, the evangelical Christianity which he practised dated back to the first and second centuries AD, and had been nurtured in Britain, a new if temporary Jerusalem, ever since. There it had been preserved from those later, mutant forms of Christianity which had established themselves in Jerusalem during the ensuing centuries. Islam had also come, asserting its own religious priorities and severing the Holy Land from Christian control. Now, in the mid-nineteenth century, with the encouragement and endorsement of British power, evangelicals could return their plant to its soil.

There are delicious ironies in this rhetoric. Evangelicals in England were drawn to the affinities between themselves and the Jews of the Old Testament. They were also fired by a gentile Zionism, encouraging Jews to move back to Palestine by appeals to a notion of ancient heritage. Yet, when they arrived in a country returned to Ottoman rule in 1841, every effort was made by missionaries to convert these Jews to the religion of Henry VIII, and, more specifically, to the Old Testament-inspired piety of evangelicalism.

Jerusalem itself was no mere neutral plot for this evangelical and non-orientalist colonial project, but a city of intense rivalries and enormous political and religious symbolism. Its potent place in the imagination and mythology of several cultures was matched by the potency of space in the city, especially of its quarters and their key buildings. Any addition was bound to carry an extraordinary symbolic weight. Like Alexandria and Cairo it had, since the sixteenth century, suffered a period of official neglect by Istanbul. But from the mid-nineteenth century, following a period of occupation by Muhammad Ali, construction boomed, modern building technologies were imported, and European countries at the highest level of state assumed a direct interest in the city. Religious communities, with their characteristic close-knit and inward-looking compounds and quarters, dominated it but they now assumed an expansionist attitude that entailed the growth of facilities for pilgrim-tourists, the refurbishment and extension of philanthropic buildings, and often an active interest in the members of other communities. Some new sects even joined the fray. Amongst the first and most influential of these were the evangelical Anglicans, unofficial representatives of the British government.

EVANGELICAL DISCOURSE ON PALESTINE

Evangelicalism became a powerful force in early nineteenth-century English society, spreading through the middle classes and infiltrating the institutions of the Anglican Church. Its faith was based on the literal truth of the Bible, on intuition and feeling, and consequently on a personal, non-institutionalized relationship with God arrived at through Atonement. Evangelicals believed they had a mission to save the unconverted and often used their public positions to this end. They believed in Britain's special role in restoring Jews to the Holy Land, and restoration was also one of the conditions predicted in scriptural prophecy for the Second Coming, an essential part of evangelical eschatology, the realization of inevitable narrative drives. A typical example of this belief was Matthew Habershon's *A Dissertation on the Prophetic Scriptures* (1834). Habershon was one of the Jews Society's architects and was to play an important part in building the society's church in Jerusalem. His book presented an exegetical account of how the prophesied 'Signs of the Times' could be accurately dated. His objective was 'to refer the important scenes and momentous events amidst which we are living, to their proper place in the prophetic page'.[1] The prophecies were calculated so precisely that the restoration of the Jews was dated to 1843, leaving less than a decade for the job to be done.[2] But it could be quickened through the efforts of missionary societies and the conversion of Jews to Christianity, both of which were seen by Habershon as other Signs of this Second Coming.

Lord Ashley (later the Seventh Earl of Shaftesbury), known as the pope of the Low Church, was one of the best-known public promoters of Jewish restoration in the middle decades of the nineteenth century, and his evangelicalism was combined with a shrewd political sense. Ashley argued that a consul in Jerusalem would provide greater security for settling Jews, who in turn would improve the economy of the land.[3] Writing to Palmerston he described these Jewish settlers as 'the cheapest and safest mode of supplying the wastes of those depopulated regions'.[4] For Ashley and other influential evangelicals, religious beliefs could provide a sacred authority and a philanthropic face for policies of surrogate colonization. The belief in restoration, combined with the missionary impulse, also underpinned the Jews Society's desire to build a church in Jerusalem. In Ashley's terms the church project was an essential vessel both of restoration doctrine and conversion:

> Our soul-stirring and soul-satisfying Liturgy – in Hebrew – its deep
> and tender devotion – the evangelical simplicity of its ritual – will
> form, in the mind of the Jew, an inviting contrast to the idolatry and
> superstition of the Latin and Eastern Churches; its enlarged charity

will affect his heart, and its Scriptural character demand his homage.[5]

Later I shall show that this notion of simplicity offering an inviting contrast was particularly crucial to the architectural form of the new church, but before that the evangelical interest in Judaism and the city of Jerusalem must be seen in the context of a renewed interest in the Holy Land as a place still bearing witness to the authenticity of the Bible. Like the Egyptomania of these same decades, this bibliolatry – and its accompanying cultural tourism – was encouraged by the improving accessibility of the Ottoman Empire to westerners. The interest was widespread. There was already, of course, the ritual invocation of Biblical geography in sermons and hymns, giving many people a mental map of the Holy Land, and elementary schools often set their children to learn by rote the details of Biblical history and particularly the place-names of Palestine in topographical order.

A different form of Biblical interest was epitomized by Thomas Hartwell Horne's *Landscape Illustrations of the Bible* (1836). Horne's work provided over a hundred engravings of Biblical sites taken from recent views by such oriental specialists as Charles Barry (Plate 81), Frederick Catherwood, Joseph Bonomi and David Roberts, and adapted by artists like William Turner and Samuel Prout. The illustrated views were both topographical and picturesque, fitting

PLATE 81 J. M. W. Turner, based on a sketch by Charles Barry. 'Jerusalem', *c.* 1836. Engraving. (Horne, *Landscape Illustrations of the Bible*)

information about the place into established aesthetic conventions about the ideal landscape whilst ignoring any signs of agricultural labour. Each illustration was accompanied by a text recounting its Biblical associations and something of its present-day fate, itemizing the country's fall from grace and its present Muslim decadence. Scriptural sequence organized the narrative and legitimated what was otherwise straightforward travel literature. Thus the sedentary reader could imaginatively travel through the Holy Land while enjoying devotional replenishment and cultural superiority. Despite Edward Said's notion of the orientalist's desire for otherness, what these works predominantly celebrate and reiterate is a deeply laid cultural familiarity, even through a familiar form of moral outrage.

There was clearly a market in Britain for this kind of cheap, devotional and exotic work. In 1837, for example, the Jews Society exploited the popularity of this subject to raise funds for their new church in Jerusalem by publishing a set of views of the Holy Land.[6] The topographical landscape painter David Roberts was also to employ this combination of genres in several works directed at a similar audience. In his *The Holy Land* (1842–9), Roberts's prints were accompanied by notes on Biblical incidents, botany, Jewish history, recent events, and excerpts from the artist's own travel journal. Roberts was also to use the same type of landscape view to illustrate the Bible itself in 1857. The illustrations in these works have a scenographic quality that may owe something to Roberts's work as a theatre painter. More importantly, their empty stages conveyed a historical moral. Typically they show barely populated 'present-day' scenes (Plate 82), where Arab culture was either little more than a distant minaret and a colourful costume, or, when it did intrude, it was implied that this 'religion of barbarism', in Roberts's words, was to blame for current decay, idleness and ruination.[7]

In Roberts's work, in Horne's, and in that of a number of photographers who worked in Palestine,[8] geography – the land itself – became textual. This purportedly factual landscape imagery served to underline textual truth, and also provided an iconography suited to Protestant beliefs: to the experience of religion through traces and not through idols. These works supported that attitude to the Bible which was summed up when one writer called it 'the very best of all Guides to Palestine – the book which cannot err', or when Ashley himself claimed that 'a traveller may be guided by Holy Writ with all the minuteness and accuracy of a road-book'.[9] If Britons could travel to Jerusalem they might there employ Catherwood's map, itself annotated with all the relevant sites of Biblical recollection.

It is important to emphasize that the meaning of works like Horne's, and even Roberts's Bible, was not simply devotional. Most carried a more or less implicit message for modern English Christians. Echoing Ashley's view that

'The tide of action seems to be rolling back from the west to the east',[10] Roberts's catalogue predicted:

> If it is natural to regard the scenes of remarkable events in heathen history with classic emotion, how much more natural, powerful, and solemn must be the feelings excited by scenes among which lay the greatest events of human nature from the beginning of time, and which shall probably be again the theatre of events still more influential, superb, and comprehensive.[11]

Missionary groups, political interests, the work of publishers and artists, and the activities of travellers and archaeological groups (including the Syro-Egyptian Society and the Palestine Exploration Fund), all contributed to this discourse. Britain's modern role in Palestine was sanctioned by the inevitabilities of history and religion.

PLATE 82 David Roberts. 'Jerusalem from the North', 1838. Lithograph. (*The Holy Land, Syria, Idumea, Arabia, Egypt and Nubia*, 1842)

THE JEWS SOCIETY IN JERUSALEM

Established in 1809, the Jews Society was one amongst many evangelical mission societies set up at the turn of the eighteenth century.[12] It was active on both home and foreign fronts: by 1813 it had set up a church and school complex known as 'Palestine Place' in Bethnal Green, London, mission work was begun amongst Jews in Holland, Russia and Germany, and by 1820 it was sending missionaries to Palestine.

In the early nineteenth century missionary work multiplied in the Near East. The Church Missionary Society set up missions at Malta in 1800, Istanbul in 1819, Egypt in 1825 and Izmir in 1830,[13] all of which were aimed at members of the oriental churches. In the 1820s British and American missionaries began to converge on Syria and Palestine. The Jews Society decided that its own interests were at stake in this movement, but it also realized early on that diplomatic assistance was crucial.

After the First Syrian War of 1831–3, Muhammad Ali's occupation of Syria and Palestine relaxed some of the restrictions on travelling and residing in the Holy Land.[14] (It was after the war, for example, that – as discussed in Chapter 1 – Catherwood, Arundale and Bonomi visited the country.) In 1834 the Jews Society could begin planning to build a church there.[15] Its appeal for building funds was characteristically evangelical in its vision of aesthetic austerity as a measure of religious purism. Jews visiting the city must surely despise Christians as 'worshippers of images', and thus they could easily be drawn to the society's scheme: 'let a Protestant temple there erect its holy front – let a verse from the Hebrew Bible, engraved on its walls, attract the attention of the wandering Jew'.[16] The church would 'exhibit practically what Christianity is, as distinguished from the corruptions of the Romish, Greek, and Armenian Churches, which are so peculiarly offensive to the Jews'.[17] Protestants were presented, using Hebrew liturgy, as the truest descendants of those Jews in Jerusalem who had first converted to Christianity at the time of Christ. While this offered no formal guidelines for an architect, a kind of asymbolic programme had been established for the new church. It was to be a demonstration of scripturally ordained values and a haven for simple Christian practices. By its very negation, it was hoped, the church would be distinct from idolatrous representations.

The society's interest in Jerusalem was paralleled by a growing British governmental concern with that city. Britain had already established an official presence in Syria when the government took over the duties of the Levant Company in 1825. Consul-generals were established at Damascus and Beirut and a consul at Aleppo. In the late 1830s they also moved into Palestine, setting up a consular agent at Acre in 1837 and in Jerusalem in 1838.[18]

Palmerston and the British government believed that Jews would play a role in modernizing the Ottoman Empire as well as acting as agents of British commerce.[19] They were to be formally protected by the new consul, especially in their attempts to purchase land for settlement. The Jews thereby became a British-protected group, just as the French had taken over the interests of Roman Catholics and the Russians those of the Greek Orthodox. Although not a major commercial centre itself, Jerusalem was valued for its strategic and symbolic importance in the Holy Land at a time when the Porte's weakness threatened to leave these markets and cotton-producing lands in the hands of a powerful modern Egyptian empire.

THE CHURCH PROJECT

In September 1838 plots started to be bought piecemeal at a site near the Jaffa Gate (Plate 83) and registered in the name of an Armenian Christian who was an Ottoman citizen.[20] The next year, despite uncertainty about acquiring permission, Nicolayson felt able to press ahead with his building plans.[21] He produced a scheme in which the site was envisaged as a compound, with a group of very simple houses for missionaries, all one room deep and predominantly one storey high, arranged around a rectangular courtyard (Plate 84).[22] The proposed church, a rectangular preaching box intended to seat 350 people, was set back from the eastern side of the courtyard, hemmed in by a mosque and the garden of a neighbouring Armenian convent. The clasping buttresses evident in the plan indicate that a Gothic style was probably intended. Nicolayson's was a simple and untutored scheme, but the very fact that he produced it demonstrates the multifarious roles demanded of such missionaries: Nicolayson also negotiated the purchase of properties, inspected quarries, took on labour and supervised the clearing of the site and digging of foundations. He directed the masons to adopt local models, and recounted one such exercise:

> [I] went with Aboo Selameh to Bethlehem to see the plain style of building of the Greek Convent there erected in 1820. This will serve very well to give Aboo Selameh and the Mason, who himself worked on that, a general idea of the sort of building I wish. The details I must direct myself.[23]

But with the prospect of building the church now looming, more professional skills had to be employed. In July 1840 the society sent out William Curry Hillier, a 25-year-old architect and civil engineer, who

PLATE 83 John Murray.
Map of Jerusalem,
1858. Arrow indicates
location of Anglican
church. (*A Handbook for
Travellers in Syria and
Palestine*).

brought with him a small library of essential books: Palladio, Britton, Chambers on perspective, works on engineering, mortar and cement, and *Hints for Labourers*.[24] He brusquely reported that a lower storey of the mission house had been nearly completed,

> In the rude style of masonry generally adopted in the better class of Arab houses – a style which consumes a very large quantity of materials, and which I conceive it will be highly expedient to abandon . . . on the ground of economy, convenience, and sightliness.[25]

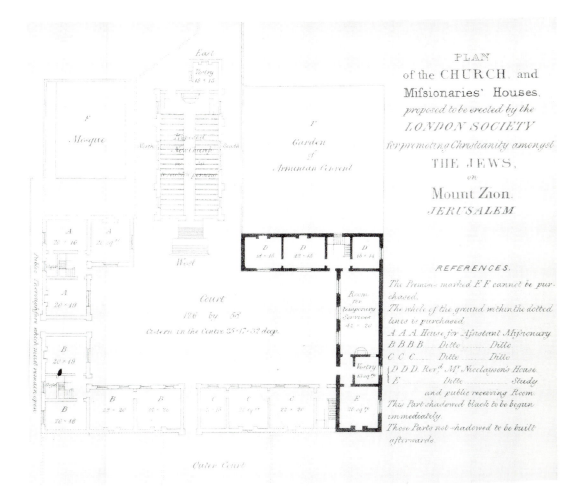

PLATE 84 John Nicolayson. Christ Church, Jerusalem, 1840. Plan. (*JI*)

This comment marks a turning-point in the evolution of the church. Until then Nicolayson had been attempting to adapt his notion of Gothic to the sources and skills available in the locality. Hillier wanted none of this. He desired a style of construction gauged 'with a view to meeting, so far as may be practicable, the expectations of contributors'.[26] He judged that better masons would be required than the Arabs whom Nicolayson had employed, and he decided to find them in Malta.[27] (There are shades here of what Street expected for the Crimean church, though the specific example – masonry rather than freestone walling – was the opposite of Street's.) Although Hillier was not to see this through, dying barely a month after his arrival, with his entry the project had become not only more professional but also more concerned with architectural and hence representational prestige. In addition the call for Maltese masons, albeit on a small scale, hitched the project into an imperial economy. The other step initiated by Hillier was to address the project as much or more to a British public as to its putative context.

NEW DEVELOPMENTS IN 1841

Britain achieved a new pre-eminence in Near Eastern affairs with her successful intervention in the Second Syrian War, which ended the Egyptian occupation of Palestine in February 1841. Encouraged by this, the vigour of the society's approach to finding a new architect demonstrates the increased importance that was attached to the church in Jerusalem. By 1841 the priorities for an architect were strict adherence to the society's religious line and a design to fit the demands of evangelicals at home rather than the conditions of Palestine. The Jerusalem church had thereby become a double-facing object; a mask presented as much to Britain as to Jerusalem.

The implications of the increased charge given to the project are worth detailing. When James Wood Johns (*c.* 1810–?) was appointed he was given an annual salary and sent out with an assistant 'to train him in his profession, for the future service of the Mission in that Department'.[28] Habershon would act as an agent in England. On the way to Palestine Johns stopped at Malta to secure the services of a foreman and two Maltese masons. The society now specified its ambitions: 'the style of building [would] be plain Gothic or Norman ... the plan be so formed as to admit of enlargement by future addition of transept, side aisle and chancel'. They allowed Johns to arm himself with 'Pugin's Examples, Pugin's Specimens, and Pugin's Gothic Ornaments'. Evidently Johns intended to use these stringent illustrations of Gothic architecture to provide him with at least the details for his 'plain' church. But, as I will demonstrate, plainness was a difficult concept for Johns, at least, to grasp. Plainness for his clients meant a kind of speaking modesty, a practical exhibition of religious, and hence political, value.

It was also decided to establish what was called a 'School of Industry' as part of the mission complex. Here 'moral and religious instruction combined with useful practical knowledge in all the various branches of medical science, mechanical arts and handicraft trades' would be taught to converts who would also be given a 'temporary asylum'.[29] They would have both 'a means of earning their future livelihood by their own industry' and an indoctrination into evangelical belief.[30] Such schools or houses of industry were common in evangelical missions and epitomized their belief in work as a technique of salvation.

An embarrassing problem in Malta, then a British colony, would have warned the Tory government about too close an identification with the church in Jerusalem.[31] In 1839 a church designed by Richard Lankersheer had been built in Valletta. This had soon developed serious structural problems and was condemned. The failure of the building was attributed to the incompetence of the Director of Public Works, adding fuel to a Maltese campaign opposing the English monopoly of Maltese government posts. All this had come to a head in 1841 when Lankersheer died and the British government commissioned William Scamp, civil architect to the Admiralty, to repair the church and thereby their own prestige.[32] It could not have escaped the government's notice that the British reputation in Palestine was even more delicately balanced, and that to stake it on a church was perhaps to risk too much.

But another cause focused British public attention on Jerusalem in 1841 and drove the church ahead of it. The story of the Jerusalem bishopric, one of the most controversial issues of the day, needs no retelling here except insofar as it affected the church in Jerusalem.[33] Inevitably Ashley and others saw the establishment of a bishopric as an essential tool of their predictive theology, as well as a way of strengthening the mission in Jerusalem. But the stakes were upped when the king of Prussia, Frederick William IV, proposed that the bishopric should be a joint venture centred on the new building in Jerusalem. It would thus establish Prussian interests in the Holy Land, while fulfilling the king's personal aim to achieve a Teutonic alliance of the Lutheran and Anglican Churches.[34] This belief in racial destiny was exemplified by the king's ambassador to Britain, the orientalist Baron Christian Bunsen. Bunsen had written as early as 1814 of how he sought 'to draw the East into the study of the entire Course of Humanity (particularly of European and more especially of Teutonic humanity)'.[35] Although this parallels Saint-Simonian interests, it can also be seen as a riposte to French influence, and it was certainly not to adopt any orientalizing garb. It seems, then, that in the early 1840s it was hoped that some form of Anglo-Prussian axis might be established to promote Protestant interests in the Levant, and that one pivot for this axis was Baron Bunsen.[36] It was Bunsen who completed the negotiations supported by £15,000 of Prussian money to help endow the bishopric.

By November 1841 a converted rabbi, Michael Alexander, was made bishop of Jerusalem, and from then until the Prussians withdrew from the scheme in 1886, bishops were alternately nominated by the English and Prussian monarchs. The Prussian intervention ensured that the significance of what was still a modest building project had become fantastically overinflated. Even before it had been started the church was set to bear a huge weight of significance and it was this burden, arguably, that influenced the miniature grandiosity of Johns's designs, and then the swing to the straitened modesty of the final building.

THE WORK OF J. W. JOHNS

Johns published an account of his experiences in Jerusalem and presented his design for the church in his book *The Anglican Cathedral Church of Saint James, Mount Zion, Jerusalem* (1844). It seems from this account that his initial plan to use concrete foundations was frustrated by the debris discovered beneath the surface of the site. This included not only the normal urban detritus but also ancient remains: segments of arches, broken floors, ruined chambers and fragments of sculpture. Consequently Johns had to dig down to the base rock, and when a foundation stone was laid on 28 February 1842, it was at a depth of 35 feet below the surface. The massive foundations that were built over the next nine months, between depths of 30 and 42 feet, consisted of great piers with connecting arches and walls (Plate 85). These elements traced out a plan that could be added to but not altered despite the vagaries of changing architects and restricted funds over the next few years.

PLATE 85 J. W. Johns. Building work on Christ Church, Jerusalem, *c.* 1842. (*The Anglican Cathedral Church of St. James, Mount Zion, Jerusalem,* 1844)

Johns imagined a more grandiose building than was suggested by these foundations. For instance, the foundations did not provide for the long chancel with a semicircular apse that Johns had drawn in his plans (Plate 86). If it had been built, this would have provided for the third of three nearly separate

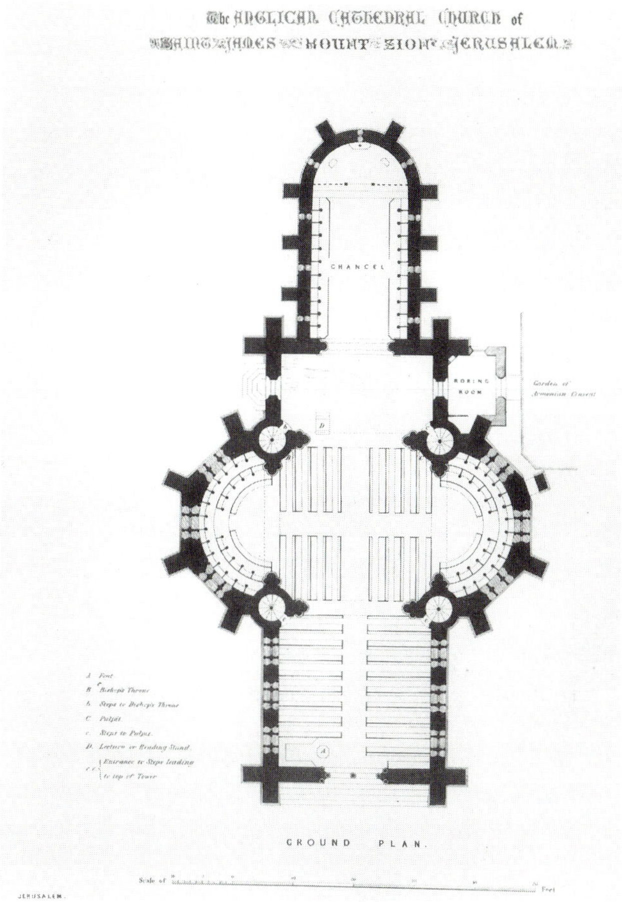

PLATE 86 J. W. Johns. Christ Church, Jerusalem. Plan. (*The Anglican Cathedral Church of St. James, Mount Zion, Jerusalem,* 1844)

ecclesiastic functions. Johns envisaged the church as the seat of a bishop and a large body of attending clergymen who would be separated from the rest of the congregation in the chancel, while the transepts with their curved benches formed a kind of tribune in the central part of the building, separate in its turn from the western end of the nave. The seating in this tribune was intended for children from the mission schools,[37] while the nave proper was probably intended for the planned Anglican community of Jewish converts and British citizens. The seating arrangement in the central tribune may not have been the only attempt to establish a distinct evangelical aspect in the design. Curiously, the chancel – a feature retained, despite truncation, from this moment onwards – may reflect a new recognition of its role by Prussian Lutherans who had passed rules in 1835 and 1842 upholding its importance.[38]

Johns's drawings show a church displaying an Early English Gothic vocabulary of triple lancets and rose windows (Plate 87). Yet rather than the crispness of detail and deftness in the use of archaeological reference identified

PLATE 87 J. W. Johns.
Christ Church,
Jerusalem. Perspective.
(*The Anglican Cathedral
Church of St. James,
Mount Zion, Jerusalem,*
1844)

with the work of A. W. N. Pugin at this time, Johns's design – even considering its 'popular character'[39] – had little refinement in its ornament, no apparent concern for texture, and a confused sense of proportion. This handling did not aid the grander elements of the design such as the central tower, barely higher than the steep nave roof, and – the design's most idiosyncratic feature – the four elongated pinnacles that rose from the corners of this tower. Johns also published an interior view looking down the greatly exaggerated length of the nave with its scissor-beamed roof, past the toplit crossing with a pavement decorated with five crosses in mosaic, and into a chancel flooded with light (Plate 88).

Evidently, Johns wanted to create a cathedral-like symbolism on a small scale, hoping that the paucity of his aesthetic and material resources would be hidden by his dramatic presentation. But his critics seized on these contradictory effects: 'the anomalies of the design arise from the architect having attempted to give an extraordinary effect with very humble means', wrote one.[40] Nevertheless, the significance of Johns's design lies in its extraordinary attempt to make evangelical presence architecturally manifest in a city where there were still only the seeds of a political influence to justify it. It was doomed to be a fantasy of paper architecture which attracted more

PLATE **88** J. W. Johns.
Christ Church,
Jerusalem. Interior. (*The
Anglican Cathedral
Church of St. James,
Mount Zion, Jerusalem,*
1844)

interest from political and religious circles than from the architectural establishment in England.

Johns's scheme was finally defeated by the unsolved problem of permission and the manoeuvrings that this still required. Just as building work had got under way the society decided that, to circumvent the lack of a firman, the church should be linked with the bishop's residence and so arranged as to seem only one part of a larger edifice. The initiation of the work and the prospect of Johns's strident scheme had brought the question of legality dangerously near to the surface. Also at this time Nicolayson's original idea of integrating the church into a compound was adopted in some anonymous and now lost plans that were prepared by order of the king of Prussia and included the new bishop's residence. These plans, conveyed to the society by Baron Bunsen, clearly fitted the new requirements, and in June 1842 Johns was told to adopt them. Bunsen further involved himself in the project by suggesting that German carpenters in Rome should be engaged.

Johns's position was made impossible, and in October 1842 he was dismissed.[41]

THE WORK OF MATTHEW HABERSHON

Johns's replacement was the society's own architect, Matthew Habershon (1789–1852). With the exception of his most prestigious work, Derby Town Hall (1828), Habershon's architecture was largely undistinguished and unnoticed. As has been shown, Habershon was also an exponent of evangelical theology, and his *Dissertation on the Prophetic Scriptures* (1834) accorded well with the aims of Lord Ashley and the Jews Society.

It was not until 1844 that Habershon made any progress with his design, and not until 1846, when the local city governor accepted Istanbul's granting of permission for a chapel attached to a consulate, that building work was restarted. Work proceeded relatively quickly, despite obstacles thrown in the way of procuring stone and labour by the authorities stopping the market then raising prices.[42] A roof and other wooden fittings were sent out from England, and the church was finally consecrated in January, 1849.[43]

Habershon's church, with its consulate and bishop's residence oddly attached, was substantially the same as the building that stands in the Anglican compound today (Plate 89). Additions in 1911 hardly changed the severe and rather dull structure that Habershon placed atop the foundations for Johns's idiosyncratic scheme. Despite the limitations imposed by these foundations, all of the exterior features of Johns's design, save the plan of his shallow transepts, were ignored. Instead a box with a shallow-pitched roof was

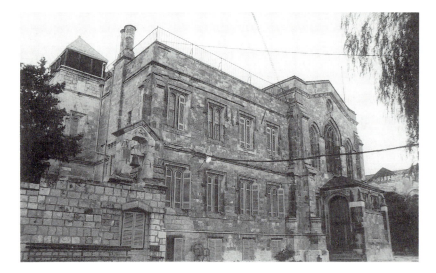

PLATE 89 J. W. Johns and M. Habershon. Christ Church, Jerusalem, 1839–49

built. As can be seen from Francis Frith's photograph, published in 1858, the
west front with its pierced, low gable, had five windows with reticulated
tracery and a simple doorway with a flat hood-moulding (Plate 90). The
consulate and bishop's residence formed a four-bayed two-storey building
attached to the north of the church and continuing the line of its west front.
The secular building was simply articulated with hood-mouldings and
stringcourses, but otherwise the exterior of both church and consulate were
unadorned. Together they formed a curiously terraced image (perhaps with
collegiate reminiscences) rising above a scattering of lower buildings grouped
around a courtyard. Here was an apt subject for Francis Frith's camera and one
that works across the grain of images like those of Roberts and Horne
discussed earlier. Although we are clearly placed in the city, once again its
eastern elements of domes and inward-looking houses are kept distanced. The
foreground is now occupied, through a combination of Habershon's design
and Frith's photography, with the newly dominant church, wide-eyed and
evenly fenestrated, facing out over a cleared site. This is a Christianized
Orient, an antidote to the 'terribly debased and defiled city' encountered by
Frith.[44]

PLATE 90 Francis Frith.
Photograph of Christ
Church, Jerusalem in *c.*
1858. (*Egypt and
Palestine Photographed
and Described*)

The interior of the church exhibited the unresolved differences between

Habershon's and Johns's conceptions (Plate 91). Johns's image of a soaring nave leading into the theatrically lit transverse and longitudinal volumes of crossing and chancel was lost, and with it the architecturally enshrined hierarchy within the congregation. Instead the nave was an unadorned, flat-ceilinged passage attached to the oddly expansive crossing and what was originally a somewhat truncated chancel. The wide eastern piers of the crossing and the shallow, apsidal transepts provided the only elements of visual interest. The altar itself was originally very bare; instead of a cross there were 'two tablets of black marble, on which the Ten Commandments [were] engraven in Hebrew characters of gold'.[45] At the front of the church a wooden screen, which in a synagogue would hold the ark, provided a vestigial narthex underneath a gallery. However schematically, the interior thus attached tokens of Judaism to its evangelical programme, marking out its intended target.

Not only were the dramatic cathedral-like aspects of Johns's design lost but also many of its Gothic trappings. It has to be remembered that in the previous decade, through the work of A. W. N. Pugin, there had developed a widespread identification between a fully revived Gothic architecture and Roman Catholicism. If Gothic was to be used by evangelicals to signal Englishness it had also to be distanced from its Puginian associations. Thus with Johns's design shorn of its hints of Roman Catholicism, only its openness and uncluttered quality remained. This unobstructed, unsymbolical space was typical of evangelicalism. The chapel built for the Jews Society at Bethnal Green in 1813 had been designed in a markedly austere Greek Revival style.

PLATE 91 J. W. Johns and M. Habershon. Christ Church, Jerusalem, 1839–49. Interior looking east.

Later, when the Gothic Revival was more widespread, simplicity remained the ruling notion in Protestant writing about church architecture. George Wightwick, for example, wrote in 1840, 'We require, for our Protestant Cathedral, no internal piers nor arcades; free space, and as large a number of sitters as can be accommodated ... being the chief desiderata'.[46] In 1849 James Fergusson, in overt opposition to Pugin's vision of Catholic architecture, called for a Protestant church architecture not dogmatically attached to one style but open to progressive evolution, and, crucially, centred on the concept of open spaces free of obstruction to sight or sound.[47]

Coming through all these evangelical buildings and statements is a relative lack of concern for style. And what this suggests in turn is that the overall disposition of the architecture – its interior openness, its emphatic but simple exterior – was more significant than any style that it adopted. At Jerusalem the result might be read as a statement of Low Church values: modestly English in style, austere in its surfaces, accessible in its spaces and marking itself out from Catholic and Orthodox persuasions while hopefully appealing to Jews.

This restraint was clearly seen by evangelicals as the key to the church's meaning. W. H. Bartlett described it as

> Without any pretensions to architectural beauty or decorative elegance ... neat, plain, and sufficiently appropriate, presenting, in its chaste simplicity, a striking contrast to the tinsel splendour of the Greek church of the Holy Sepulchre.[48]

For evangelicals, architecture was not to distract from the private inward conviction which was the only form of judgement in religious matters. The house of worship was neither to represent a corporate Church nor overly to stimulate the imagination, particularly not through idolatry and symbolism. It was to be an arena for the display of devout and exemplary evangelical practice.

But inevitably High Church critics found only meanness in this austerity. In his book *Palestine As It Is* (1858), George Bridges described how 'sadly defaced and disfigured it appears, if not desecrated, by a Mansion and domestic offices ... built in the angle of its Latin Cross', and therefore how it reflected badly upon British and Prussian power.[49] One High Church critic described its builders as incapable of 'divesting themselves of their innate propensity to Proprietary Chapels and Pew Rents'.[50] The desire to be distinct and 'to exhibit practically what Christianity is', combined with the contingencies of its construction history, account for something of this effect.

*

Despite all its other difficulties, the British church in Alexandria had benefited both from the good relations between the British community and Muhammad Ali, and, paradoxically, from Britain's defeat of Muhammad Ali in the Second Syrian War. The British church in Jerusalem had no such good fortune. First, there was no British community in Jerusalem. Second, Jerusalem was alternately occupied by Ottoman and Egyptian forces and was continuously kept in a position of legal ambiguity, particularly regarding laws relating to foreigners. Finally, its clients, the Jews Society, were the representatives neither of any British community nor of British government policy; in fact Britain's diplomats were often instructed to keep their distance from the church project. As a result an intricate net of considerations ensnared the very idea of building a church and forced it, literally, into line with the consulate.

Yet the differences between the churches in Jerusalem and Alexandria were primarily differences between what might be termed a militant evangelicalism and a liberal and less dogmatically defined approach. Where the latter resulted in an experimental oriental eclecticism invoking a Muslim public, the former produced an exercise in exemplary propriety directed at Jews and ignoring Palestinians entirely. Where the one evoked alliance or assimilation, the other expressed a Spartan adherence to the evangelical ethic: to conversion, not to engagement. The evangelical colonial project was, then, as much aimed against some interests (notably all forms of Catholicism, Roman or Anglican) as it was intended to attract a set of other interests (those of Jews in England and Jerusalem).

THE MISSION HOSPITAL

Around the new consulate and church stood some of the elements of the compound that had already been erected by 1849. To the south was the one-storey mission house that Nicolayson had built before Johns arrived on the scene and in which a temporary chapel had been set up. This was later replaced by a symmetrical, two-storeyed schoolhouse designed by Conrad Schick, a Swiss architect resident in Jerusalem who became head of the House of Industry and involved with the society's building plans in the late 1850s.[51] The other buildings accommodated a hospital, an elementary school, and the House of Industry. Thus by 1849 a small Protestant evangelical compound had come into being, but one whose central courtyard and main buildings remained relatively visible to the rest of the city. In the following years the community steadily increased.[52] In 1853 a boys' school was established just outside the city walls, and the society opened two farms and a training project for stonemasons at Talbiyeh. Another Anglican church was consecrated in 1874, built by the Church Missionary Society, which also erected churches in Shefamar, Nazareth and Mejedel.[53] And in 1894 an Anglican collegiate church was designed by George Jeffrey based on New College, Oxford, and finally completed in 1910. It was not, however, until the British Mandate was imposed after the First World War that any more consistent pattern of British building started in Palestine.

Of the British buildings that were built between the time of Christ Church and the Mandate, much the most interesting was the hospital built for the Jews Society by Arthur Beresford Pite (1861–1934) between 1892 and 1900. Pite's building points to important developments within what might be termed the 'mission aesthetic'.[54] Although it belongs to a later date than other buildings in this study, at a time when the British Empire was at its apogee elsewhere, in Palestine imperial influence was only beginning to assert itself with full architectural confidence.

By the 1890s Jerusalem, whose population had trebled since the 1830s, and which had expanded way beyond the Ottoman walls, had become a modern city. After 1892 tourists could arrive by train from Jaffa, travel by carriage along the newly paved roads of the suburbs, and, aided by the recent guidebooks of Cook or Baedeker, choose to stay at the New Imperial Hotel just inside the Jaffa Gate or one of the other modern hotels. Once settled, they could perhaps stroll out to acquire photographic souvenirs of the city from the establishments of Fiorillo or Bonfils. Two buildings stood out as having particular imperial significance from afar. On the prestigious site of the Mount of Olives overlooking the city, the Russians had built a cathedral distinguished by its five onion domes. Even more prestigious was the site within the old city, near the Holy Sepulchre, where the Germans were able to mark the consecration of their Church of the Redeemer in 1898 with the much-fêted visit of the Kaiser (even enlarging an entrance in the city walls so he could enter on horseback). German unification in 1871 and the dissolution of the joint bishopric in 1887 demanded an architectural statement of the new power. The Church of the Redeemer, designed by Friedrich Adler, was round-arched and domed, established continuity with the past by reusing some of the Crusader ruins around it, and affirmed Lutheran presence through its distinctive tower, the highest in the old city.

Amongst the various parties competing in the new city, British interests were largely preoccupied with the expanding suburbs on the western side of the old city. It was here, along the road to the new station, that Sir Moses Montefiore (1784–1885), a wealthy British-born Jewish philanthropist, established the parallel roads of the Yemin Moshe neighbourhood with the British government's help. Montefiore, who acted as a kind of roving ambassador for Jewish interests but whose concerns often meshed well with those of the British government, was able to buy a site in his own name, possibly because of his prominent mediating role and possibly as a mark of the alliance that in 1855 was engaged in war in the Crimea.[55] A windmill and a long line of almshouses known as Mishkenot Sha'ananim (or 'Montefiore's cottages') were built from 1857 to 1860, designed by William Edward Smith (Plate 92).[56] These almshouses became the straight-terraced basis for the later Yemin Moshe quarter. Placed in relatively open space, philanthropically intended half for Sephardi Jews and half for Ashkenazi Jews (each with a synagogue at the end of the terrace), and given an emphatic low rectilinear form, these almshouses set up a rhetorical contrast of enlightened modernity with the cramped, airless warren of streets in the old city and perhaps even with the intimate communities and clustered houses of Jewish and Muslim settlements outside it. If the old city was still the place where imperial power found its best expression in religious buildings, the new city springing up outside its walls was the site where the lessons of modernity could best be spelt out.

The most prestigious hub of the extramural suburban building boom was the Jaffa Road, and it was here that the Jews Society acquired a site for a new hospital. Since the 1870s both sides of this road had seen the development of new Jewish quarters, built using locally cut stone and with roofs often supported by iron girders. A great influx of Russian Jews arrived in Jerusalem

PLATE 92 W. E. Smith. 'Montefiore's cottages', Jerusalem, 1860. (S. Manning, *Those Holy Fields*, 1874)

in the early 1880s, settling mostly outside the city, and helping to revive the activities of the Jews Society.

The society's journal, *Jewish Intelligence*, was revamped in 1885 and kept a close eye on the new Jewish colonies in Jerusalem. In 1890 the journal's cover was redesigned to combine an engraved view of the sun rising over Jerusalem together with images of Palestine Place (the society's base in London) and the sunlit interior of Christ Church; signalling a new ambitiousness and sense of achievement (Plate 93). This theme of a linked circuit of home and foreign locations, a kind of contrapuntal geography, runs through many missionary activities; it was essential, for instance, to the whole project of 'return'. It can also be found in the methods used to raise funds and moral support for the hospital. *Jewish Intelligence* reported how a 'Palestine and Eastern Exhibition' toured England in 1892, including a 'Street in Jerusalem':

> At intervals Dr D'Erf Wheeler, aided by various friends in Eastern costumes, practically demonstrated many Biblical and modern Oriental costumes; and under the experienced guidance of Mrs S. Schor, the weird sounds of Arabic wedding and funeral chants, with the twang of strange Eastern instruments and the persistent tom-toms, so familiar to the Palestinian traveller, broke in upon the animated talk in Jerusalem Street and around the Bedouin Encamp-ment, and evoked an intensity of silence, which only ended in delighted applause.[57]

Like other missionary societies, the Jews Society had seen early on that one of the best ways to exert missionary influence was under the cover of medical relief (it was because these aims were so transparent that rabbis opposed and boycotted such missionary hospitals).[58] They saw that the location of the hospital was crucial to its success, and that it had to be able to compete with the other hospitals (German, French, Russian, Jewish and Turkish) standing on the same ridge as the Jaffa Road.[59] Through professional architectural expertise they also saw that the new building had to address its context and audience, Jews who might use the hospital, in a more carefully measured manner than hitherto, yet also to break out of the sterile and unambitious mission architecture that the society had built previously.

Arthur Beresford Pite would have identified closely with much of this. He was first commissioned to design a hospital in 1892, at a time when he was serving on the society's general committee (as Street had been when he gained the Crimean church commission).[60] The project allowed him to follow both family tradition and his devoutly evangelical beliefs.[61] In 1892 Pite, who had studied at the South Kensington School of Art, was working in the office of

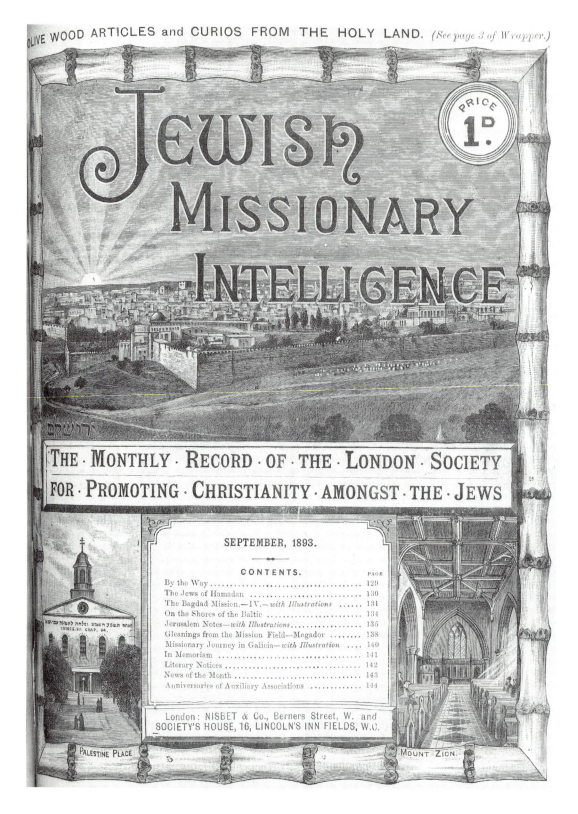

OLIVE WOOD ARTICLES and CURIOS FROM THE HOLY LAND. *(See page 3 of Wrapper.)*

JEWISH MISSIONARY INTELLIGENCE

PRICE 1^D

ירושלם

THE · MONTHLY · RECORD · OF · THE · LONDON · SOCIETY · FOR · PROMOTING · CHRISTIANITY · AMONGST · THE · JEWS

SEPTEMBER, 1893.

CONTENTS.

London: NISBET & Co., Berners Street, W. and
SOCIETY'S HOUSE, 16, LINCOLN'S INN FIELDS, W.C.

PALESTINE PLACE.

MOUNT ZION.

John Belcher. He and his friend William Lethaby, both keen activists in the Arts and Crafts movement, had begun to question the picturesque eclecticism of the prevalent 'Queen Anne' style, and, in Pite's case, to reconsider the now unfashionable High Victorian architecture of Burges, Cockerell and Street, particularly for its demonstrative tectonic effects, its feeling for materials, and its preference for functional expression over formal order. Like many evangelicals Pite held these to be virtues above adherence to any one style, and in his later career he would cast them in Baroque, Byzantine, Greek or Gothic form. In Jerusalem he had a commission of peculiar potency, one where he might establish himself as an independent architect, making these still nascent ideas congruent with the religious and political imperatives of the project.

Pite's first scheme for the hospital, exhibited at the Royal Academy in 1892, drew on several references to the architecture of the region. The components of the hospital were planned on what was called the 'pavilion principle' (Plate 94): grouped as separate elements linked by their gridlike placement as well as by long covered passageways across the site. In effect, the Nightingale ward had remarried the military cantonment, but was now dressed in a new and exotic set of clothes. The service and administration wings fronting the site were given pentroofs and picturesque towers with wide balconies, such as Pite would later observe in Damascus.[62] In the centre of the

PLATE 93 (opposite) *Jewish Missionary Intelligence.* Cover, September 1893.

PLATE 94 A. Beresford Pite. First design for English mission hospital for Jews, 1892. (*Builder*, 1893)

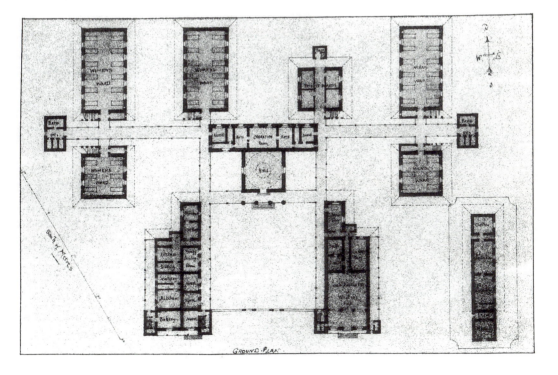

GROUND PLAN

plan was a square domed hall, with the dome supported on eight pointed brick arches and fronted by a large polychrome arch. Although it was made much more modest in the final scheme, this dome was a clear sign of Pite's interest in Byzantine architecture.

This interest in Byzantine must be placed at a very early stage in the late nineteenth-century 'Byzantine Revival', since it predates the most important work in that style, J. F. Bentley's Catholic cathedral in Westminster (1895). Unlike Lethaby, who was at this time working on his and Henry Swainson's key book on Hagia Sophia, to be published in 1894, Pite's interest in this architecture seems to have had a distinct religious flavouring. As another friend later put it, in Pite's work 'a tendency can be observed for Protestantism to turn to the forms of the Eastern Church for its expression rather than to those of the Church in the West'.[63] An identification with the forms, it should be emphasized, rather than the *practices* of the Orthodox Church, which Pite would probably have been appalled by. The reasons for this are perhaps better sought in terms of a desired affinity with the architecture that accompanied the earliest centuries of Christianity, and that in Pite's view could be seen as

PLATE 95 A. Beresford Pite. English mission hospital for Jews, Jerusalem, 1894. (*Builder*, 1896)

ENGLISH MISSION HOSPITAL FOR JEWS SITUATED ON THE HILL GAREB JERUSALEM BIRD'S EYE-VIEW LOOKING NORTHWARD 1893 BERESFORD PITE ARCH

the earliest distinctively Christian architecture.[64]

Although its large dome was reduced, on first sight the finished Jerusalem hospital, unlike the society's earlier church, still has the capacity to shock and disorientate. In 1894 the architect was forced to abandon the first scheme because its outer units came too near the precincts of a mosque, and he reacted by gathering in all the units from the corners of the site and joining them with a curved arcade.[65] The centripetal forces symbolically exerted by the first scheme's domed hall were now replaced by an immediate, almost autocratic visual unity, achieved by having the wards and other buildings radiate outwards from a central open hub. In a bird's-eye view (Plate 95) Pite pictured the hospital as an extraordinary amalgam of images: to one pair of eyes a radial compound centred on a trim circle of lawn, like a crescent of bungaloid almshouses; to another, a Baroque semicircular courtyard harbouring a miniature ideal city of cupolas and gable ends; to a third, a frontier town of cubic blocks and pillared huts set down on a rocky wasteland occupied only by a couple of camels, their minders, and a distant, dilapidated mosque. This was Pite's embodied and rather theatrical idea of evangelical munificence. And

it was both more and less than a vision: a new Jerusalem outside the old city of God.

Opened in 1897, but only completely finished in 1900, the hospital was substantially built using local stone and the masonry skills locally encouraged by the Jews Society since the mid-century.[66] Pite, who had visited most of the hospitals in Jerusalem, emphasized how the detachment of the wards and the provision of numerous doors and windows would help 'cure patients with as little medicine as possible', through the effects of light and ventilation. Modern enlightenment was to be supported by Hebrew inscriptions over the doors.[67]

Although Pite's hospital matched the solemn qualities of local construction and stonework, what was extraordinary about it in this context was not any symbolic or associative surface style or details. Even more than the other architecture discussed in this book, it established its sense of radical difference from anything oriental by its dynamic spatial disposition. Both the hospital and the church were place-clearing buildings that attempted to assert a new sense of spatial form against the organic, tight-knit quarters of the city. Pite's was an architecture which, despite its clear allusions to a Levantine vernacular, aimed to go beyond the meanings of style. If there were messages in the hospital building then they were intended as much or more for the subjects of evangelicalism as for Pite's architectural culture in Britain. Pite's architecture had to steer a course between some merely didactic and wishful demonstration of British distinctiveness, and an associative charade of respect and understanding for local styles, crafts and histories. It wanted to show rather than to display: to draw general affinities with the place and culture in which it was built, in order to convert both space and souls. It could be said, then, that its primitivism intimated a newer kind of modernism than had been known by the nineteenth-century architects of empire.

CONCLUSION

•

Although there are a number of redolent images of British architecture in the Near East, there is no definable form of colonial architecture that was specific to the British in this location. There might be two linked reasons for this. First, despite the domestic imaginings of orientalism, there was no simple target, no even notionally unified public, to be aimed at in the Islamic city. Instead there was an extraordinary range of groups – arguably far wider than in India and certainly wider than in Britain – to be considered in deliberations over design. To list only the major ones, there were the rival French, Italians or Russians, British expatriates and British tourists, Prussian Lutheran allies, ruling Ottomans or Egyptians, various mediating groups, and the Jewish and Muslim subjects of proselytism, to any of whom some form of address might be deemed necessary.

Perhaps the very range of styles and attitudes within a suddenly visible architectural presence could be said to be one condition of Victorian architecture in the informal empire. Architecture had to address a number of specific audiences, such as the groups that provided its funding, or the intended users of the building (groups in the immediate urban setting or groups in Britain), whilst also conjuring up more amorphous constituencies such as the generalized ideas of a Muslim or a Jewish public. (It is a notable comment on the last of these ideas that the number of actual religious conversions was remarkably low.) As this architectural endeavour became more and more inflated and overdetermined in its attempt to address myriad audiences and to represent the different aspirations of clients, so these ambitions were encouraged by the rich variety and flexibility of Victorian eclecticism. The resources of stylistic choice and synthesis might seem to have led to a bewildering range of responses to this situation, but they also resulted in an identification of conflicting interests that could have more specific or more multifarious meanings than was possible in, say, the relatively mute versions of international neoclassicism seen in Smith's buildings in Istanbul or than might have been possible in a single established and doctrinaire imperial style.

The second reason for this problem in defining British architecture in the Near East is that, although we can find the established and elaborated tropes and schemata of orientalism in writing about architecture of the region, there was no uniform western culture, no single and irreducible interest at stake over all this activity, and therefore no all-commanding colonial discourse – as Said would have us believe. To take one instance, there was in fact a range of institutionalized Anglican bodies that had to be catered for and distinguished, both from each other and from other religious interests: High Church in Istanbul; evangelical in Jerusalem; and liberal broad church in Alexandria. These were often linked to the strategic local concerns of British communities, which might match or conflict with a number of formal political concerns. We can say that Radical interests were involved in Donaldson's orientalist consulate design, and more tentatively that Whig concerns may have been influential in the British consulate buildings of Istanbul. Local British interests in Jerusalem and Alexandria in the 1840s, as we saw in their churches, were sometimes at odds with those of the British government. Yet the Crimean Memorial Church was clearly more the manifestation of powerful High Church and Tory interests in England than of a transient political moment in Istanbul. Also worthy of mention are those figures who promoted modernization and reform, and who had links with both local and European interests: Montefiore and Hekekyan, amongst others. It is when these different kinds of interests cohered, and especially when architecture seemed to establish an identity around which cohesion could occur, that we can talk of certain colonial projects, often unconsummated and often in friction with one another.

But in terms of construction strategies, even with a relatively small number of buildings erected in this period, one trend is discernible. Very broadly, while indigenous solutions to problems set by the climate were increasingly adopted or at least considered, it can also be said that builders drew more on British methods of organizing labour and on British sources of technology and materials, including prefabricated items, towards the end of this period than at its onset, and, more specifically, that they even tended to take this option during the course of the various buildings. There was some flirtation with the idea of using local skills for the Crimean church, and possibly some actual use of them in St Mark's, but otherwise when skilled work had to be done craftsmen were either imported to instruct local workmen, or the work was executed in England and shipped out. Unskilled labour was often the only substantial resource that was supplied locally.

On a local level, then, and given a limited number of examples, the policies adopted in construction can be seen to move towards the patterns of distribution and specialization that came to characterize the global economy. This certainly supports Brian Taylor's stripping of the myth that western methods 'promoted a desirable restructuring of traditional building trades to modern industrial commissions'. Instead, as Taylor has argued, there was

> a destructuring of traditional know-how and methods of organization which, in many instances where colonial powers had trained local technicians and cadres, subsequently left many countries at independence with a building industry incapable of doing anything other than meet demands of the modernist sector.[1]

Despite the several distinct approaches to architecture, shared attitudes towards the oriental city can be found. Over and above the enormous symbolic significance attached to sites, there was a recurring desire to form compounds, or compound-like groupings of buildings, particularly in Istanbul, Jerusalem and Alexandria. Compounds came about partly because of the rivalry between European communities in these cities, and partly as a consequence of the restrictive religious and property laws regarding foreigners that had generally been abolished in Europe but still prevailed in the Near East during this period. These compounds were both inward- and outward-looking. Their most significant buildings manifest a desire to announce themselves through facades, disjunctive form, bell-towers, sheer height, or a new spatial relationship to the city. They are very visible presences that assert themselves with and against those orientalist tropes about the 'Islamic city' commonly reiterated at the time, if not yet to achieve codified form.[2] The questions are really about what kind of power they visualize, with what confidence, and to what effect?

The larger European-style replanning of these cities had little obvious British involvement in this period. It was usually carried out under the direction of local elites (Cairo), or European groups with only marginal British participation (Beyoglu and Alexandria). The British tended to regard most of the Near East and especially Egypt more in terms of its access to India than of its own large-scale reorganization. Besides, what they saw as its Picturesque qualities still prevailed, sometimes even in the organization of their own architectural spaces. It was only after this period, with the need to create an apparatus of control, that the British started to regard urban design as part of the regulation of physical resources, to involve themselves in its adminstration and to transfer on a more wholesale basis the skills they had gathered in India.

This book has emphasized how the practice of informal imperialism was made to seem a benevolent or inevitable force through ideological constructs of alliance, identity, philanthropic reform, or modernization, and the role that architecture played both as a functional material object and as representation. This was not a one-sided matter. Near Eastern rulers often desired both the means and the forms of western culture and industry. The skills and products of the West were therefore imported as much as they were forced on the area (and not necessarily for modernization – the Fossati brothers, Catherwood, and others, for example, were employed to restore mosques).

But the question of dissent and resistance needs to be addressed more explicitly here. Although mediating acts should not be forgotten, there are also examples in most of this architecture of blocking, delaying, demonstrating, boycotting and generally harassing tactics from the indigenous population and rulers, to both the activities of building and those of recording architecture, and, through them, to what those activities might institute. Sometimes these resistances were orchestrated from above, sometimes they arose spontaneously from local slights, sometimes they were an institutional defence of enshrined legal and religious prohibitions, and sometimes they simply arose from a refusal to kowtow to a foreign power. Always, they inscribed themselves on the histories of these buildings, if not directly shaping their architectural form. Though 'resistance' might seem too strong a term, it usefully corrects the tendency to explain away such acts as merely the xenophobic reflexes of traditional groups. They should be seen as cases where British architecture came into mostly silent but sometimes open conflict with those pre-established social patterns and forces that refused, opposed, or simply failed to recognize its various rhetorical postures, and perhaps saw it within a different kind of world-view, as an imposition of foreign influence and methods; a harbinger of unwelcome change.

Almost inevitably, each of these buildings had a long gestation period and encountered enormous difficulties in construction. The Crimean church was finished eleven years after it was first mooted, and only after many changes and reductions; W. J. Smith's embassy in the same city took fifteen years to build, his consulate six years and his seaman's hospital eight years; John's and Habershon's church in Jerusalem took nine years to build; Wild's church in Alexandria took nine years and even then was incomplete; and the Alexandria consulate, for which designs were shuffled around for ten years, was never built. One exception to this pattern is itself exemplary. St Helena's Chapel in Istanbul was built very quickly in 1856 due to the employment of British sappers and miners staying in the city during the Crimean War, and the use of British army materials. Otherwise the history of the architecture of informal empire is largely a history of the disappointment or insufficiency of orientalist ambitions. It was a much less coherent and a much more multivocal activity than we might have imagined from Said's thesis. Yet the informal empire was proving to be an essential part of the British economy. Why were there these disparities?

Some light might be shed on the difficult experience of this architecture by the easy execution of the few buildings that British architects designed for Ottoman clients, especially the buildings designed by W. J. Smith, and perhaps the kiosks designed by Owen Jones and Robert Stephenson. Clearly more research is needed here, yet it can be said that these were buildings in which certain commodities, meanings and skills were clearly sought out and acquired, and in which economic co-operation was closely related to the gathering of cultural values. In the buildings erected by and for the British, there was little or no such exchange. In addition to, and partly as a result of, the acts of resistance outlined earlier, there was little continuity or accumulation of practical knowledge between these projects, in sharp contrast to the apparently mounting data and certainties of orientalism. There were simply not the mechanisms or, with the slow and convoluted funding arrangements, those mechanisms were insufficiently greased to enable British architects to work in harmony with the local building industry.

To compare British buildings with British involvement in the development of railways (which, like banking, prospered under the conditions of informal imperialism) would expose what a fragile and symbolically overloaded relationship building had with local cultures. The local economy had little to gain from such an occasional encounter, and the British could not make local conditions simulate those at home. Only under the extreme conditions of war, where resources could be managed within military organizations, could a project be quickly completed. Otherwise building histories are riddled with compromise and incomprehension to a far greater degree than the normal frustrations of this work.

Following from this, it could be said that, although this British architecture held before it ideal images of imperial control, religious conversion or quasi-alliance, there was in fact little fit between its form and the development of informal imperialism. The contrast with India is telling. There, since the late seventeenth century, military engineers had taken on much of the early building work of the East India Company, and after 1857 a Public Works Department was set up as part of the apparatus of imperial government. After the mid-century increasing numbers of British Royal Engineers, civilian engineers and professional architects worked in the subcontinent, and their work was supported by newly established engineering colleges and, more generally, functioned within the imperial administration of capital, law and labour, as well as a developing colonial sociology.[3] Through these formations building work could often be managed in this alternative centre of the empire much as it was directed in Britain. The only similar example of this situation in the Near East was in Istanbul, where the British maintained Office of Works architects for some years. Even then, of course, these architects had to adapt themselves to a system which was not controlled by the British. British building activity was in a curious position: nearer to British debates and practices than in India because most of its architects were still firmly lodged in the British context, and yet further away from that familiar setting because the infrastructure for building was so different and in such different hands.

Victorian architecture in the Near East was thus an inefficient and often contradictory matter. It is hard to argue that Britain's power was embodied in its architecture, in any comparable way to what happened in India, but it could be said that its buildings were an expression of British aspirations and often a site or record of their frustration. Certainly from these buildings we arrive at a very different and much more fragmented idea of colonial discourse than we might have assumed.

If these detailed studies of buildings have exposed the disordering experience of architecture, the discussion of the more distanced, British-based representation of the Near East's architecture has shown its greater success in imposing order. It was particularly in the accounts of Islamic architecture, rather than in what the British saw as the culturally and historically more equivocal architecture of Byzantium, that there seems to have been a congruence between the growing influence exerted by the British over the region and the scholarly ordering of new knowledge. This can be attributed to two major causes: first the availability of racial theories or, to put it more broadly, the recourse to racial categorization as a cognitive and evaluative armature; and second, the important role of Islamic models to debates about industrial design and design education. Yet, in more specific areas, building and orientalist knowledge were not distinct, even if they were unable to claim the same form of success. At many points building activity touched on the enterprise of understanding Islamic architecture: in particular cases like the use of a neo-Islamic style in St Mark's and in Donaldson's 'eastern' consulate design for Alexandria; in the manner in which Jones, Burges, Wild and Donaldson studied the architecture of the area; or in the various attempts to find forms suitable to the climate. Furthermore, all of these buildings were conceived in relation to certain ideas that were held about their oriental settings: particularly notions of Islamic display, of the essential elements of Islamic urbanism and architecture, and of what constituted a Muslim public. Beyond these areas of contact were the motivating forces of religion and imperialism, and the drive to define nation and race, which underlay architecture as an area of knowledge and a form of representation. Without an understanding of these forces the buildings and the writing seem unconnected and each is left without its fuller context. If, for instance, Ruskin's cultural critique is shorn of its racial themes it is left without that more equivocal, shifting set of oppositions that enabled him to invest his work with the thematics of imperial struggle; just as Wild's church in Alexandria, if separated from contemporary orientalist thought or considered without its nineteenth-century Egyptian setting, becomes either an example of associationist aesthetics or an exercise in answering the conundrum of nineteenth-century style and a signpost on the road to modernism.

The mission both of this architectural practice and of architectural history was to identify and differentiate, to set up a notion of what was definitively oriental and Islamic, and to align or contrast Britain with that notion as needs demanded. Imitations of Islamic architecture at home made the contrasts more pointed while straining out what seemed either too similar or too complex from the original. The international exhibition was an important symbolic machine, relating centre and periphery, nation and colony. It was also around this orbit that the debate between Jones and Ruskin moved, swaying from rationalism and geometry to empiricism and naturalism. This mission also enabled connections between, for example, Ruskin deliberating on Islamic ornament and a clerk of works struggling to train a workforce in Istanbul, or Lord Ashley pronouncing on Jewish restoration and an architect importing Maltese masons into Jerusalem.

Such formulations of the relation between ethnography and architecture of James Fergusson or Edward Freeman, or a debate like that between Ruskin and the Cole group over the relevance of Islamic art to design education, were not simply insular affairs, but gathered together many of the notions by which contemporary Islamic society was understood, and thereby helped to focus the policy and architectural approach taken towards it. Eclecticism was itself an appropriately flexible aesthetic approach for this imperial mission. However, coherent representations, in whatever style, demand accessible and malleable resources – whether buildings, workforces or audiences – and these were not so apparent or so easily regulated in the Near East as they were in theoretical work and historical analysis. Herein lay the problem that was not only at the heart of these buildings, but which must also be seen as central to architectural discourse as a whole. Orientalism was never interested in nor adequate to the job of describing architecture as an ensemble of properties, representations and practices. Orientalism, and writing about Islamic architecture in particular, never attempted to analyse the contradictions and complexities of particular oriental settings. Architecture had to resolve or bypass these difficulties in order to be built.

NOTES

•

INTRODUCTION

1 This term was first formulated in John Gallagher and Ronald Robinson, 'The Imperialism of Free Trade', *Economic History Review*, 6, 1953, pp. 1–15. For theories of imperialism see R. Owen and B. Sutcliffe (eds), *Studies in the Theory of Imperialism*, London: Longman, 1972; Anthony Brewer, *Marxist Theories of Imperialism*, London: Routledge & Kegan Paul, 1980; Tony Smith, *The Pattern of Imperialism*, Cambridge: Cambridge University Press, 1981; Giovanni Arrighi, *The Geometry of Imperialism*, London: Verso, 1983.

2 British exports to the Near East increased more than fourfold, from 3.5 million in 1848 to 16 million in 1870: Eric Hobsbawm, *The Age of Capital, 1848–1875*, London: Cardinal, 1988, p. 66.

3 Edward Said, *Orientalism*, New York: Vintage Books, 1979, p. 58.

4 See Nicholas Thomas, *Colonialism's Culture: Anthropology, Travel and Government*, Cambridge: Polity Press, 1994, pp. 105–7. Apart from Thomas's, the most useful recent books in this area are Homi K. Bhabha, *The Location of Culture*, London: Routledge, 1994; Lisa Lowe, *Critical Terrains: French and British Orientalisms*, Ithaca and London: Cornell, 1991; John MacKenzie, *Orientalism: History, Theory and the Arts*, Manchester: Manchester University Press, 1995; Robert J. C. Young, *Colonial Desire: Hybridity in Theory, Culture and Race*, London: Routledge, 1995; Bill Ashcroft, Gareth Griffiths and Helen Tiffin (eds), *The Post-Colonial Studies Reader*, London: Routledge, 1995.

5 Thomas, *Colonialism's Culture*, p. 105. See also Stephen Slemon, 'The Scramble for Post-Colonialism', in Ashcroft, Griffiths and Tiffin (eds), *Post-Colonial*, pp. 45–52.

6 Said, *Orientalism*, p. 52. Several books have recently addressed this subject: Timothy Mitchell, *Colonising Egypt*, Cambridge: Cambridge University Press, 1988; Thomas R. Metcalf, *An Imperial Vision: Indian Architecture and Britain's Raj*, London: Faber & Faber, 1989; Nezar Alsayyad (ed.), *Forms of Dominance: On the Architecture and Urbanism of the Colonial Enterprise*, Aldershot: Avebury, 1992;

Zeynep Celik, *Displaying the Orient: Architecture of Islam at Nineteenth-Century World's Fairs*, Berkeley and Los Angeles: University of California Press, 1992.

7   Edward Said, 'East Isn't East – The Impending End of the Age of Orientalism', *Times Literary Supplement*, 3 February 1995, p. 4.

8   Edward Said, *Culture and Imperialism*, London: Vintage Books, 1994, p. 87; Paul Rabinow, *French Modern: Norms and Forms of the Social Environment*, Cambridge, Mass. and London: MIT Press, 1989, p. 290.

9   Oleg Grabar, *The Formation of Islamic Art*, New Haven and London: Yale University Press, 1987, pp. 55–64.

10 S. A. Nilsson, *European Architecture in India, 1750–1850*, London: Faber, 1968, p. 105.

11 Timothy Mitchell's *Colonising Egypt* makes extremely interesting use of responses to modernization. For the problem of 'subaltern' reception see Gayatri Spivak, 'Can the Subaltern Speak?', in Ashcroft, Griffiths and Tiffin (eds), *Post-Colonial*, pp. 24–8.

12 T. J. Clark, *Image of the People: Gustave Courbet and the 1848 Revolution*, London: Thames & Hudson, 1973, p. 15.

13 Thomas, *Colonialism's Culture*, pp. 57–8.

14 See James Fergusson, *An Historical Enquiry into the True Principles of Beauty in Art, Especially with Reference to Architecture*, London: Longman, 1849; John Ruskin, *Works*, 9, p. 61; *Edinburgh Review*, 105, January–April 1857, p. 112.

15 See Gwendolyn Wright, *The Politics of Design in French Colonial Urbanism*, Chicago and London: University of Chicago Press, 1991; Rabinow, *French Modern*; S. Hamadeh, 'Creating the Traditional City – a French Project', in Alsayyad, *Forms of Dominance*, pp. 241–59. On urban apartheid see J. Abu-Lughod, *Rabat: Urban Apartheid in Morocco*, Princeton: Princeton University Press, 1980.

1   USEFUL KNOWLEDGE

1   See Kerry Downes, *Hawksmoor*, London: Zwemmer, 1979, p. 29.

2   Aaron Hill, *A Full and Just Account of the Present State of the Ottoman Empire*, London: John Mayo, 1709, p. 131.

3   Ibid., p. 130.

4   Richard Pococke, *A Description of the East*, London: W. Bowyer, 1743–5, vol. 1, pp. 28ff.; vol. 2, pp. 121ff. Pococke's manuscript shows that he wrote from older accounts rather than from direct observation: BM Add. 22995. Another writer who should be mentioned here is Thomas Shaw. Shaw commented on the Islamic buildings that he saw in his travels in North Africa and the Near East, but he was mainly interested in building materials: Thomas Shaw, *Travels, or Observations, Relating to Several Parts of Barbary and the Levant* (1757), 3rd edn, Edinburgh: J. Ritchie, 1818, 2 vols.

5   Pococke, *Description*, vol. 1, p. 37.

6   J. B. Fischer von Erlach, *A Plan of Civil and Historical Architecture*, London: published and translated by T. Lediard, 1737, preface.

7   S. P. Cockerell (ed.), *Travels in Southern Europe and the Levant, 1810–17. The Journals of C. R. Cockerell RA*, London: Longmans, Green & Co., 1903, pp. 26–7.

8   See M. Archer, *Indian Architecture and the British*, London: RIBA, 1968, pp. 32ff.

9   Martin Bernal argues that 'Egypt exerted more influence on Europe from the 15th to the 18th century than it did in the 19th': M. Bernal, *Black Athena: The Afroasiatic Roots of Classical Civilisation*, London: Free Association, 1987, p. 267.

10 RIBA: Barry Journals, vol. 5. See also M. Binney, 'The Travels of Sir Charles Barry', *Country Life*, 146, 28 August, 4 and 11 September, 1969.

11 Revd A. Barry, *The Life and Works of Sir Charles Barry, RA, FRS*, London, 1867, pp. 38, 26.

12 RIBA: Barry Journals, vol. 5.

13 Ibid., entry dated 2 November 1818.

14 Ibid., vol. 9, entry dated 30 May 1819.

15 Edward Said, *Orientalism*, New York: Vintage Books, 1979, p. 43.

16 Ibid., p. 85.

17 These illustrations appear in the 'État moderne' plate volumes 1 (1809) and 2 (1817): Commission des sciences et arts d'Égypte, *Description de l'Égypte*, Paris: Imprimerie impériale, 1809–28.

18 E.-F. Jomard, 'Description abrégée de la ville et de la citadelle du Kaire': ibid, 'État moderne' vol. 2, part 2, pp. 579–764.

19 For this see A. Godlewska, 'Map, Text and Image. The Mentality of Enlightened Conquerors: A New Look at the *Description de l'Égypte*', *Transactions of the Institute of British Geographers*, 20, 1995, pp. 5–28.

20 Selwyn Tillett, *Egypt Itself: The Career of Robert Hay*, London: SD Books, 1984, pp. 14, 17.

21 For their drawings see BM Add. 29812–29860. Several of the group (Scoles, Bonomi, Catherwood and Parke) were in Rome together in 1821, and many (Parke, Catherwood, Scoles, Arundale and Bonomi) attended Sir John Soane's Royal Academy lectures.

22 G. B. Belzoni, the Egyptologist, had been brought to Egypt by Muhammad Ali in 1815 to work as an engineer. A. C. T. E. Prisse d'Avennes, the French Islamicist, held an engineering post there from 1826 to 1836. Pascal Coste also worked for Muhammad Ali. Linant de Bellefonds, who went to Egypt in 1818, was employed as an engineer and was made Minister of Public Works in 1837. See V. W. von Hagen, *Frederick Catherwood: Architect-Explorer of Two Worlds*, Barre, Mass.: Barre Publications, 1968, p. 32.

23 This became the subject of Francis Arundale's *Illustrations of Jerusalem and Mount Sinai*, London: Henry Coulburn, 1837.

24 Catherwood's own account of his work was published in W. H. Bartlett, *Walks about the City and Environs of Jerusalem*, London: George Vertue, 1844, pp. 161–78. For other works using Catherwood's drawings see V. W. von Hagen, *Frederick Catherwood Archt*, New York: Oxford University Press, 1950, p. 50 n. 34. See also Y. Ben Arieh, 'The Catherwood Map of Jerusalem', *Quarterly Journal of the Library of Congress*, 1974, pp. 150–60.

25 BM Add. 29812.

26 Stanley Lane Poole, *Life of Edward William Lane*, London and Edinburgh: Williams & Norgate, 1877, p. 39.

27 E. W. Lane, *An Account of the Manners and Customs of the Modern Egyptians*, London: Charles Knight, 1836, vol. 1, p. iii.

28 T. Mitchell, *Colonising Egypt*, Cambridge: Cambridge University Press, 1988, pp. 23ff.

29 The 'Islamic city' as a codified orientalist construct only fully emerged in this century: see J. Abu-Lughod, 'The Islamic City, Historic Myth, Islamic Essence and Contemporary Relevance', *International Journal of Middle East Studies*, 19, 1987, pp. 155–76.

30 Lane, *Account*, vol. 2, pp. 9–11, 35–45.

31 Ibid., vol. 2, p. 3.

32 See Said, *Orientalism*, pp. 41, 169–70.

33 Hay bought Coste's drawings of Cairo in 1828 and negotiated forlornly to publish them himself: see Tillett, *Egypt*, pp. 43–5. These drawings are now in the V&A, Searight Collection. For this correspondence see BP.

34 Ibid.

35 See C. Mango, 'Constantinopolita', *Jahrbuch des Deutschen Archäologischen Instituts*, 80, 1965, 305–36.

36 Vulliamy's drawings are in the V&A, Searight Collection. See Michael Darby, 'Owen Jones and the Eastern Ideal', unpublished Ph.D. thesis, University of Reading, 1974, pp. 9–14; D. Van Zanten, 'Architectural Polychromy, Life in Architecture', in Robin Middleton (ed.), *The Beaux-Arts and Nineteenth-Century French Architecture*, London: Thames & Hudson, 1982, p. 209.

37 V&A, 8273A, 8276A and 8271A.

38 Van Zanten, 'Polychromy', pp. 209ff. See also R. Middleton, 'Hittorff's Polychrome Campaign', in Middleton (ed.), *Beaux-Arts*, pp. 174–96.

39 Owen Jones, *Lectures on Architecture and the Decorative Arts*, London: privately published, 1863, p. 18.

40 Thomas Hope, *An Historical Essay on Architecture*, London: J. Murray, 1835, p. 24. For Hope's views on ethnography see his *Essay on the Origin and Prospects of Man*, London: J. Murray, 1831.

41 M. A. Laugier, *Essai sur l'architecture*, Paris: Duchesne, 1753. William Hodges, writing in 1793, had compared the different prototypes of Greek, Gothic, Hindu and Islamic architecture, and argued that there could only be a theory of beauty relative to each of these prototypes. However, although Hodges cited Lodoli, there was no hint of the theory of apparent utility in his writing: William Hodges, 'Dissertation on the Prototypes of Architecture, Hindoo, Moorish and Gothic', in his *Travels in India during the Years 1780, 1781, 1782 and 1783*, London: J. Edwards, 1793, pp. 63–77.

42 Hope, *Essay*, p. 25.

43 Jones, *Lectures*, pp. 20–1.

44 See, for example, Samuel Johnson's *History of Rasselas* (1759), William Beckford's

Vathek (1787), and Benjamin Disraeli's *Tancred* (1847).

45 As in his No. 8 Kensington Palace Gardens (1843–6), and No. 24 Kensington Palace Gardens (1845–9 – demolished), London.

46 See Darby, 'Owen Jones', 1974; D. Van Zanten, *The Architectural Polychromy of the 1930s*, New York and London: Garland, 1977; Van Zanten, 'Polychromy', pp. 211–15; and Michael Darby and D. Van Zanten, 'Owen Jones's Iron Buildings of the 1850s', *Architectura*, 4, 1974, pp. 53–75.

47 Darby, 'Owen Jones', p. 81. Jones knew César Daly, Henri Labrouste and Prosper Merimée.

48 W. Benjamin, *Charles Baudelaire – A Lyric Poet in the Era of High Capitalism*, London: Verso, 1989, p. 165.

49 Particularly in the 1820s and 1830s, but also later, and most dramatically, with F.-M. de Lesseps and the Suez Canal: see Bernal, *Black Athena*, pp. 268–9; and Said, *Orientalism*, pp. 88–95.

2 SOUTH-SAVAGE

1 For racial theory see J. W. Burrow, 'The Uses of Philology in Victorian Britain', in Robert Robson (ed.), *Ideas and Institutions of Victorian Britain*, London: Bell & Sons, 1967; Martin Bernal, *Black Athena*, London: Free Association, 1987; Robert J. C. Young, *Colonial Desire: Hybridity in Theory, Culture and Race*, London: Routledge, 1995, pp. 65–6.

2 Edward A. Freeman, *A History of Architecture*, London: Joseph Masters, 1849, pp. 270–1.

3 Ibid.

4 Ibid., p. 313. For a discussion of the evolution of Freeman's theory and its relation to the theology of J. H. Newman see David B. Brownlee, 'The First High Victorians: British Architectural Theory in the 1840s', *Architectura*, 15, 1985, pp. 33–46.

5 See Thomas Hope, *An Historical Essay on Architecture*, London: J. Murray, 1835, vol. 1, pp. 144, 147; Joseph Gwilt, *An Encyclopaedia of Architecture*, London: Longman, Brown, Green, & Longmans, 1842, p. 52; A. B. Orlebar, 'Observations on the Mahomedan Architecture in Cairo', *Journal of the Bombay Branch of the Royal Asiatic Society*, 2, 1845, p. 137.

6 Similarly, J. H. Newman, on whom Freeman's theory of development was based, denied that the Turks had any 'internal history' or 'inward development': J. H. Newman, 'The Turks in Their Relation to Europe' (1853), *Historical Sketches*, Westminster, Md.: Christian Classics, 1970, vol. 1, pp. 213–14. See also E. A. Freeman, *The History and Conquests of the Saracens*, Oxford: J. H. and J. Parker, 1856.

7 Freeman, *History of Architecture*, p. ix.

8 Ibid., p. 16.

9 Ibid., p. 18.

10 Lecture given on 12 November 1845, *Proceedings of the OSPSGA*, Michaelmas term, 1845, p. 24.

11 Freeman, *History of Architecture*, pp. 271–2.

12 Ibid., p. 291.

13 James Fergusson, *The Illustrated Handbook of Architecture*, London: J. Murray, 1855, vol. 1, pp. 408–9. This is a curious comment given Ibn Tulun's many remarkably un-Egyptian features.

14 Ibid., p. 389.

15 Ibid., pp. 469–70.

16 Ibid., p. 469. Very similar remarks can be found about Indian architecture in Fergusson's *History of Indian and Eastern Architecture*, London: J. Murray, 1876, pp. 4–6.

17 James Fergusson, *A History of Architecture in All Countries*, London: J. Murray, 1865, p. 43.

18 Ibid., pp. 54–9.

19 Ibid., p. 70.

20 This was a widely held view: see, for example, E. A. Freeman, 'Creasy's History of the Ottoman Turks', *Saturday Review*, 2, 1856, p. 61.

21 Compare James Fergusson, *An Historical Inquiry into the True Principles of Beauty in Art*, London: Longman, Brown, Green & Longmans, 1849, p. 166.

22 Fergusson, *A History*, p. 72. Fergusson also found Comte's classification of knowledge useful for his *An Historical Inquiry*, p. 21.

23 Fergusson, *A History*, p. 73.

24 Ibid., p. 46.

25 Ibid., p. 42.

26 On Lyell see Roy Porter, 'Charles Lyell and the Principles of the History of Geology', *British Journal for the History of Science*, 9, July 1976, pp. 91–104; and Mott T. Greene, *Geology in the Nineteenth Century*, Ithaca and London: Cornell University Press, 1982.

27 See G. W. Stocking, 'What's in a Name? The Origins of the Royal Anthropological Institute (1837–71)', *Man*, 6:3, September 1971, pp. 369–90.

28 The review is actually of the appendix to Fergusson's *History of Modern Architecture* (1862), titled 'Ethnology from an Architectural Point of View'; however, this is very close to the introduction that appeared in *A History of Architecture in All Countries*.

29 *Anthropological Review*, 1:2, August 1863, pp. 216–27. The reviewer was probably James Hunt, the founder of the society.

30 The catch-all use of Turanian was particularly objectionable. The Turanians, properly speaking, were tented nomads. By enlarging this category and by including Egyptians within it, the *Anthropological Review* argued, Fergusson implied that black races were capable of building monumental architecture: ibid., pp. 221–2. This should be placed within Martin Bernal's thesis about the rise of an 'Aryan Model' of Greek and Egyptian culture: Bernal, *Black Athena*.

31 Ruskin, *Works*, 35, p. 403.

32 Ibid., 9, p. 34.

33 Ibid., 9, p. 39.

34 Ibid., 1, p. 118.

35 Ibid., 7, pp. 175–6. In arguing for the continuity of this geographic determinism I am deliberately cutting across the more common account of Ruskin's aesthetic development which sees his early 'Picturesque' work as giving way in the 1850s to analyses of detail, craft and labour.

36 Ibid., 9, p. 282. In an appendix Ruskin was careful to distinguish these comments from his view of the Alhambra which, having experienced the building through Owen Jones's book and clearly identifying it with that book's limitations, he found a decadent and detestable example 'fit for nothing but to be transferred to patterns of carpets or bindings of books, together with their marbling and mottling, and other mechanical recommendations': ibid., 9, p. 469.

37 Ibid., 9, p. 427.

38 Ibid., 22, p. 343.

39 It was not unusual for Islamic architecture to be included under Byzantine: see, for example, Jules Gailhabaud, *Ancient and Modern Architecture*, London: Firmin Didot, 1846, where the Byzantine section includes both San Miniato and the Mosque of Cordoba. Ralph Wornum had called Islamic 'only a Mahomedan development of Byzantine art': Ralph Wornum, 'Romanesque and Saracenic Art. Mosques and Moorish Palaces', *Builder*, 7, 1849, p. 328.

40 *Works*, 9, p. 41.

41 Ibid., 9, p. 38.

42 Ibid., 33, p. 94.

43 Ibid., 9, p. 40.

44 See Young, *Colonial Desire*, pp. 11, 17, 67.

45 See, for instance, *Works*, 10, pp. 176–7.

46 Owen Jones, *The Alhambra Court in the Crystal Palace*, London: Bradbury & Evans, 1854, p. 9.

47 Jones's principles had appeared in 'An Attempt to Define the Principles Which Should Regulate the Employment of Colour in the Decorative Arts' (lecture given on 28 April 1852 at the Society of Arts), and in four lectures 'On the True and False in the Decorative Arts' (given in June 1852 at Marlborough House): all were published in Owen Jones, *Lectures on Architecture and the Decorative Arts*, London: privately published, 1863. See also his article 'On the Distribution of Form and Colour Developed in the Articles Exhibited in the Indian, Egyptian, Turkish, and Tunisian Departments of the Great Exhibition', *Journal of Design*, 5, 1851, pp. 89–93.

48 See Eric Stokes, *The English Utilitarians and India*, Oxford: Clarendon Press, 1959.

49 Hans Aarsleff, *The Study of Language in England 1780–1860*, London: Athlone Press, 1983, pp. 139–41.

50 Jones's model for this presentation may have been F. M. Hessemer's *Arabische und alt-italienische Bau-Verzierungen*, Berlin: G. Reimer, 1842.

51 Owen Jones, *The Grammar of Ornament*, London: Day & Son, 1856, pp. 70–2.

52 Ibid., p. 78.

53 For a summary of M. D. Wyatt's views see his contribution after J. D. Crace's lecture, 'On the Ornamental Features of Arabic Architecture in Egypt and Syria', *Sessional Papers of the RIBA*, 1870, p. 85.

54 Ruskin's attention had been particularly drawn to this work: see *Works*, 16, p. 304 n.

55 See R. W. Lightbown, 'The Inspiration of Christian Art', in S. Macready and F. H. Thompson (eds), *Influences in Victorian Art and Architecture*, London: Society of Antiquaries, 1985.

56 *Works*, 10, p. 232.

57 Ibid., 12, p. 97.

58 Ibid., 16, p. 262. On Ruskin and India see Partha Mitter, *Much Maligned Monsters*, Oxford: Clarendon Press, 1977, pp. 238–51. For a related discussion of these issues see W. Vaughan, 'The Englishness of English Art', *Oxford Art Journal*, 13:2, 1990, pp. 11–23.

59 *Works*, 16, p. 263.

60 Ibid., 16, pp. 265–6.

61 Ibid., 16, p. 268. See also Ruskin's *Inaugural Address Delivered at the Cambridge School of Art, October 29, 1858*, Orpington: G. Allen, p. 23.

62 The issue of naturalism did not always separate Islamic experts from Ruskin and his supporters. T. H. Lewis, for example, regretted the apparent absence of nature in his subject as a severe curtailment of its aspirations: T. H. Lewis, 'Saracenic Architecture', *Building News*, 5, April 1859, p. 363.

63 *Works*, 16, p. 268.

64 Robert Young has argued that by the mid-1860s – fuelled by the Mutiny, the American Civil War, and the Jamaica Insurrection – cultural hostility to other races reached a new height: Young, *Colonial Desire*, p. 119. The question of support for Governor Eyre, who brutally suppressed the Jamaica Insurrection of 1865, polarized British opinion. Ruskin supported Eyre and has been accused of rightwing racism for doing so by Young and Edward Said: ibid., p. 87; Edward Said, *Culture and Imperialism*, London, Vintage Books, 1994, p. 157. Yet while undoubtedly Eyre's supporters were mostly rabid imperialists, Ruskin's position (and that of Charles Dickens) was more inflected, if inappropriately subtle. Here, as in his conflict with the Cole group, he was prepared to risk accusations of racism because he was more interested in exposing the hypocrisy of many of the utilitarian Radicals who opposed Eyre, arguing that their ideas produced white slavery in industrialism, his prime concern: Bernard Semmel, *The Governor Eyre Conspiracy*, London: MacGibbon & Kee, 1962, pp. 108–14. While Said has oversimplified this issue, his detractors have failed to notice or account for Ruskin's equivocal – to say the least – position on imperialism. On this issue John MacKenzie's counter-polemic, for instance, is guilty of the same distortive simplification of which he accuses Said: John MacKenzie, *Orientalism: History, Theory and the Arts*, Manchester: Manchester University Press, 1995, pp. 35–6.

65   See Peter Fuller, *Theoria*, London: Chatto & Windus, 1988, pp. 45–51.

66   Compare MacKenzie, *Orientalism*, pp. 35–6. MacKenzie accuses Said of ignoring Hobson's anti-Semitism and overplaying Ruskin's imperialism, yet his own account merely inverts this.

67   *Works*, 16, p. 307.

68   Ibid.

69   I am thinking particularly of the work of Ruskin's disciple Sir George Birdwood: see Annie E. Coombs, *Reinventing Africa: Museums, Material Culture and Popular Imagination in Late Victorian and Edwardian England*, New Haven and London: Yale University Press, 1994, pp. 43–62.

70   See Thomas R. Metcalf, *An Imperial Vision*, London: Faber & Faber, 1989, pp. 149–75. For Ruskin's later explicit views on Britain's duty to expand its rule, see Said, *Culture*, pp. 123–6.

71   Mitchell, *Colonising*, pp. 15–17.

72   See Tony Bennett, *The Birth of the Museum*, London: Routledge, 1995, p. 81.

73   *Journal of Design*, 5, 1851, p. 39; C. Hobhouse, *1851 and the Crystal Palace*, London: J. Murray, 1950, p. 133.

74   The others were Pompeian, Egyptian, Greek, Roman, Medieval, Renaissance, Elizabethan, Italian.

75   Samuel Phillips, *Guide to the Crystal Palace and Park*, London: Crystal Palace Library, 1855, p. 66. It was quite possible that these arrangements were too subtle and that both here and in the 1851 exhibition, as William Whewell argued, the proximity of exhibits would 'produce a spectacle in which is annihilated the time which separates one stage of a nation's progress from another': W. Whewell, 'The General Bearing of the Great Exhibition on the Progress of Art and Science', in *Lectures on the Results of the Great Exhibition of 1851*, London: G. Barclay, 1852, p. 14.

76   See *The Natural History Department of the Crystal Palace Described*, London: Crystal Palace Library, 1854.

77   Jones, *Alhambra Court*, p. 30.

78   Ibid., p. 32.

79   Ibid., pp. 34–42.

80   *Illustrated London News*, 17 June 1854, p. 585; *Catalogue of the Oriental Museum*, London: James Wyld, 1857; *The Times*, 9 August 1854.

81   On Lewis's Panopticon see *Builder*, 9, 1851, pp. 802–3; *Builder*, 11, 1853, pp. 290–1, 308–9; *Builder*, 12, 1854, pp. 137, 143; *Illustrated London News*, 31 January 1852, p. 96; *CEAJ*, 16, 1853, p. 161; Richard Altick, *The Shows of London*, Harvard and London: Harvard University Press, 1978, pp. 491–6; *Survey of London*, London: GLC & Athlone, 1966, vol. 34.

82   Desmond Ray, *The India Museum, 1801–1879*, London: HMSO, 1982, p. 42. For an illustration see *Illustrated London News*, 6 March 1858, p. 229.

83   For neo-Islamic architecture see Michael Darby, *The Islamic Perspective*, London: Scorpion Books, 1983; and John Sweetman, *The Oriental Obsession*, Cambridge: Cambridge University Press, 1988.

84 *Builder*, 12, 1854, p. 137.

85 *Illustrated Handbook of the Royal Panopticon of Science and Art*, London: Hotson, 1854, p. 6.

86 Ibid., pp. 7, 14, 15.

87 Ibid., p. 13.

88 Victor Horeau, who won the original competition to design the Crystal Palace, later made designs for an iron and glass theatre in Cairo: V&A, 7929.1,2.

89 Quoted in Raymond Head, *The Indian Style*, London: George Allen & Unwin, 1986, p. 121.

90 Bennett, *Birth*, p. 82.

91 See Paul Greenhalgh, *Ephemeral Vistas: The Expositions Universelles, Great Exhibitions and World's Fairs, 1851–1939*, Manchester: Manchester University Press, 1988, pp. 30ff.

92 Alfred Normand made a comparative study on this basis: see his *L'Architecture des nations étrangères . . . à l'Exposition Universelle de Paris*, Paris, 1870. See also Z. Celik, *Displaying the Orient: Architecture of Islam at Nineteenth-Century World's Fairs*, Berkeley: University of California Press, 1992, pp. 51ff.

93 Also at the 1889 exposition was Charles Garnier's History of Human Habitation, a street of 39 houses representing a taxonomy of housing across cultures: see Deborah Silverman, 'The 1889 Exposition', *Oppositions*, Spring 1977, pp. 70–91; Celik, *Displaying*, pp. 75–8; Mitchell, *Colonising*, pp. 1–13.

94 See W. Benjamin, *Charles Baudelaire – A Lyric Poet in the Era of High Capitalism*, London: Verso, 1989, pp. 164–7.

3 ORIENTAL BYZANTIUM

1 C. Mango, 'Approaches to Byzantine Architecture', *Muqarnas*, 8, 1991, p. 40.

2 David B. Brownlee, 'Neugriechisch/Néo-Grec: The German Vocabulary of French Romantic Architecture', *Journal of the Society of Architectural Historians*, 50, March 1991, pp. 18–21.

3 Charles Texier's Byzantine researches were published as 'Sainte-Sophie de Constantinople', *Revue Française*, 2, 1839, pp. 43ff., 275ff.; *Description de l'Asie Mineure*, Paris: Ministère de l'instruction publique, 1839–49, 5 vols.; and *Description de l'Arménie, la Perse, et la Mésopotamie*, Paris: Institut de France, 1842–52. His drawings were presented to the RIBA in 1867, where they still reside.

4 Félix de Verneilh, *L'Architecture byzantine en France*, Paris: Librairie archéologique de Victor Didron, 1851. For the French interest in Byzantine see Robin Middleton, 'The Rationalist Interpretation of Classicism of Léonce Reynaud and Viollet-le-Duc', *AA Files*, 11, 1986, pp. 29–48.

5 The best-known of these works was J.-I. Hittorff and L. Zanth's *Architecture moderne de la Sicile*, Paris: P. Renouard, 1835. On these issues see Neil Levine, 'Architectural Reasoning in the Age of Positivism: the Néo-Grec Idea of Henri

Labrouste's Bibliothèque Sainte-Geneviève', unpublished Ph.D. thesis, Yale University, 1975; Neil Levine, 'The Romantic Idea of Architectural Legibility: Henri Labrouste and the Néo-Grec', in A. Drexler (ed.), *The Architecture of the Ecole des Beaux-Arts*, New York and Cambridge, Mass.: Museum of Modern Art and MIT Press, 1977; Barry Bergdoll, '"The Synthesis of All I Have Seen": The Architecture of Edmond Duthoit (1834–89)', in R. Middleton (ed.), *The Beaux-Arts and Nineteenth-Century French Architecture*, London: Thames & Hudson, 1984; and Middleton, 'Rationalist Interpretation'.

6   T. L. Donaldson, *Preliminary Discourse on Architecture*, London: Taylor & Walton, 1842, p. 29.

7   *Ecclesiologist*, May 1842, p. 121.

8   George Godwin jun., 'Pen and Pencil Sketches in Poitiers', *CEAJ*, 5, May 1842, pp. 150–1.

9   *Ecclesiologist*, September 1845, p. 222.

10 Ibid., p. 223.

11 *Ecclesiologist*, May 1845, p. 108.

12 J. M. Neale, *A History of the Holy Eastern Church*, London: Masters, 1847–51, vol. 1, p. 166.

13 Anon., 'Churches of Palestine No. II', *Ecclesiologist*, December 1846, p. 206.

14 For instance, *Ecclesiologist*, March 1842, pp. 91–105; October 1842, pp. 5–16.

15 W. Kemp, *The Desire of My Eyes: The Life and Work of John Ruskin*, London: HarperCollins, 1991, p. 195.

16 R. W. Lightbown, 'The Inspiration of Christian Art', in S. Macready and F. H. Thompson (eds), *Influences in Victorian Art and Architecture*, London: Society of Antiquaries, 1985, p. 33; Hugh Brigstocke, 'Lord Lindsay and the *Sketches of the History of Christian Art*', *Bulletin, John Rylands Library*, 64, 1981, p. 28. See also William Vaughan, *German Romantic Painting*, London: Yale University Press, 1986, pp. 163–7.

17 See J. Steegman, 'Lord Lindsay's *History of Christian Art*', *Journal of the Warburg and Courtauld Institutes*, 10, 1947, pp. 123–31.

18 Lord Lindsay, *Sketches of the History of Christian Art*, London: J. Murray, 1847, vol. 1, p. 60.

19 Ibid., p. 69.

20 Ibid.

21 W. R. W. Stephens, *The Life and Letters of Edward Freeman*, London: Macmillan, 1895, vol. 1, p. 109. On Niebuhr see Martin Bernal, *Black Athena*, London: Free Association Press, 1987, pp. 297–307. The classic account of the impact of German historiography on British historians is Duncan Forbes, *The Liberal Anglican Idea of History*, Cambridge: Cambridge University Press, 1952.

22 Stephens, *Freeman*, vol. 1, p. 107.

23 E. A. Freeman, *A History of Architecture*, London: Joseph Masters, 1849, p. 7.

24 Ibid., pp. 164–5.

25 Ibid., pp. 165–6.

26 Ibid., p. 18.

27 See, for instance, Anon, 'Byzantium and Its Architecture', *Builder*, 17, 1859, pp. 354–6, 404–6, 644–6, 691–3, 852–5 – this refers to Niebuhr and traces a historical cycle of infancy, culmination and decline. See also Linda Dowling, 'Roman Decadence and Victorian Historiography', *Victorian Studies*, 28, Summer 1985, pp. 579–609.

28 James Fergusson, *The Illustrated Handbook of Architecture*, London: John Murray, 1855, vol. 2, p. 962.

29 See Bernal, *Black Athena*, p. 220.

30 George Finlay, *Greece under the Romans*, Edinburgh and London: W. Blackwood, 1844, p. xi.

31 Ibid., pp. 226, 492–3.

32 George Finlay, *History of the Byzantine Empire from 716 to 1453*, Edinburgh and London: W. Blackwood, 1853, vol. 1, p. 6.

33 See Lightbown, 'Inspiration', p. 27; Brigstocke, 'Lord Lindsay', p. 46.

34 *Works*, 9, p. 35 n. For other accounts of this subject see John Unrau, *Ruskin and St. Mark's*, London: Thames & Hudson, 1984; Jeanne Clegg, *Ruskin's Venice*, London: Junction Books, 1981.

35 Robert Curzon, *Visits to Monasteries in the Levant*, London: John Murray, 1849, p. 26.

36 *Works*, 10, pp. 146–8, 176.

37 Ibid., 10, pp. 78–9.

38 Ibid., 10, pp. 82–4.

39 Ibid., 10, pp. 91–3.

40 Ibid., 10, p. 93.

41 Ibid., 10, p. 98.

42 Ibid., 10, p. 117.

43 Ibid., 10, pp. 140–1.

44 Ibid., 10, p. 129.

45 Michael W. Brooks, *John Ruskin and Victorian Architecture*, New Brunswick and London: Rutgers University Press, 1987, pp. 57–9.

46 *British Almanac*, 1854, p. 239.

47 Pullan made three journeys to the Near East: see Charles Texier and R. P. Pullan, *Byzantine Architecture*, London: Day & Son, 1864, p. v. For Burges's visit see Chapter 5. The most important, if relatively late, architect to follow this path eastwards was W. R. Lethaby, whose visit to Istanbul resulted in his and Henry Swainson's *The Church of Sancta Sophia, Constantinople*, London: Macmillan, 1894.

48 For other strands and examples of this greater interest in Byzantine at this period see Mark Crinson, 'Victorian Architects and the Near East: Studies in Colonial Architecture, Architectural Theory and Orientalism, 1840–70', unpublished Ph.D. thesis, University of Pennsylvania, 1989, pp. 234–6.

49 G. E. Street, 'Architectural Notes in France', repub. in *Unpublished Notes and Reprinted Papers*, New York: Hispanic Society of America, 1916, p. 135.

50 David B. Brownlee, 'The First High Victorians: British Architectural Theory in the 1840's', *Architectura*, 1985, pp. 33–46. Freeman had used this theory as early

as 1843 in describing the history of Gothic architecture, but significantly he did not extend it to his analysis of Byzantine.

51 George Gilbert Scott, 'The Study of Medieval Architecture', *Building News*, 3, 1857, p. 279.

52 For Scott's designs see Rylands Library, Manchester, E. A. Freeman correspondence, Scott–Freeman, 11 October and 16 October 1856.

53 E. A. Freeman, 'Finlay on the Byzantine Empire', *North British Review*, 22, 1855, p. 343.

54 Freeman, 'Finlay'. Freeman criticized such 'Philo-Mahmoudism' in E. S. Creasy's *History of the Ottoman Turks* (1854), which, by contrast with Finlay, was castigated for continuing its history up to the present day: E. A. Freeman, 'Creasy's History of the Ottoman Turks', *Saturday Review*, 2, 1856, pp. 61–2, 88–9.

55 Stephens, *Life and Letters*, p. 149. Another prominent Oxford thinker who supported the Russians was J. H. Newman: see his 'The Turks in Their Relation to Europe' (lectures give in Liverpool, 1853), *Historical Sketches*, Westminster, Md.: Christian Classics, 1970.

56 E.-E. Viollet-le-Duc, *Entretiens sur l'architecture*, Paris: Morel, 1863–72, vol. 1, p. 195.

57 Ibid., p. 216.

58 Ibid., p. 199.

59 See also A. Solomon-Godeau, *Photography at the Dock*, Minneapolis: University of Minnesota Press, 1991, p. 157; Y. Nir, *The Bible and the Image: The History of Photography in the Holy Land, 1839–99*, Philadelphia: University of Pennsylvania Press, 1985, pp. 53–8.

60 'Renan saw it as his mission to bring science, which was Aryan, to religion, which was Semitic': Bernal, *Black Athena*, p. 346. On Renan see also Edward Said, *Orientalism*, New York: Vintage Books, 1979, pp. 130–48; Bergdoll, 'Edmond Duthoit', pp. 221–2.

61 See Bernal, *Black Athena*.

62 See his 'First Lecture at the Ecole des Beaux-Arts' (1864), reprinted and translated in *Architectural Design Profile – Eugène-Emmanuel Viollet-le-Duc*, London: Architectural Design, 1980, p. 25. In his *Histoire de l'habitation humaine* (1875), Viollet took up some of the Comte de Gobineau's notions of racial inequality, as expressed in his notorious *Essai sur l'inégalité des races humaines*: see Jacques Gubler, 'In Search of the Primitive', *Architectural Design Profile*, p. 83.

63 Viollet-le-Duc, *Entretiens*, vol. 1, pp. 215–26.

64 For an example of this belief see James Fergusson, *An Historical Inquiry into the True Principles of Beauty in Art*, London: Longman, Brown, Green & Longmans, 1849, p. 293. See also Bernal, *Black Athena*, pp. 341–2, 345.

65 Viollet-le-Duc, *Entretiens*, vol. 1, p. 226.

66 'The Churches of Palestine', *Ecclesiologist*, December 1846, pp. 206–14. There seems to have been little consideration at this time of the need for mosques to be aligned according to accurate compass orientations.

67 The works by Fergusson were: *An Essay on the Ancient Topography of Jerusalem*,

London: J. Weale, 1847; *Notes on the Site of the Holy Sepulchre in Jerusalem*, London: J. Murray, 1861; *The Holy Sepulchre and the Temple of Jerusalem*, London: J. Murray, 1865; and *The Temple of the Jews and the Other Buildings in the Haram Area at Jerusalem*, London: J. Murray, 1878. Fergusson first visited Palestine in 1864. His theory was partly based on Edward Robinson and E. Smith's *Biblical Researches in Palestine*, London, 1841.

68 George Williams, *The Holy City*, London: J. W. Parker, 2nd edn, 1849 (this included Robert Willis's 'An Architectural History of the Church of the Holy Sepulchre'). Ermete Pierotti explored the conduits under the Haram al-Sharif and published a refutation of Fergusson under the title *Jerusalem Explored*, London: Bell & Daldy, 1864, 2 vols. See also George Williams, *Dr. Pierotti and His Assailants, or a Defence of 'Jerusalem Explored'*, Cambridge: Deighton, Bell & Co., 1864; Comte Melchior de Vogüé, *Le Temple de Jérusalem*, Paris: Noblet & Baudry, 1864. It was Warren's survey in 1868 that finally scotched Fergusson's theory: see Charles Warren, *The Temple or the Tomb*, London: R. Bentley, 1880. On Pierotti see N. A. Silberman, *Digging for God and Country: Exploration, Archeology and the Secret Struggle for the Holy Land, 1799–1917*, New York: Alfred Knopf, 1982, pp. 73–4.

69 Silberman, *Digging*, p. 74.

70 Ibid., pp. 74–7.

71 W. Burges, 'The Church of the Holy Sepulchre', *Builder*, 21, 1863, p. 386.

PREFACE TO PART II

1 Nicholas Thomas, *Colonialism's Culture: Anthropology, Travel and Government*, Cambridge: Polity Press, 1994, p. 106.

4 ARCHITECTURE IN CAPTIVITY

1 Published sources on Wild have been either brief or fragmentary: they include C. Purdon Clark's Obituary in *RIBAJ*, 9, 30 March 1893, pp. 275–6; J. Summerson, 'An Early Modernist. James Wild and his Work', *Architect's Journal*, 69, 9 January 1929, pp. 57–62; H. S. Goodhart-Rendel's 'Rogue Architects of the Victorian Era', *RIBAJ*, 56, April 1949, pp. 251–9. In the 1970s, work on Owen Jones and architectural polychromy cast a passing light on Wild: see David Van Zanten, *The Architectural Polychromy of the 1830s*, New York and London: Garland, 1977, and Michael Darby, 'Owen Jones and the Eastern Ideal', unpublished Ph.D. thesis, University of Reading, 1974.

2 Michael Darby, *The Islamic Perspective*, London: Scorpion Communications, 1983, p. 65; Darby, 'Owen Jones', p. 24.

3 See Van Zanten, *Polychromy*, p. 347. Jones designed the interior decoration, which was completed in 1851, although only his painted capitals and apse mosaic survive.

4   GLRO P95/CTC1/139–51.

5   Summerson, 'An Early Modernist'; for Pevsner see his *Pioneers of Modern Design* (1936), Harmondsworth: Penguin, 1974, pp. 128, 151.

6   BIHR A2.42.5. Wild–Wood, 14 December 1841.

7   C. R. Lepsius, *Letters from Egypt, Ethiopia, and the Peninsula of Sinai*, trans. by L. and B. Horner, London: Henry G. Bohn, 1853, p. 35. Another member was the architect Georg Erbkam, who later designed the German Evangelical church in Alexandria (1867).

8   V&A, E3705-1938 to E3768-1938. One of these drawings, E3768-1938, is signed and dated 'Cairo Oct.(42)'.

9   S. Lane-Pool, *Life of E. W. Lane*, London and Edinburgh: Williams & Norgate, 1877, p. 114. See also BP, file of correspondence for 1843.

10 *Athenaeum*, 12 November 1842, p. 971; W. Thackeray, *Notes of a Journey from Cornhill to Grand Cairo*, London: Smith Elder, 1869, p. 506. The following drawings were all taken at Lewis's house: V&A, E3764-1938 to E3768-1938.

11 Obituary, *RIBAJ*, p. 276. Michael Darby has made these links to Fourierist and Saint-Simonian teaching: Darby, 'Owen Jones', p. 85.

12 V&A, E3845-1938 – this is dated May 1844.

13 Owen Jones drew upon Wild's studies for his *Grammar of Ornament*, London: Day & Son, 1856. They were also used by E. S. Poole in his appendix on 'Arabian Architecture' published in the 5th edition of E. W. Lane's *An Account of the Manners and Customs of the Modern Egyptians*, London: J. Murray, 1871, 2 vols..

14 *Athenaeum*, 15 June 1844, pp. 549–50. Wild's measured drawings of the tombs at Giza still exist: GI IA 20–22 – these are signed and dated November 1842.

15 It is not known whether the design was executed. FO 78/583, Barnett–Aberdeen, 23 March 1844. The site was off the Shari al-Dujara, to the south of present-day Garden City.

16 GI ID 27.

17 GI IC 13–16.

18 *Works*, 35, p. 405; ibid., 12, p. 363.

19 GI IC 17. A notebook (possibly of the same period as it includes studies of Theban decoration) contains notes on human proportion: GI IIA 49. Another notebook has sketches of male nudes: GI III.

20 See Kenneth Bendiner, 'David Roberts in the Near East: Social and Religious Themes', *Art History*, 6, 1983, p. 69.

21 See P. Rabinow, *French Modern: Norms and Forms of the Social Environment*, Cambridge, Mass. and London: MIT Press, 1989, pp. 64–5.

22 See J. Bonomi, *Project of an Instrument for the Identification of Persons in Military Establishments, Police Offices, etc. . . .*, London: Longmans, Green & Co., 1872; E. B. Tylor, *Anthropology: An Introduction to the Study of Man and Civilisation*, London: Macmillan, 1881, p. 79.

23 For his travels during these years see Mark Crinson, 'Leading into Captivity: James Wild and His Work in Egypt', *Georgian Group Journal*, 1995, p. 134 n. 25.

24 David Roberts, *The Holy Land, Syria, Idumea, Arabia, Egypt, and Nubia*, London:

Day & Son, 1855–6, vol. 6.

25   Edward W. Lane, *An Account of the Manners and Customs of the Modern Egyptians*, London: Charles Knight, 1836, vol. 1, pp. 29–30.

26   M. A. Serageldin, 'Urbanization and Social Change in a Foreign Dominated Economy: Cairo, 1805–1930', unpublished Ph.D. thesis, Harvard University, 1972, p. 31; A. L. A. Marsot, *Egypt in the Reign of Muhammad Ali*, Cambridge: Cambridge University Press, 1984, pp. 78–9. In 1830 Muhammad Ali imported power looms and a British engineer set up steam engines at Shubra and Qalat al-Kabsh: Marsot, *Egypt*, p. 171. See also A. Abdel-Malek, *Idéologie et renaissance nationale: l'Égypte moderne*, Paris: Éditions Anthropos, 1969, p. 31.

27   H. Dodwell, *The Founder of Modern Egypt: A Study of Muhammad Ali*, Cambridge: Cambridge University Press, 1931, p. 170. For a contemporary account of these good relations see R. R. Madden, *Egypt and Mohammad Ali*, London: Hamilton, Adams & Co., 1841, pp. 27–9, 50.

28   *Westminster Review*, 53, January–April 1841, p. 111.

29   Peter M. Fraser, 'Alexandria from Mohammed Ali to Gamal Abdal Nasser', in N. Hinske (ed.), *Alexandrien: Kulturbegegnungen dreier Jahrtausande im Schmelztiegel einer mediterranen Grossstadt*, Mainz am Rhein: Philipp von Zabern, 1981, p. 66. For Italians in nineteenth-century Egypt see L. A. Balboni, *Gli italiani nell civilità egiziana*, Alexandria: Società Dante Alghieri, 1906; M. Volait, 'La Communauté italienne et ses édiles', *Revue de l'Occidente Musulman et de la Mediterranée*, 46, 1987, pp. 137–55.

30   W. Furniss, *Waraga, or the Charms of the Nile*, New York: Baker & Scribner, 1850, pp. 14–15.

31   Gabriel Baer, 'Social Change in Egypt: 1800–1914', in W. R. Polk and R. L. Chambers (eds), *The Beginnings of Modernization in the Middle East: the Nineteenth Century*, Chicago: University of Chicago Press, 1968, p. 158. For figures of European communities in 1840 see M. J. Reimer, 'Colonial Bridgehead: Social and Spatial Change in Alexandria, 1850–82', *International Journal of Middle East Studies*, 20, November 1988, pp. 531–53.

32   FO 78/542 Stoddart to Aberdeen, 27 February 1843.

33   There have been two attempts at a history of St Mark's: R. Massie Blomfield, 'St. Mark's Anglican Church, Alexandria', *Bible Lands*, 2, 1904–7, pp. 81–3, 101–3, 116–18, 146–9, 176–9, 204–9, 217–21, 232–3; and an anonymous account in the *Egyptian Gazette*, 6 February 1902.

34   FO 78/375 Campbell–Palmerston, 28 July 1839 and 7 August 1839. Not surprisingly Campbell was replaced by the pro-Palmerstonian Colonel Hodges.

35   The *hodget* is in the SMDB together with a translation. It grants the land to 'General Campbell H.B.M.'s Consul at Alexandria'.

36   *Builder*, 5 September 1846, p. 421.

37   FO 78/503, Barnett–Foreign Office, 16 January 1842.

38   Act 6 George IV Cap. 87 – later known as 'The Consular Advances Act, 1825'; CMJ, c.15, 23 July 1839.

39   *CEAJ*, 6, March 1843, p. 107. J. L. Pearson, who worked for Salvin at about this

time, made tracings of the design: see J. Allibone, 'Anthony Salvin', unpublished Ph.D. thesis, University of London, 1977, p. 299.

40　Benjamin Webb, 'On the Adaptation of Pointed Architecture to Tropical Climates', *Transactions of the Cambridge Camden Society*, 1845, p. 216.

41　Ibid., p. 215. Derick's design was originally requested from the OSPSGA: *Proceedings of the OSPSGA*, Lent term 1843, pp. 14–16. Salvin was also asked for a design for the Colaba church, but a church was eventually completed in 1848 to the design of Henry Conybeare.

42　For example, V&A, E3840-1938, pp. 21, 26, 27, 32, 33, 36–45; E3800 and E3801.

43　V&A, E3759-1938 and E3782-1938.

44　*Builder*, 4, 5 September 1846, p. 421. See also *Athenaeum*, 11 April 1846, p. 373.

45　FO 78/583, Barnett–Bidwell, 22 March 1844. Similar claims of historical lineage had been made by the residents in 1840 when they noted in a resolution that 'British Protestants should be without a Church in the City of Alexandria, the scene of the labours of St. Mark, St. Athanasius, and many other primitive Christians': FO 78/542, Stoddart–Aberdeen, 27 February 1843.

46　*Proceedings of the OSPSGA*, Easter and Act terms 1845, p. 10.

47　Ibid., pp. 11, 13.

48　*Ecclesiologist*, November 1846, pp. 166–9.

49　FO 78/663, leaflet included in Barnett–Aberdeen, 4 April 1846.

50　See Thomas R. Metcalf, *An Imperial Vision: Indian Architecture and Britain's Raj*, London: Faber & Faber, 1989, p. 1.

51　This will also be discussed in relation to the Anglican church in Jerusalem – see Chapter 7.

52　For its construction history see Mark Crinson, 'Victorian Architects and the Near East: Studies in Colonial Architecture, Architectural Theory and Orientalism, 1840–70', unpublished Ph.D. thesis, University of Pennsylvania, 1989.

53　See GLRO P95/CTC1/139–51.

54　Bayle St. John, *Two Years Residence in a Levantine Family*, London: Chapman & Hall, 1850, pp. 24–5.

55　J. J. Auchmuty, *The Early Days of the Anglican Church in Egypt*, typescript in Middle East Centre (St. Antony's College, Oxford), Jerusalem and the East Mission, Box CIII, File IV.

56　There was one other neo-Islamic building on the square by 1882 – the 'Moorish' Zizinia Palace. Ruins of this building were photographed in 1882 by L. Fiorillo (photograph in the Royal Commonwealth Society Library).

5　THE SPECTACLE OF ALLIANCE

1　*Times*, 1 November 1858, p. 8. The ceremony was illustrated by a woodcut in *Illustrated London News*, 27 November 1858, p. 511.

2　Stratford hinted at this when he referred to how the church had been imposed on the Turkish quarters in Beyoglu through an act of 'requisition': *The Times*, 1 November 1858.

3   Works 10/4/773 – in 1845 there were 185 British nationals in Istanbul; in 1846, 207; in 1847, 249; and in 1848, 301. Estimates put the number of British seamen visiting Istanbul annually before the war at 2,000: *Building News*, 3 April 1857, p. 332.

4   *Architectural Magazine*, 1, 1834, p. 208. Barlow had been sent by the firm of Maudsley and Field to Istanbul to manufacture ordnance for the Turkish government. He later became better known for designing the immense single-span train shed at St. Pancras (1862–9).

5   H. M. Colvin (ed.), *The History of the King's Works*, London: HMSO, 1973, vol. 6, p. 635. Smith returned to England in October 1842, but by 1844 he was back in Istanbul: Works 10/4/810.

6   FO 97/406.

7   For many years Barry was thought to have been the designer – a mistake due to these resemblances and to Barry's having been brought in to revise Smith's design and investigate his accounts: Colvin, *King's Works*, p. 636.

8   For a description of the use to which this arrangement was put see Dowager Marchioness of Dufferin and Ava, *My Russian and Turkish Journals*, London: John Murray, 1917, p. 133. See also Works 10/3/718, 10/24/54.

9   Colvin, *King's Works*, p. 636.

10 Works 10/2/412.

11 Colvin, *King's Works*, p. 637.

12 Works 10/5/1065, 1161.

13 See, for instance, Revd Robert Walsh, *Constantinople and the Scenery of the Seven Churches of Asia Minor*, London: Fisher & Son, 1839, vol. 1, preface. See also Julia Pardoe, *Beauties of the Bosphorus*, London: Virtue, 1837.

14 FO 78/2067, Cumberbatch–Russell, 23 December 1862; USPG D29B, correspondence dated November 1860.

15 FO 78/341, 78/2067.

16 Works 10/42/1, FO–Trevelyan, 2 November 1847. The old chapel was located across a small road from Smith's new one. It was an apse-ended structure with galleries: PRO MFQ 167(2).

17 FO 78/3207, Canning–Clarendon, 28 June 1856.

18 Works 10/44/1. The chapel still stands. The prison, consulate and seaman's hospital were all destroyed when a new hospital designed by Charles Holden was started in 1901.

19 FO 78/3207; Works 10/4/1002; Ayse Nasir, 'Türk Mimarliginda Yabanci Mimarlar', unpublished Ph.D. thesis, Technical University of Istanbul, 1991, p. 104.

20 Works 10/3/464; Works 10/3/532; Works 10/5/1054–6; Nasir, 'Türk', pp. 51–2; *Builder*, 24 September 1853, p. 606.

21 Works 10/5/1054–6. In fact, according to Ayse Nasir, Smith was paid monthly by the Ottoman authorities.

22   Works 10/2/181–2; Nasir, 'Türk', p. 48.

23   *Builder* published extensive and admiring reviews of it: *Builder*, 6 September 1862, pp. 631–2, and 27 September 1862, pp. 690–2.

24   See Geoffrey Goodwin, *A History of Ottoman Architecture*, London: Thames & Hudson, 1971, p. 419.

25   See Z. Celik, *Displaying the Orient: Architecture of Islam at Nineteenth-Century World's Fairs*, Berkeley: University of California Press, 1992, pp. 139–40; H. Sumner-Boyd and J. Freely, *Strolling through Istanbul*, Istanbul: Redhouse, 1973.

26   Many Ottoman statesmen regarded such reforms simply as measures designed to mollify foreign opinion; Roderic H. Davison, *Reform in the Ottoman Empire*, Princeton: Princeton University Press, 1963, p. 57.

27   Steven T. Rosenthal, *The Politics of Dependency, Urban Reforms in Istanbul*, Westport, Conn., and London: Greenwood, 1980, p. 106.

28   It was built for £400–£600, and no longer exists: USPG D2, Stothart–SPG, 16 January 1856, and Stothart–SPG, 26 February 1856; USPG CLR 90, Curtis–SPG, 5 June 1856; Mrs Edmund Hornby, *Constantinople during the Crimean War*, London: Bentley, 1863, p. 295; *The Times*, 20 February 1856, p. 7.

29   Quoted in G. M. Young, *Victorian England. Portrait of an Age*, Oxford: Oxford University Press, 1977, p. 112.

30   Nassau W. Senior, *A Journal Kept in Turkey and Greece in the Autumn of 1857 and the Beginning of 1858*, New York: Arno Press (reprint), 1977, 72–3.

31   Steven T. Rosenthal, 'Minorities and Municipal Reform', in Benjamin Braude and Bernard Lewis (eds.), *Christians and Jews in the Ottoman Empire*, New York: Holmes & Meier, 1982, vol. 1, p. 370.

32   Senior, *Journal*, p. 74.

33   See C. Stolpe's map of Istanbul (*c.* 1854) reproduced in Rosenthal, *Politics*. See also Zeynep Celik, *The Remaking of Istanbul*, Seattle and London: University of Washington Press, 1986.

34   Rosenthal, 'Minorities', pp. 373–4.

35   For the history of the SPG see J. P. Thompson, *Into All Lands: The History of the Society for the Propagation of the Gospel in Foreign Parts, 1701–1900*, London: SPCK, 1951.

36   See, for example, *Missionary Herald*, 53, 1857, pp. 194–5; Richter, *History*, p. 173.

37   For a history of the competition and Burges's designs see J. Mordaunt Crook, *William Burges and the High Victorian Dream*, Chicago and London: University of Chicago Press, 1981, pp. 175–7; *Missionary Herald*, 60, 1864, p. 311; FO 78/1851. For the original proposal, resolutions of the committee and instructions for the competition, see *Building News*, 3 April 1857, pp. 332–5.

38   *Ecclesiologist*, August 1856, pp. 294–6.

39   USPG D29B, undated paper by Hope. In this prohibition of Byzantine Hope was supported by Robert Willis when he joined the judges in May 1856: USPG D2, Hope–SPG, 30 May 1856.

40   *Ecclesiologist*, November 1846, p. 166. For Webb see the discussion in Chapter 4,

and also B. Webb, 'On the Adaptation of Pointed Architecture to Tropical Climates', *Transactions of the Cambridge Camden Society*, 1845, pp. 199–218.

41   See David B. Brownlee, 'The First High Victorians', *Architectura*, 15, 1985, pp. 33–46.

42   See, for example, G. E. Street's 'The True Principles of Architecture and the Possibility of Development', *Ecclesiologist*, August 1852, p. 254.

43   On Hope's theory see J. Mordaunt Crook, 'Progressive Eclecticism: The Case of Beresford Hope', *Architectural Design*, 53, 1983, pp. 56–62.

44   *Saturday Review*, 1, 1856, pp. 234–6.

45   A. J. B. Beresford Hope, *The English Cathedral of the Nineteenth Century*, London: J. Murray, 1861, p. 90.

46   USPG D29B, Hope's undated notes on proposed church.

47   This was noticed in *Builder*, 28 February, 1857, p. 115.

48   George Gilbert Scott also adopted this view: Rylands Library, Manchester, E. A. Freeman Correspondence, Scott–Freeman, 25 November 1859.

49   *Saturday Review*, 6, 28 August 1858, p. 208.

50   The reasons for the judges' decisions were published in *Building News*, 6 February 1857, p. 145.

51   See *Building News*, 27 March 1857, p. 298; *CEAJ*, 20, 1857, p. 124; *Ecclesiologist*, April 1857, p. 112.

52   RIBA V19/89, 91; *Builder*, 21 March 1857, pp. 162–3.

53   Use of an outer cloister can be found in Roskell Bayne's Thornhill and Mayne Memorial, Allahabad (*c.* 1878) and G. G. Scott's Senate Hall, University of Bombay (*c.* 1876).

54   G. E. Street, 'On Colour as Applied to Architecture', in *Associated Architectural Societies Reports and Papers*, 1855, p. 355.

55   Hope, *Cathedral*, p. 93; *Building News*, 6 February 1857, p. 145.

56   *Ecclesiologist*, April 1857, pp. 104–5.

57   *Gentleman's Magazine*, 202, April 1857, pp. 422–3.

58   This was pointed out in *The Saturday Review*, 3, 7 March 1857, p. 219.

59   *Saturday Review*, 2, 3 May 1856, p. 11.

60   Hope, *Cathedral*, p. 14.

61   Ibid., p. 91.

62   Burges's information was probably taken from Ludwig Grüner, *Specimens of Ornamental Art*, London: T. McLean, 1850, 2 vols, of which he owned a copy: see Crook, *Burges*, p. 379 n. 64.

63   *Builder*, 28 February 1857, p. 115.

64   RIBA W16 Set no. 1. There are detail drawinmgs in R. P. Pullan, *Architectural Designs of William Burges*, London: B. T. Batsford, 1887.

65   *Building News*, 3 April 1857, p. 335.

66   *Building News*, 6 February 1857, p. 145.

67   *Ecclesiologist*, April 1857, p. 102.

68   *Builder*, 28 February 1857, p. 115.

69   Ibid.

70   *Building News*, 6 March 1857, p. 240.

71   *Ecclesiologist*, April 1857, p. 104.

72   *Gentleman's Magazine*, 202, April 1857, pp. 423–5.

73   W. Burges, 'Comte de Vogüé on the Holy Places at Jerusalem', *Gentleman's Magazine*, 214, 1863, p. 563.

74   See Linda Nochlin, 'The Imaginary Orient', *Art in America*, 71, May 1983, pp. 119–31, 187–91. The engravings are in *Building News*, 3 April 1857, p. 333; and *Builder*, 14 March 1857, p. 151.

75   Harold Temperley, 'The Last Phase of Stratford de Redcliffe', *English Historical Review*, 47, 1932, pp. 226–331.

76   Davison, *Reform*, p. 71.

77   RIBA Burges Small Notebook no. 24.

78   USPG CLR 90, Burges–SPG, 14 July 1857.

79   USPG CLR 90, Burges–SPG, 9 June 1857; D2, Gordon–SPG, 21 August 1856; RIBA Burges Small Notebook nos. 22 and 23.

80   According to Burges the Russian embassy (1836–43) was £40,000, the French embassy (1838–45) was £35,000, and the British embassy (1842–54) was £86,000: RIBA Burges Small Notebook no. 23.

81   W. Burges, 'Architectural Experiences at Constantinople', *Building News*, 12 February 1858, pp. 163–7. This article is almost identical to Burges's 'Turkish Art and Architecture', in Walter Thornbury, *Turkish Life and Character*, London: Smith & Elder, 1860, vol. 2.

82   RIBA Burges Small Notebook no. 22.

83   USPG D2, Hawkins–Burges, 14 May 1857. He also noted that building costs were half as much again as in England, partly due to more expensive building materials, but also because 'every artisan is paid at least five shillings a day, and does one-half the work of an Englishman': *Building News*, 12 February 1858, p. 167.

84   See Brian Hanson, 'Mind and Hand in Architecture: Ideas of the Artisan in English Architecture from William Chambers to John Ruskin', unpublished Ph.D. thesis, University of Essex, 1987, pp. 79ff.

85   On this see P. Kohane, 'Architecture, Labor and the Human Body: Fergusson, Cockerell and Ruskin', unpublished Ph.D. thesis, University of Pennsylvania, 1993.

86   *Building News*, 12 February 1858, p. 166. For the similar if later views of William Morris and Christopher Dresser see John MacKenzie, *Orientalism: History, Theory and the Arts*, Manchester: Manchester University Press, 1995, p. 118.

87   W. Burges, 'The Japanese Court in the International Exhibition', *Gentleman's Magazine*, 213, 1862, p. 243.

88   USPG CLR 90, Burges–SPG, 9 June 1857.

89   Edward Said, *Orientalism*, New York: Vintage, 1979, p. 177.

90   USPG CLR 90, Burges–SPG, 3 July 1857. The mosque is the Haci Mimi Celebi Cami.

91   Ibid.

92 See C. Stolpe's map of Istanbul (*c.* 1854) reproduced in Rosenthal, *Politics*.

93 USPG D2, Hanson–Burges, 3 November 1858; USPG D2, Curtis–SPG, 29 October 1858.

94 USPG D2, Burges–SPG, 10 October 1858; USPG D2, Nadin–Burges, 30 November 1859; D2, Baines–Burges, 14 December 1859; D29B, Nadin–Burges, November 1860 correspondence; D29B, Sarell–SPG, 5 February 1861.

95 USPG C/EUR/22, Taylor–SPG, 5 October 1860.

96 Davison, *Reform*, 112. It was a significant year also for the rising control of European banks over the Ottoman economy; see Issawi, *Economic History*, p. 100.

97 USPG D29B, Notes of building committee meeting, 3 July 1861. The design is RIBA W16, Set no. 5.

98 USPG D29B, Street–SPG, 8 December 1863.

99 USPG D29B, Street–SPG, 12 March 1864; *SPGL*, 48, p. 396.

100 USPG C/EUR/22, drafts of contracts.

101 USPG D29B, Street–SPG, 14 January 1864.

102 K. Bell, 'The Constantinople Embassy of Sir Henry Bullwer, 1858–65', unpublished Ph.D. thesis, University of London, 1961, p. 5.

103 USPG D29B, Curtis–SPG, 10 September 1863; D29C, Curtis–SPG, 3 October 1865; D29C, Wood–SPG, 16 December 1867. The photographs of capitals and stringcourses are still in the USPG archives.

104 USPG D33, Rogers and Booth–SPG, 2 October 1868.

105 See Henry A. Millon, 'G. E. Street and the Church of St. Paul's in Rome', in Helen Searing (ed.), *In Search of Architecture. A Tribute to Henry-Russell Hitchcock*, Cambridge, Mass.: MIT Press, 1982, p. 87; and Judith Rice Millon, *St. Paul's within the Walls Rome: A Building History and Guide, 1870–1980*, Dublin, N.H.: William A. Bauhan, 1982, p. 29.

106 David B. Brownlee, *The Law Courts. The Architecture of George Edmund Street*, Cambridge, Mass. and London: The Architectural History Foundation and MIT Press, 1984, pp. 291–3.

107 USPG D33, Rogers and Booth–SPG, 2 October 1868.

108 Nicholas Thomas, *Colonialism's Culture: Anthropology, Travel and Government*, Cambridge: Polity Press, 1995, p. 106.

6 DIGNIFIED PROGRESS

1 On this issue see the discussion of Cairo in Michael Gilsenan, *Recognizing Islam*, London and Canberra: Croom Helm, 1982, pp. 198–200. See also Timothy Mitchell, *Colonising Egypt*, Cambridge: Cambridge University Press, 1988, pp. 21ff., 46–61.

2 The classic Arabic source for a description of Alexandria in this period is Ali Pasha Mubarak, *al-Khitat al-tawfiqiyya al-jadida*, Cairo: Bulaq, 1887–9, vol. 7.

3 *Building News*, 3 July 1857, p. 683; Arnold Wright (ed.), *Twentieth Century Impressions of Egypt*, London: Lloyd's, 1909, p. 179 (for photograph); *Illustrated*

London News, 23 January 1858, pp. 73–4 – this includes an engraving. Robert Stephenson (1803–59) was the only son of the great engineer George Stephenson. He had arrived in Egypt in 1850 as a member of the International Commission reporting on the Suez Canal, and was engaged on the Cairo–Alexandria railway from 1851 to 1856.

4   Daniel Panzac gives the following population figures: 1846 – 139,359 Egyptians and 25,000 foreigners; 1882 – 181,703 Egyptians and 49,693 foreigners. Foreigners here presumably includes consular protégés, while Egyptians includes all Ottoman subjects: D. Panzac, 'Alexandrie: évolution d'une ville cosmopolite au XIXe siècle', *Annales Islamologiques*, 14, 1978, p. 197.

5   A European-run commission was set up to oversee these improvements in 1876: see M. F. Awad, 'Le Modèle européen: l'évolution urbaine de 1807 à 1958', *Revue de l'Occident Musulman et de la Mediterranée*, 46, 1987, p. 101.

6   See Anthony King, 'The Language of Colonial Urbanization', *Sociology*, 8, 1974, pp. 81–110.

7   See J. Millie's 1868 map in Gaston Jondet, *Atlas historique de la ville et des ports d'Alexandrie*, Cairo: Institut Français, 1921, plate 39.

8   On these *okelles* see Awad, 'Le Modèle', p. 79; and Mercedes Volait, 'La Communauté italienne et ses édiles', *Revue de l'Occident Musulman et de la Mediterranée*, 46, 1987, p. 146.

9   See Mohammad A. Chaichian, 'The Effects of World Capitalist Economy on Urbanization in Egypt, 1800–1970', *International Journal of Middle East Studies*, 20, 1988, p. 28; P. J. Vatikiotis, *The Modern History of Egypt*, London: Weidenfeld & Nicolson, 1969, pp. 84–5.

10 In 1873 there were 19,120 foreigners in Cairo compared with 47,316 in Alexandria. Of these there were 1,000 Britons in Cairo and 4,500 in Alexandria: M. A. Serageldin, 'Urbanization and Social Change in a Foreign Dominated Economy: Cairo, 1805–1970', unpublished Ph.D. thesis, Harvard University, 1972, p. 83.

11 D. Behrens-Abouseif, *Azbakiyya and Its Environs from Azbak to Ismail*, Cairo: Institut Français, 1985, p. 87. On Cairo's development see Mitchell, *Colonising Egypt*; Janet Abu-Lughod, *Cairo: 1001 Years of the City Victorious*, Princeton: Princeton University Press, 1971.

12 Abu-Lughod, *Cairo*, p. 102.

13 Wray had built the railway terminus at Kanpur and St. James's Church, Calcutta (1864). For all the information on this building see *Builder*, 20 November 1869, pp. 925–7. Carved stone, terracotta, woodwork and fittings were sent out from England.

14 For Donaldson's post office see BM Add. 37463, Donaldson–Hekekyan Bey, 22 July 1861; FO 78/1714, Donaldson–Works, 16 December 1862. Collyer's hospital was published in *Builder*, 11 April 1868, p. 266. There must have been other British buildings erected in Egypt between 1850 and 1870, but records of them are hard to come by.

15 *Building News*, 5 August 1859, p. 708; *Builder*, 4 February 1860, pp. 72–3. As

a neo-Islamic iron kiosk intended for an eastern setting this was not unique. Another, designed by Owen Jones, was sent to Bombay: *Builder*, 10 November 1866, pp. 832–5; 1 December 1866, pp. 885, 887.

16 See R. Ilbert and M. Volait, 'Neo-Arabic Renaissance in Egypt, 1870–1930', *Mimar*, 13, July–September 1984, p. 30. For an illustration of the palace as built see G. Ebers, *Egypt: Descriptive, Historical and Picturesque*, London: Cassell, Petter, & Galpin, 1879, vol. 2, p. 32.

17 These drawings are in the possession of the V&A: V&A, 8277 A-M, A.204. Information from Kresten Jespersen. Matthew Digby Wyatt designed panels for the Pasha's train: J. D. Crace, 'The Ornamental Features of Arabic Architecture in Egypt and Syria', *Sessional Papers of RIBA*, 1870, pp. 71–90.

18 *Builder*, 9 May 1874, p. 385. Marriotts Hotels took over the palace and in their 'renovation' stripped the interiors of their original decoration. The V&A have two designs for friezes which may have been part of this project: V&A, D 30 and D 31 – 1888. B.3.C.

19 See M. Scharabi, *Kairo*, Tübingen: Wasmuth, 1989, pp. 59–61; Ilbert and Volait, 'Neo-Arabic', p. 34.

20 Michael Darby, *The Islamic Perspective*, London: Scorpion Communications, 1983, p. 125; *RIBAJ*, 14 January 1899, pp. 126–30.

21 T. H. Lewis, 'Cairo', *Builder*, 12 March 1859, p. 203. He repeated these comments in the entry on 'Architecture' for the *Encyclopaedia Britannica*, 9th edn, vol. 2, p. 398.

22 There had been a British consulate in Alexandria since at least the early years of Muhammad Ali's rule. By the mid-century this consulate occupied a rented building on the rue de la Bourse, to the north-east of the Anglican church. It is marked on Müller's 1855 map: see Plate 61.

23 SMDB, Minute Book vol. 2, 3 December 1859.

24 SMDB, Minute Book vol. 2, 29 April 1857; FO 78/1714, FO–Green, 16 September 1857.

25 FO 78/1714, Colquhoun–FO, 24 April 1860.

26 FO 78/1714, Sofio–Colquhoun, 18 June 1860.

27 FO 78/1714, Colquhoun–FO, 18 June 1860.

28 *Oxford English Dictionary*. See also A. W. N. Pugin, *The True Principles of Pointed or Christian Architecture*, (1841) London: Henry Bohn, 1853, p. 48.

29 See John Sweetman, *The Oriental Obsession*, Cambridge: Cambridge University Press, 1988, p. 188.

30 FO 78/1714, Donaldson–Works, 16 December 1862.

31 Linant de Bellefonds (1799–1883) was a French engineer who arrived in Egypt in 1818 and lived there for the next sixty-five years travelling, surveying, working on irrigation projects, and in 1837 becoming Minister of Public Works. Yusuf Hekekyan Bey (1807–75) was born in Istanbul of Armenian parentage. From 1817 to 1830 he was educated in England, first with Samuel Briggs, the former consul-general and merchant in Egypt, then at Stonyhurst College, and finally studying hydraulics and canal construction with a civil engineer. His

friendship with Donaldson is recorded in letters preserved amongst the Hekekyan Papers at the British Museum: Add. 37463. He was also friendly with Gardner Wilkinson, Joseph Bonomi and Linant de Bellefonds: Ahmed Abdel-Rahim Mustafa, 'The Hekekyan Papers', in P. M. Holt (ed.), *Political and Social Change in Modern Egypt*, London: Oxford University Press, 1968, pp. 68–75; see also Mitchell, *Colonising Egypt*, pp. 69–71, 191 n. 25.

32 FO 78/1714, Donaldson–Works, 26 April 1861. On Donaldson's study of ancient Egyptian and fellahin domestic architecture see *Building News*, 22 February 1861, pp. 167–9.

33 FO 78/1714, Donaldson–Works, 26 April 1861.

34 FO 78/1714, FO–T, 17 December 1861; T–FO, 14 January 1862.

35 A. H. Layard, *Autobiography and Letters*, ed. by W. N. Bruce, London: John Murray, 1903, vol. 2, p. 199.

36 Ibid., p. 212.

37 Ibid., p. 218.

38 *Quarterly Review*, 29, 1859, p. 558.

39 On Layard's part in the Law Courts saga see David B. Brownlee, *The Law Courts: The Architecture of George Edmund Street*, Cambridge, Mass. and London: Architectural History Foundation and MIT Press, 1984. In the late 1870s, when he was ambassador in Istanbul, Layard called W. J. Smith's embassy 'a monument of lavish expenditure of public money, combined with false economy, ignorance and bad taste': Gordon Waterfield, *Layard of Nineveh*, London: John Murray, 1963, p. 360. James Fergusson briefly held the post of secretary or advisor to Layard at the Office of Works.

40 FO 78/1714, Donaldson–Layard, 21 December 1861.

41 FO 78/1714, Donaldson–FO, 27 December 1861.

42 T. L. Donaldson, *Preliminary Discourse on Architecture*, London: Taylor & Walton, 1842, p. 28. See also T. L. Donaldson, *A Review of the Professional Life of Sir John Soane*, London: John Williams, 1837, p. 20.

43 *Architect*, 7 July 1885, p. 76. According to his journal, when Hekekyan came to England in 1862 to see the International Exhibition he visited both Donaldson and Austen Layard: BM Add. 37456.

44 Interior decoration can be seen in FO 925/3012 Part 2.

45 Although there is no other known Islamic design by Donaldson, his interest at this time in polychromatic brick and terracotta facades can also be seen in his Shaw's Printing Office, Fetter Lane, London (1857).

46 Mitchell, *Colonising Egypt*, p. 27.

47 T. R. Metcalf, *An Imperial Vision*, London: Faber & Faber, 1989.

48 Ibid. Robert Chisholm was using this style in the late 1860s and 1870s. Donaldson's design and Wild's church might also be compared to the neo-Islamic buildings that appeared in Istanbul from the 1860s onwards, and with the neo-Islamic style used in Cairo in the 1870s initially for rich Europeans or princes and then later, in the 'neo-Arabic renaissance': see Z. Celik, *Displaying the Orient: Architecture of Islam at Nineteenth-Century World's Fairs*, Berkeley: University of

California Press, 1992, p. 157; Ilbert and Volait, 'Neo-Arabic', p. 34.

49 FO 78/1714, Colquhoun–Layard, 1 September 1862.

50 FO 78/1714, Donaldson–Works, 16 December 1862.

51 See FO 78/2212, FO Memo, 16 May 1865; FO 78/2212, Gladstone–Russell, 12 June 1865; FO 78/2212, FO–T, 19 May 1865; FO 78/2212, FO Memo, 10 June 1865; FO 78/2212, FO–Stanton, 4 July 1865.

52 PRO MPK/433; FO 78/2212, FO Memo written on Stanton–FO, 3 March 1868.

53 *DNB*; *RIBAJ*, 30 March 1893, pp. 275–6; John Physick, *The Victoria and Albert Museum*, Oxford: Phaidon, 1982, pp. 82–3.

54 FO 78/2212, Wild–FO, 31 July 1869. Wild had first submitted schematic plans to the Foreign Office in October 1867: these are mentioned in FO 78/2212, Stanton–FO, 26 June 1868.

55 *Building News*, 20 May 1870, p. 370; *Architect*, 7 May 1870, p. 219; *Builder*, 7 May 1870, p. 358.

56 *Architect*, 7 May 1870, p. 219.

57 See Ronald McFadzean, *The Life and Work of Alexander Thomson*, London: Routledge & Kegan Paul, 1979, p. 147.

58 V&A, E.3964-4083 – 1938.

59 For Tehran at this time see George Curzon, *Persia and the Persian Question*, London: Longmans, 2 vols, 1892; *Building News*, 15, 24 April 1868, p. 279.

60 Persian masons and plasterers were used, but many components, including the iron roof, were shipped out from Britain. Wild's drawings for these items can be found in Works, 10/34/2 and 10/34/3. The building was commissioned by Charles Allison, the British envoy to Persia and a close friend of A. H. Layard. For correspondence on it see FO 249/52. One of the interesting aspects of the project was its close links to the South Kensington Museum; apart from Wild, both its supervisors – Caspar Purdon Clarke and Robert Murdoch Smith – were buyers or keepers of eastern art for the museum.

61 For a plan and elevation of the old Mission House see PRO MPK 396.

62 FO 78/2212, Wild–FO, 31 July 1869.

63 FO 78/2212, FO Memos of 22 August 1869 and September 1869; FO 78/2212, FO Memo, 15 August 1871.

64 SMDB, Minute Book vol. 3, 6 July 1871, 14 February 1872.

65. See S. Lane Poole, *Cairo. Sketches of Its History, Monuments and Social Life*, London: Virtue, 1892, pp. 282–304.

7 NEW JERUSALEMS

1 Matthew Habershon, *A Dissertation on the Prophetic Scriptures*, London: James Nisbet, 1834, p. xvi.

2 Ibid., p. 199. See also Michael Ragussis, *Figures of Conversion: The Jewish Question and English National Identity*, London: Duke University Press, 1995, which unfortunately appeared too late to be used here.

3 Lord Ashley, Review of *Letters on Egypt, Edom and the Holy Land* by Lord Lindsay, *Quarterly Review*, 58, 1839, p. 189.

4 Edwin Hodder, *The Life and Work of the Seventh Earl of Shaftesbury*, London: Cassell, 1886, vol. I, p. 314.

5 Ashley, Review, p. 187.

6 ITAC, PMJ, 2, 23 January 1837.

7. Helen Guiterman and Briony Llewellyn, *David Roberts*, London: Phaidon and Barbican Art Gallery, 1986, p. 81. Roberts's statement expresses a standard trope of westerners visiting the Near East. Recent research has argued, on the contrary, that the Ottomans were in fact active keepers of Jerusalem and its monuments throughout the eighteenth and nineteenth centuries: B. St Laurent and A. Riedlmayer, 'Restorations of Jerusalem and the Dome of the Rock and Their Political Significance, 1537–1928', *Muqarnas*, 10, 1993, pp. 76–84.

8 For photographers see Yeshayahu Nir, *The Bible and the Image: The History of Photography in the Holy Land, 1839–99*, Philadelphia: University of Pennsylvania Press, 1985. Francis Frith used photographs to illustrate the Bible in 1862.

9 Quoted in Nir, *Bible*, p. 48; Ashley, Review, p. 167.

10 Ashley, Review, p. 166.

11 Roberts, *Holy Land*, preface.

12 For histories of the Jews Society see Gidney, *History*; T. D. Halsted, *Our Missions: Being a History ... of the LSPCJ*, London: W. Macintosh, 1866; A. L Tibawi, *British Interests in Palestine, 1800–1901*, London: Oxford University Press, 1961.

13 See Julius Richter, *A History of Protestant Missions in the Near East*, New York: AMS Press, 1970, pp. 89–96.

14 On Egypt's rule see A. L. Tibawi, *A Modern History of Syria*, London: Macmillan, 1969.

15 CMJ, c.14, General Committee Minutes, 25 November 1834; *JI*, 1, 1835, pp. 1–3.

16 *JI*, 1, 1835, p. 2.

17 CMJ, c.15, 16 December 1836.

18 In 1836 Britain had fourteen consuls in the Ottoman Empire; by 1842 they had twenty-five, of whom seven were in Syria and Palestine.

19 Jasper Ridley, *Lord Palmerston*, London: Panther, 1972, p. 397; Tibawi, *British Interests*, 33; *Times*, 20 May 1840, p. 6.

20 CMJ, c.125.

21 For a full history of the machinations behind the church see Mark Crinson, 'Victorian Architects and the Near East: Studies in Colonial Architecture, Architectural Theory and Orientalism, 1840–70', unpublished Ph.D. thesis, University of Pennsylvania, 1989.

22 For the original plan see CMJ, c.15, 14 November 1839. This is reproduced in *JI*, 6, 1840, opp. p. 61.

23 ITAC, PMJ, 3, 30 July 1839.

24 *JI*, 6, 1840, p. 165; ITAC, Large Box, list of Hillier's effects.

25 J. W. Johns, *The Anglican Cathedral Church of Saint James, Mount Zion, Jerusalem,*

London: n.p., 1844, p. 4.

26 Ibid.

27 ITAC, PMJ, 3, 16 July 1840. In fact the importation of Maltese masons, together with Greek masons from Istanbul imported to work on Jewish synagogues, had a big impact in turning the city's building industry towards more precise masonry methods: see Conrad Schick, 'Die Baugeschichte der Stadt Jerusalem', *Zeitschrift des deutschen Palästina-Vereins*, 17, 1894, p. 267; Y. Ben Arieh, *Jerusalem in the Nineteenth Century: The Old City*, New York: St. Martin's Press, 1984, p. 139.

28 ITAC, Letters, 1, Cartwright–Jerusalem Mission, 21 April 1841.

29 CMJ, c.16, 10 April 1841; see also CMJ, c.20, 28 June 1848. On the introduction of western forms of education into the Near East, see Timothy Mitchell, *Colonising Egypt*, Cambridge: Cambridge University Press, 1988, pp. 69–94.

30 *JI*, 15, 1849, p. 205.

31 Hodder, *Shaftesbury*, vol. 1, p. 377. See also FO 78/501, FO–Young 3 May 1842; Hansard, *Parliamentary Debates*, 3rd series, pp. 68, 853.

32 H. M. Colvin, 'Victorian Malta', *Architectural Review*, June 1946, p. 179.

33 On the bishopric see Tibawi, *British Interests*; W. H. Heckler, *The Jerusalem Bishopric*, London: Trübner, 1883; R. W. Greaves, 'The Jerusalem Bishopric', *English Historical Review*, 64, July 1949, pp. 328–52; P. J. Welsh, 'Anglican Churchmen and the Establishment of the Anglican Bishopric', *Journal of Ecclesiastical History*, 8, 1957, pp. 193–204.

34 Heckler, *Bishopric*, p. 30.

35 Greaves, 'Bishopric', p. 333.

36 This axis could also be contrasted with the links established at about this time between Roman Catholic and High Church architects and politicians in the two countries: see Michael J. Lewis, *The Politics of the German Gothic Revival – August Reichensperger*, New York: Architectural History Foundation, 1993, pp. 87ff.

37 Seating plan in ITAC, Large Box.

38 See Lewis, *Politics*, p. 222.

39 *JI*, 10, 1844, p. 190.

40 *Gentleman's Magazine*, 176, 1844, p. 619.

41 CMJ, c.17, 30 April 1842; 21 June 1842; 26 July 1842; ITAC, Letters, 1, Cartwright–Nicolayson, 11 October 1842.

42 *JI*, 12, 1846, pp. 409–10.

43 *JI*, 13, 1847, pp. 220–1; CMJ, c.19, 23 March 1847; *JI*, 15, 1849, p. 97.

44 See Bill Jay, *Victorian Cameraman*, Newton Abbott: David & Charles, 1973, pp. 18, 20. G. G. Wheelhouse, who photographed the church in 1849–50, and August Salzmann, in 1856, present it with similar starkness.

45 Heckler, *Bishopric*, p. 60.

46 G. Wightwick, *Palace of Architecture*, London: James Fraser, 1840, p. 185.

47 J. Fergusson, *An Historical Enquiry into the True Principles of Beauty in Art Especially with Reference to Architecture*, London: Longmans, 1849, pp. 156–68.

48 W. H. Bartlett, *Jerusalem Revisited*, London: Hall & Virtue, 1855, p. 26.

49 Quoted in Nir, *Bible*, p. 49.

50 USPG, D2, W. Willis–SPG, 26 May 1856.

51 In 1862 Conrad Schick was employed to design a physician's home: CMJ, c.125/15. See also Ben Arieh, *Jerusalem*, p. 9.

52 Arieh, *Jerusalem*, pp. 190–4.

53 Heckler, *Bishopric*, pp. 75, 89, 93, 101.

54 On Pite's other missionary architecture see Mark Crinson, 'Pite and the Mission Aesthetic', in Brian Hanson (ed.), *The Golden City: Essays on the Architecture and Imagination of Beresford Pite*, London: Prince of Wales's Institute of Architecture, 1993.

55 See Martin Gilbert, *Jerusalem – Rebirth of a City*, London: Chatto & Windus, 1985, p. 84. Montefiore had approached English and foreign architects to make designs for a Jewish hospital in 1852. See also David Kroyanker, *Jerusalem Architecture – Periods and Styles*, Jerusalem: Domino Press, 1983; James Finn, *Stirring Times*, London: Kegan Paul, 1878, vol. 2, p. 335.

56 *The Architect's, Engineer's, and Building-Trades' Directory*, London: Wyman, 1868, p. 137.

57 *JI*, January 1892, pp. 3–4.

58 Tibawi, *British Interests*, p. 76; Gilbert, *Jerusalem*, pp. 216–22.

59 For photographs of some of these see *JI*, February 1901, pp. 22–3.

60 CMJ, c.32. On Pite see Hanson (ed.), *Golden City*.

61 See *RIBAJ*, 42, 7 December 1935, p. 125.

62 Drawings from Pite's 1897 trip to the area survive in RIBA.

63 *RIBAJ*, 42, 7 December 1935, p. 125.

64 See *Architect and Contract Reporter*, 99, 25 January 1918, p. 63.

65 RIBA. These drawings are dated May–June 1894; *Builder*, 70, 9 May 1896, pp. 404–5.

66 *JI*, September 1895, pp. 144–6 – this includes photographs of the building under construction. In 1900 Pite produced designs for a block containing a lecture room and operating room to be placed so that it closed the semicircle: CMJ, c.250/3.

67 *JI*, July 1897, p. 105; *JI*, May 1898, pp. 72–4.

CONCLUSION

1 B. B. Taylor, 'Rethinking Colonial Architecture', *Mimar*, 13, 1984, pp. 22–5.

2 See J. Abu-Lughod, 'The Islamic City – History, Myth, Islamic Essence and Contemporary Relevance', *International Journal of Middle East Studies*, 19, 1987, pp. 155–76; and Aziz Al-Azmeh, 'What Is the Islamic City?', *Review of Middle East Studies*, 2, 1977, pp. 1–12.

3 See B. Cohn, 'The Census, Social Structure, and Objectification in South Asia', in B. Cohn, *An Anthropologist among the Historians and Other Essays*, Delhi: Oxford University Press, 1987.

SELECTED BIBLIOGRAPHY

•

ARCHIVES

Bodleian Library, Oxford: Archives of the Church's Mission to the Jews.

Borthwick Institute of Historical Research, York: Hickleton Papers.

British Museum: Manuscripts.

Christ Church, Jerusalem: Papers and Photographs.

Collection of Mrs Vivien Betti: Bonomi Papers.

Collection of Mrs de Cosson: Bonomi Papers.

Diocesan Office, Diocese of Gibraltar in Europe, London: Crimean Memorial Church Papers.

Greater London Record Office, London: Records of Christ Church, Streatham.

Griffith Institute, Oxford: James Wild Papers.

Guildhall Library, London: Archives of Diocese of London.

Israel Trust of the Anglican Church, Jerusalem: Palestine Mission Journal, Drawings and Other Papers.

Middle East Centre, St. Antony's College, Oxford: Photographs and Papers.

Public Record Office, London: Foreign Office Papers, Treasury Papers, Board of Works Papers.

Rhodes House Library, Oxford: Archives of the United Society for the Propagation of the Gospel.

Royal Commonwealth Society Library, Cambridge University: Photographic Collection.

Royal Institute of British Architects, London: British Architectural Library Archives; Drawings Collection.

Rylands Library, Manchester: Letters of E. A. Freeman.

St Helena's Chapel, Istanbul: Various Papers.

St Mark's Church, Alexandria: Deed Box.

Victoria and Albert Museum, London: Prints and Drawings Collection.

BOOKS AND ARTICLES

Aarsleff, Hans. *The Study of Language in England 1780–1860*, London: Athlone Press, 1983.

Abdel-Malek, A. *Idéologie et renaissance nationale: l'Égypte moderne*, Paris: Editions Anthropos, 1969.

Abu-Lughod, Janet. *Cairo: 1001 Years of the City Victorious*, Princeton: Princeton University Press, 1971.

——'Cairo: Perspective and Prospectus', in L. Carl Brown (ed.), *From Madina to Metropolis*, Princeton, N.J.: Darwin, 1973.

——*Rabat: Urban Apartheid in Morocco*, Princeton: Princeton University Press, 1980.

——'The Islamic City, Historic Myth, Islamic Essence, and Contemporary Relevance', *International Journal of Middle East Studies*, 19, 1987, pp. 155–76.

Ahmed, Leila. *Edward W. Lane*, London and New York: Longman, 1978.

Al-Azmeh, Aziz. 'What Is the Islamic City?', *Review of Middle East Studies*, 2, 1977, pp. 1–12.

Allibone, Jill. 'Anthony Salvin', unpublished Ph.D. thesis, University of London, 1977.

AlSayyad, Nezar. *Forms of Dominance: On the Architecture and Urbanism of the Colonial Enterprise*, Aldershot: Avebury, 1992.

Altick, Richard. *The Shows of London*, Cambridge, Mass. and London: Harvard University Press, 1978.

Archer, Mildred. *Indian Architecture and the British, 1780–1830*, London: RIBA, 1968.

Arnold, Thomas. *Introductory Lectures on Modern History*, Oxford: J. H. Parker, 1842.

Arrighi, Giovanni. *The Geometry of Imperialism*, London: Verso, 1983.

Arundale, Francis. *Illustrations of Jerusalem*, London: Henry Coulburn, 1837.

Asad, Talal (ed.). *Anthropology and the Colonial Encounter*, London: Ithaca Press, 1973.

Ashcroft, B., Griffiths, G. and Tiffin, H. (eds). *The Post-Colonial Studies Reader*, London: Routledge, 1995.

Ashley, Lord. Review of Lord Lindsay's *Letters on Egypt . . .*, *Quarterly Review*, 63, 1839, pp. 166–92.

Awad, M. F. 'Le Modèle européen: l'évolution urbaine de 1807 à 1958', *Revue de l'Occident Musulman et de la Mediterranée*, 46, 1987, pp. 93–109.

Baer, Gabriel. 'Social Change in Egypt: 1800–1914', in P. M. Holt (ed.), *Political and Social Change in Modern Egypt*, London: Oxford University Press, 1968.

——*Studies in the Social History of Modern Egypt*, Chicago: University of Chicago Press, 1969.

Baring, Sir Thomas. *A Bibliographical Account and Collation of 'La Description de l'Égypte'*, London: London Institution, 1838.

Barker, Francis *et al.* (eds). *Europe and Its Others*, Colchester: University of Essex Press, 1985.

Barry, Rev. Alfred. *The Life and Works of Sir Charles Barry RA, FRS*, London: John Murray, 1867.

Bartlett, W. H. *The Nile Boat: or, Glimpses of the Land of Egypt*, New York: Harper & Brothers, 1851.

———*Jerusalem Revisited*, London: A. Hall, Virtue & Co., 1855.

Behrens-Abouseif, Doris. *Azbakiyya and Its Environs from Azbak to Ismail*, Cairo: Institut français d'archéologie orientale, 1985.

Bell, K. 'The Constantinople Embassy of Sir Henry Bullwer, 1858–65', unpublished Ph.D. thesis, University of London, 1961.

Ben Arieh, Y. *Jerusalem in the Nineteenth Century: The Old City*, New York: St. Martin's Press, 1984.

Bendiner, Kenneth. 'David Roberts in the Near East', *Art History*, 6, 1983, pp. 67–82.

Benedict, Burton. *The Anthropology of World Fairs*, London and Berkeley: Lowie Museum of Anthropology and Scolar Press, 1983.

Benjamin, Walter. *Charles Baudelaire – A Lyric Poet in the Era of High Capitalism*, London: Verso, 1989.

Beresford Hope, A. J. B. *The English Cathedral of the Nineteenth Century*, London: John Murray, 1861.

Bernal, Martin. *Black Athena: The Afro-Asiatic Roots of Classical Civilisation*, London: Free Association, 1987.

Bevan, Samuel. *Sand and Canvas*, London: Gilpin, 1849.

Binney, Marcus. 'The Travels of Sir Charles Barry', *Country Life*, 146, 1969, pp. 494–8, 550–2, 622–4.

Blomfield, Sir R. Massie. 'St. Mark's Anglican Church, Alexandria', *Bible Lands*, 2, 1904–7, pp. 81–3, 101–3, 116–18, 146–9, 176–9, 204–9, 217–21, 232–3.

Bourgoin, Jules. *Les Arts arabes*, Paris: Morel, 1873.

Bradley, Ian. *The Call to Seriousness: The Evangelical Impact on the Victorians*, London: Cape, 1976.

Braude, Benjamin and Lewis, Bernard (eds). *Christians and Jews in the Ottoman Empire*, New York and London: Holmes & Meier, 1982.

Brewer, Anthony. *Marxist Theories of Imperialism*, London: Routledge & Kegan Paul, 1980.

Brigstocke, Hugh. 'Lord Lindsay and the *Sketches of the History of Christian Art*', *Bulletin, John Rylands Library*, 64, 1981, pp. 27–60.

Brooks, Michael W. *John Ruskin and Victorian Architecture*, New Brunswick and London: Rutgers University Press, 1987.

Brownlee, David B. *The Law Courts: The Architecture of George Edmund Street*, Cambridge, Mass. and London: MIT Press, and New York: The Architectural History Foundation, 1984.

———'The First High Victorians: British Architectural Theory in the 1840s', *Architectura*, 15, 1985, pp. 33–46.

———'Neugriechisch/Néo-Grec: The German Vocabulary of French Romantic Architecture', *Journal of the Society of Architectural Historians* 50, March 1991, pp. 18–21.

Bruce, William N. *Sir A. Henry Layard: Autobiography and Letters*, London: John Murray, 1903.

Bunsen, Christian, Meyer, C. and Müller, M. *Three Linguistic Dissertations Read at the Meeting of the British Association in Oxford*, London: British Association for Advancement of Science, 1848.

Bunsen, Frances. *A Memorial of Baron Bunsen*, London: Longmans, 1868.

Burges, William. 'Architectural Experiences at Constantinople', *Building News*, 4, 1858, pp. 163–7.

——'Comte de Vogüé on the Holy Places at Jerusalem', *Gentleman's Magazine*, NS 14, 1863, pp. 553–663.

Burrow, J. W. 'The Uses of Philology in Victorian Britain', in Robert Robson (ed.), *Ideas and Institutions of Victorian Britain*, London: Bell & Sons, 1967.

Byrne, Leo G. *The Great Ambassador: A Study of the Diplomatic Career of the Right Honourable Stratford Canning*, Columbus: Ohio State University Press, 1964.

Carrick, John. *Evangelicals and the Oxford Movement*, Bridgend: Evangelical Press of Wales, 1984.

Carrott, Richard. *The Egyptian Revival: Its Sources, Monuments, and Meaning (1808–58)*, Berkeley and Los Angeles: University of California Press, 1978.

Celik, Zeynep. 'Impact of Westernization on Istanbul's Urban Form', unpublished Ph.D. thesis, University of California at Berkeley, 1984.

——*The Remaking of Istanbul*, Seattle and London: University of Washington Press, 1986.

——*Displaying the Orient: Architecture of Islam at Nineteenth-Century World's Fairs*, Berkeley: University of California Press, 1992.

Chaichian, Mohammad. 'The Effects of the World Capitalist Economy on Urbanization in Egypt, 1800–1970', *International Journal of Middle East Studies*, 20, 1988, pp. 23–44.

Chambers, William. *Plans, Elevations, Sections, and Perspective Views of the Gardens and Buildings at Kew Surry*, London: published for the author, 1763.

Clarke, Basil F. *Anglican Churches outside the British Isles*, London: SPCK, 1958.

Clayton, Peter. *The Rediscovery of Egypt: Artists and Travellers in the Nineteenth Century*, New York: Thames & Hudson, 1982.

Clegg, Jeanne. *Ruskin's Venice*, London: Junction Books, 1981.

Cockerell, S. P. (ed.). *Travels in Southern Europe and the Levant, 1810–17. The Journal of C. R. Cockerell RA*, London: Longmans, Green & Co., 1903.

Cohn, Bernard. *An Anthropologist among the Historians and Other Essays*, Oxford: Oxford University Press, 1987.

Colvin, Howard. 'Victorian Malta', *Architectural Review*, 1946, pp. 179–80.

Commission des sciences et arts d'Égypte. *Description de l'Égypte*, Paris: Imprimerie impériale, 1809–28.

Conner, Patrick. *Oriental Architecture in the West*, London: Thames & Hudson, 1979.

——(ed.). *The Inspiration of Egypt: Its Influence on British Artists, Travellers and Designers, 1700–1900*, Brighton: Brighton Borough Council, 1983.

Cook, E. T. and Wedderburn, A. (eds). *The Work of John Ruskin*, London: George Allen, 1903–12.

Coombes, Annie E. *Reinventing Africa: Museums, Material Culture and Popular*

Imagination in Late Victorian and Edwardian England, New Haven and London: Yale University Press, 1994.

Coste, Pascal. *Architecture arabe, ou monuments du Kaire*, Paris: Institut de France, 1837–9.

——*Monuments modernes de la Perse mesurés . . .*, Paris: Morel, 1867.

Couchaud, André. *Choix d'églises bysantines en Grèce*, Paris: Lenoir, 1842.

Crace, J. D. 'The Ornamental Features of Arabic Architecture in Egypt and Syria', *Sessional Papers of the RIBA*, 1870, pp. 71–90.

Crinson, Mark. 'Victorian Architects and the Near East: Studies in Colonial Architecture, Architectural Theory and Orientalism, 1840–70', unpublished Ph.D. thesis, University of Pennsylvania, 1989.

——'Pite and the Mission Aesthetic', in Brian Hanson (ed.), *The Golden City: Essays on the Architecture and Imagination of Beresford Pite*, London: Prince of Wales's Institute of Architecture, 1993.

——'Leading into Captivity: James Wild and His Work in Egypt', *Georgian Group Journal*, 1995, pp. 51–64.

Croly, Revd George. *The Holy Land, Syria, Idumea, Arabia, Egypt and Nubia*, London: F. G. Moon, 1842.

Crook, J. Mordaunt. 'Italian Influences on Victorian Gothic', *Academia Nazionale dei Lincei*, 375, 1978, pp. 39–65.

——*William Burges and the High Victorian Dream*, Chicago and London: University of Chicago Press, 1981.

——'Progressive Eclecticism: The Case of Beresford Hope', *Architectural Design*, 53, 1983, pp. 56–62.

——'Early French Gothic', in S. Macready and F. H. Thompson (eds), *Influences in Victorian Art and Architecture*, London: Society of Antiquaries, 1985, pp. 49–58.

——*The Dilemma of Style: Archictectural Ideas from the Picturesque to the Post-Modern*, London: John Murray, 1987.

Crook, J. Mordaunt and Port, M. H. *The History of the King's Works*, London: HMSO, 1973, vol. VI.

Curzon, George. *Persia and the Persian Question*, London: Longmans, 1892.

Curzon, Robert. *Visits to Monasteries in the Levant*, London: John Murray, 1849.

Daniel, Norman. *Islam, Europe and Empire*, Edinburgh: Edinburgh University Press, 1966.

Darby, Michael. 'Owen Jones and the Eastern Ideal', unpublished Ph.D. thesis, University of Reading, 1974.

——*The Islamic Perspective*, London: Scorpion Communications, 1983.

Darby, Michael and Van Zanten, David. 'Owen Jones's Iron Buildings of the 1850s', *Architectura*, 4, 1974, pp. 53–75.

D'Avennes, Prisse. *L'Art arabe d'après les monuments du Kaire*, Paris: Morel, 1877.

Davis, Philip. *Splendours of the Raj: British Architecture in India, 1660 to 1947*, London: John Murray, 1985.

Davison, Roderic H. *Reform in the Ottoman Empire 1856–76*, Princeton: Princeton University Press, 1963.

Deighton, H. S. 'The Impact of Egypt on Britain. A Study of Public Opinion', in P. M. Holt (ed.), *Political and Social Change in Modern Egypt*, London: Oxford University Press, 1968, pp. 231–48.

Donaldson, Thomas L. *Preliminary Discourse in Architecture*, London: Taylor & Walton, 1842.

———RIBA Lectures, *Building News*, 7, 1861, pp. 167–9.

Dowling, Linda. 'Roman Decadence and Victorian Historiography', *Victorian Studies*, 28, Summer 1985, pp. 579–609.

Downes, Kerry. *Hawksmoor*, London: Zwemmer, 1979.

Drexler, A. (ed.). *The Architecture of the Ecole des Beaux Arts*, New York and Cambridge, Mass.: Museum of Modern Art and MIT Press, 1977.

Dufferin and Ava, Dowager Marchioness of. *My Russian and Turkish Journals*, London: John Murray, 1917.

Fabian, Johannes. *Time and the Other: How Anthropology Constitutes Its Object*, New York: Columbia University Press, 1983.

Fergusson, James. *An Essay on the Ancient Topography of Jerusalem*, London: J. Weale, 1847.

———*An Historical Enquiry into the True Principles of Beauty in Art*, London: Longman, 1849.

———'On the History of the Pointed Arch', *CEAJ*, 12, 1849, p. 254.

———*The Illustrated Handbook of Architecture*, London: John Murray, 1855.

———*Notes on the Site of the Holy Sepulchre in Jerusalem*, London: John Murray, 1861.

———*A History of Architecture in All Countries*, London: John Murray, 1865.

———*The Holy Sepulchre and the Temple at Jerusalem*, London: John Murray, 1865.

———*History of Indian and Eastern Architecture*, London: John Murray, 1876.

———*The Temple of the Jews and the Other Buildings in the Haram Area at Jerusalem*, London: John Murray, 1878.

Fermor-Hesketh, Robert (ed.). *Architecture of the British Empire*, London: Weidenfeld & Nicholson, 1986.

Finlay, George. *Greece under the Romans*, Edinburgh and London: William Blackwood, 1844.

———*History of the Byzantine Empire from 716 to 1453*, Edinburgh and London: William Blackwood, 1853.

Finlayson, G. B. *The Seventh Earl of Shaftesbury 1801–85*, London: Eyre Methuen, 1981.

Finn, James. *Stirring Times or Records from Jerusalem Consular Chronicles of 1853 to 1856*, London: Kegan Paul, 1878.

Fischer von Erlach, J. B. *A Plan of Civil and Historical Architecture*, trans T. Lediard, London: Lediard, 1737.

Fleming, John. 'Cairo Baroque', *Architectural Review*, 97, 1945, pp. 75–82.

Forbes, Duncan. *The Liberal Anglican Idea of History*, Cambridge: Cambridge University Press, 1952.

Fossati, Gaspard. *Aya Sofia*, London: Colnaghi, 1852.

Fraser, Peter M. 'Alexandria from Mohammad Ali to General Nasser', in Norbert

Hinske (ed.), *Alexandrien: Kulturbegegnungen dreier Jahrtausande im Schmelztiegel einer mediterranen Grossstadt*, Mainz am Rhein: Zabern, 1981, pp. 63–74.

Freeman, Edward A. *A History of Architecture*, London: Joseph Masters, 1849.

——'Finlay on the Byzantine Empire', *North British Review*, 22, 1855, pp. 343–75.

——'Mahometanism in the East and West', *North British Review*, 23, 1855, pp. 449–80.

——'Creasy's History of the Ottoman Turks', *Saturday Review*, 2, 1856, pp. 61–2, 88–9.

——'Greece under the Ottoman Turks', *Saturday Review*, 2, 1856, pp. 206–7.

——*The History and Conquests of the Saracens*, Oxford: J. H. and J. Parker, 1856.

Friedmann, I. 'Lord Palmerston and the Protection of Jews in Palestine 1839–51', *Jewish Social Studies*, 30, 1968, pp. 23–41.

Frith, Francis. *Egypt and Palestine Photographed and Described*, London: James Virtue, 1858.

Fuller, Peter. *Theoria*, London: Chatto & Windus, 1988.

Furniss, William. *Waraga, or the Charms of the Nile*, New York: Baker & Scribner, 1850.

Gailhabaud, Jules. *Ancient and Modern Architecture*, London: Firmin Didot, 1844.

Gallagher, John and Robinson, Ronald. 'The Imperialism of Free Trade', *Economic History Review*, 6, 1953, pp. 1–15.

Geikie, Cunningham. *The Holy Land and the Bible*, London: Cassell, 1891.

Gidney, W. T. *The History of the London Society for Promoting Christianity Amongst the Jews, From 1809 to 1908*, London: LSPCJ, 1908.

Gilbert, Martin. *Jerusalem – Rebirth of a City*, London: Chatto & Windus, 1985.

Gilsenan, Michael. *Recognizing Islam*, London and Canberra: Croom Helm, 1982.

Godlewska, Anne. 'Map, Text and Image. The Mentality of Enlightened Conquerors: A New Look at the *Description de l'Égypte*', *Transactions of the Institute of British Geographers*, 20, 1995, pp. 5–28.

Godwin, Geoffrey. *A History of Ottoman Architecture*, London: Thames & Hudson, 1971.

Goodhart-Rendel, H. S. 'Rogue Architects of the Victorian Era', *RIBAJ*, 56, 1949, pp. 251–9.

Goury, Jules and Jones, Owen. *Plans, Elevations, Sections, and Details of the Alhambra*, London: Owen Jones, 1842.

Gran, Peter. *Islamic Roots of Capitalism: Egypt, 1760–1840*, Austin, Tex. and London: University of Texas, 1979.

Greaves, R. W. 'The Jerusalem Bishopric', *English Historical Review*, 64, 1949, pp. 328–52.

Greene, Mott T. *Geology in the Nineteenth Century*, Ithaca and London: Cornell University Press, 1982.

Greenhalgh, Paul. *Ephemeral Vistas: The Expositions Universelles, Great Exhibitions and World's Fairs, 1851–1939*, Manchester: Manchester University Press, 1988.

Guiterman, Helen and Llewellyn, Briony. *David Roberts*, London: Phaidon and Barbican Art Gallery, 1986.

Gwilt, Joseph. *An Encyclopaedia of Architecture*, London: Longman, Brown, Green & Longmans, 1842.

Habershon, Matthew. *A Dissertation on the Prophetic Scriptures*, London: J. Nisbet, 1834.

Hale, William and Bagis, Ali Ihsan. *Four Centuries of Turco-British Relations*, Beverley: Eothen, 1984.

Halsted, T. D. *Our Missions: Being a History of the Principal Missionary Transactions of the LSPCJ from Its Foundation in 1809 to the Present Year*, London: W. Macintosh, 1866.

Hamlin, Cyrus. *Among the Turks*, London: Sampson, 1878.

Hanson, Brian. 'Mind and Hand in Architecture: Ideas of the Artisan in English Architecture from William Chambers to John Ruskin', unpublished Ph.D. thesis, University of Essex, 1987.

Hay, Robert. *Illustrations of Cairo*, London: Tilt & Brogue, 1840.

Head, Raymond. *The Indian Style*, London: Allen & Unwin, 1986.

Heckler, W. H. *The Jerusalem Bishopric*, London: Trübner, 1883.

Herbert, Gilbert. *Pioneers of Prefabrication: The British Contribution in the Nineteenth Century*, Baltimore, Md.: Johns Hopkins University Press, 1978.

Hessemer, F. M. *Arabische und alt-italienische Bau-Verzierungen*, Berlin: G. Reimer, 1842.

Heyd, Uriel. 'The Ottoman Ulema and Westernization in the Time of Salim III and Mahmud II', *Scripta Hierosalymitana*, 9, 1961, pp. 63–96.

Hill, Aaron. *A Full and Just Account of the Present State of the Ottoman Empire*, London: J. Mayo, 1709.

Hitchcock, H.-R. 'G. E. Street in the 1850s', *Journal of the Society of Architectural Historians*, 19, 1960, pp. 145–71.

Hittorff, J. L. and Zanth, L. *Architecture moderne de la Sicile*, Paris: Paul Renouard, 1835.

Hobhouse, C. *1851 and the Crystal Palace*, London: John Murray, 1950.

Hobsbawm, Eric. *The Age of Capital 1848–75*, London: Cardinal, 1988.

Hodder, Edwin. *The Life and Work of the Seventh Earl of Shaftesbury*, London: Cassell, 1886.

Hodges, William. *Travels in India during the Years 1780, 1781, 1782, and 1783*, London: J. Edwards, 1793.

Holt, P. M. (ed.). *Political and Social Change in Modern Egypt*, London: Oxford University Press, 1968.

——*The Cambridge History of Islam*, Cambridge: Cambridge University Press, 1970.

Hope, Thomas. *An Historical Essay on Architecture*, London: John Murray, 1835.

Hornby, Mrs Edmund. *In and Around Stamboul*, London: Richard Bentley, 1858.

Hornby, Sir Edmund. *An Autobiography*, London: Constable, 1929.

Horne, Thomas H. *Landscape Illustrations of the Bible*, London: John Murray, 1836.

Hoskins, Holford L. *British Overland Routes to India*, New York, London, Toronto: Longman, Brown, Green & Longmans, 1928.

Hyamson, Albert (ed.). *The British Consulate in Jerusalem in Relation to the Jews of Palestine, 1838–1914*, London: E. Goldston, 1939–41.

Ilbert, Robert and Joutard, Philippe. *Le Miroir égyptien*, Marseilles: Jeanne Laffitte, 1984.

Ilbert, Robert and Volait, Mercedes. 'Neo-Arabic Renaissance in Egypt 1870–1930', *Mimar*, 13, July–September 1984, pp. 26–34.

Issawi, Charles (ed.). *The Economic History of the Middle East 1800–1914*, Chicago and London: University of Chicago Press, 1966.

——*The Economic History of Turkey 1800–1914*, Chicago and London: University of Chicago Press, 1980.

Johns, J. W. *The Anglican Cathedral Church of Saint James, Mount Zion, Jerusalem*, London: n.p., 1844.

Jondet, Gaston. *Atlas historique de la ville et des ports d'Alexandrie*, Cairo: Institut Français, 1921.

Jones, Owen. *The Alhambra Court in the Crystal Palace*, London: Bradbury & Evans, 1854.

——*The Grammar of Ornament*, London: Day & Son, 1856.

——*Lectures on Architecture and the Decorative Arts*, London: privately pub., 1863.

Jones, Owen and Goury, Jules. *Views on the Nile*, London: Graves & Warmsley, 1843.

Karpat, Kemal. *Ottoman Population, 1830–1914: Demographic and Social Characteristics*, Madison: University of Wisconsin Press, 1985.

Kemp, Wolfgang. *The Desire of My Eyes: The Life and Work of John Ruskin*, London: HarperCollins, 1991.

King, Anthony. 'The Language of Colonial Urbanization', *Sociology*, 8, 1974, pp. 81–110.

——*Colonial Urban Development*, London: Routledge & Kegan Paul, 1976.

Kitto, J. *Modern Jerusalem*, London: The Religious Tract Society, 1847.

Knight, Henry G. *The Normans in Sicily*, London: John Murray, 1838.

——*Saracenic and Norman Remains*, London: John Murray, 1840.

Kohane, Peter. 'Architecture, Labor and the Human Body', unpublished Ph.D. thesis, University of Pennsylvania, 1993.

Koppelkaum, Stefan. *Der imaginäre Orient: exotische Bauten des achzehnten und neunzehnten Jahrhunderts in Europa*, Berlin: Ernst & Sohn, 1987.

Kroyanker, David. *Jerusalem Architecture – Periods and Styles*, Jerusalem: Domino Press, 1983.

——*Jerusalem Architecture*, London: Tauris Parke Books, 1994.

Lane, Edward W. *An Account of the Manners and Customs of the Modern Egyptians*, London: Charles Knight, 1836.

Lane Poole, S. *Life of Edward William Lane*, London and Edinburgh: Williams & Norgate, 1877.

——*Cairo. Sketches of Its History, Monuments and Social Life*, London: Virtue, 1892.

Lepsius, Richard. *Discoveries in Egypt, Ethiopia and the Peninsula of Sinai, in the Years 1842–5*, London: Richard Bentley, 1853.

Lewis, Benjamin and Holt, P. M. (eds). *Historians of the Middle East*, London: Oxford University Press, 1962.

Lewis, Michael J. *The Politics of the German Gothic Revival – August Reichensperger*, New

York: Architectural History Foundation, 1993.

Lewis, Thomas H. 'Cairo', *Builder*, 17, 1859, pp. 185–7, 201–3.

———'On Saracenic Architecture', *Builder*, 17, 1859, pp. 262–3.

———'Saracenic Architecture', *Building News*, April 1859, pp. 361–3.

Lightbown, R. W. 'The Inspiration of Christian Art', in S. Macready and F. H. Thompson (eds), *Influences in Victorian Art and Architecture*, London: Society of Antiquaries, 1985.

Lindsay, Lord. *Sketches of the History of Christian Art*, London: John Murray, 1847.

———*Letters from Egypt, Edom, and the Holy Land*, London: Henry G. Bohn, 1858.

MacDougall, Hugh A. *Racial Myth in English History. Trojans, Teutons, and Anglo-Saxons*, Montreal: Harvest House, 1982.

MacKenzie, John M. *Orientalism: History, Theory and the Arts*, Manchester: Manchester University Press, 1995.

Madden, R. R. *Egypt and Mohammad Ali*, London: Hamilton, Adams & Co., 1841.

Mango, C. 'Constantinopolita', *Jahrbuch des Deutschen Archäologischen Instituts*, 80, 1965, pp. 305–36.

———'Approaches to Byzantine Architecture', *Muqarnas*, 8, 1991, pp. 40–4.

Manuel, F. E. *The New World of Henri Saint-Simon*, Cambridge, Mass.: Harvard University Press, 1956.

Marlowe, John. *A History of Modern Egypt and Anglo-Egyptian Relations, 1800–1956*, Hamden, Conn.: Archon Books, 1965.

Marsot, Afaf L. *Egypt in the Reign of Muhammad Ali*, Cambridge: Cambridge University Press, 1984.

Metcalf, Thomas R. *An Imperial Vision: Indian Architecture and Britain's Raj*, London and Boston: Faber & Faber, 1989.

Middleton, Robin. *The Beaux-Arts and Nineteenth-Century French Architecture*, London: Thames & Hudson, 1982.

———'The Rationalist Interpretation of Classicism of Léonce Reynaud and Viollet-le-Duc', *AA Files*, 11, 1986, pp. 29–48.

Millard, James E. 'On the Style of Architecture to be Adapted in Colonial Churches', *Proceedings of OSPGA*, Easter and Act terms 1845, pp. 7–18.

Mitchell, Timothy. *Colonising Egypt*, Cambridge: Cambridge University Press, 1988.

Mitter, Partha. *Much Maligned Monsters*, Oxford: Clarendon Press, 1977.

Müller, Max. *Lectures on the Science of Language*, London: Longmans, 1861–4.

Murray, John. *A Handbook for Travellers in Syria and Palestine*, London: John Murray, 1858.

———*A Handbook for Travellers in Constantinople . . .*, London: John Murray, 1871.

Muskau, Prince Puckler. *Egypt under Mehemet Ali*, London: Henry Colburn, 1845.

Mustafa, Ahmed Abdel-Rahim. 'The Hekekyan Papers', in P. M. Holt (ed.), *Political and Social Change in Modern Europe*, London: Oxford University Press, 1968, pp. 68–75.

Muthesius, Stefan. *The High Victorian Movement in Architecture, 1850–70*, London and Boston: Routledge & Kegan Paul, 1972.

Napier, Lord. 'Modern Architecture in India', *Builder*, 28, 1870, pp. 680–2.

Nasir, Ayse. 'Turk Mimarliginda Yabanci Mimarlar', unpublished Ph.D. thesis, Technical University of Istanbul, 1991.

Neale, F. A. *Islamism – Its Rise and Progress; or, the Present and Past Condition of the Turks*, London: James Madden, 1854.

Neale, John M. *A Few Words to Church Builders*, Cambridge: Cambridge Camden Society, 1842.

——*A History of the Holy Eastern Church*, London: Masters, 1847–51.

Newman, John Henry. *Historical Sketches* (1853), Westminster, Md.: Christian Classics, 1970.

Nilsson, S. A. *European Architecture in India, 1750–1850*, London: Faber, 1968.

Nir, Yeshayahu. *The Bible and the Image: The History of Photography in the Holy Land, 1839–99*, Philadelphia: University of Pennsylvania Press, 1985.

Nochlin, Linda. 'The Imaginary Orient', *Art in America*, 71, 1983, pp. 119–31, 187–91.

Orlebar, A. B. 'Observations on the Mahomedan Architecture of Cairo', *Journal of the Bombay Branch of the Royal Asiatic Society*, 2, 1845, pp. 119–39.

Owen, Roger. *Cotton and the Egyptian Economy, 1820–1914*, Oxford: Clarendon Press, 1969.

——*The Middle East in the World Economy*, London and New York: Methuen, 1981.

Owen, Roger and Sutcliffe, B. (eds). *Studies in the Theory of Imperialism*, London: Longman, 1972.

Panzac, Daniel. 'Alexandrie: évolution d'une ville cosmopolite au XIXe siècle', *Annales Islamologiques*, 14, 1978, pp. 195–216.

Pardoe, Julia. *Beauties of the Bosphorus*, London: Virtue, 1837.

Pascoe, C. F. *Two Hundred Years of the SPG*, London: SPG, 1901.

Pears, Sir Edwin. *Forty Years in Constantinople*, London: Herbert Jenkins, 1916.

Pevsner, Nikolaus. *Some Architectural Writers of the Nineteenth Century*, Oxford: Clarendon Press, 1972.

Phillips, Samuel. *Guide to the Crystal Palace and Park*, London: Crystal Palace Library, 1855.

Pierotti, Dr Ermete. *Jerusalem Explored*, London: Bell & Daldy, 1864.

Pococke, Richard. *Description of the East*, London: W. Bowyer, 1743.

Poliakov, Léon. *The Aryan Myth: A History of Racist and Nationalist Ideas in Europe*, translated by E. Howard, London: Chatto & Heinemann, 1974.

Polk, William R. and Chambers, Richard L. *The Beginnings of Modernization in the Middle East*, Chicago and London: University of Chicago Press, 1968.

Poole, Edward S. 'Arabian Architecture', Appendix F II of E. W. Lane, *An Account of the Manners and Customs of the Modern Egyptians*, London: John Murray, 1860.

Porter, Roy. 'Charles Lyell and the Principles of the History of Geology', *British Journal for the History of Science*, 9, 1976, pp. 91–104.

Prangey, Girault de. *Monuments arabes et moresques de Cordoue, Séville et Grenade*, Paris, 1836–9.

——*Monuments arabes d'Égypte, de Syrie et d'Asie Mineure*, Paris: G. de Prangey, 1846–55.

Proceedings of the General Conference on Foreign Missions, London: John F. Shaw, 1879.

Rabinow, Paul. *French Modern: Norms and Forms of the Social Environment*, Cambridge, Mass., and London: MIT Press, 1989.

Ragussis, Michael. *Figures of Conversion: The Jewish Question and English National Identity*, New Orleans and London: Duke University Press, 1995.

Ray, Desmond. *The India Museum, 1801–79*, London: HMSO, 1982.

Reimer, M. J. 'Colonial Bridgehead: Social and Spatial Change in Alexandria, 1850–82', *International Journal of Middle East Studies*, 20, 1988, pp. 531–53.

Richter, Julius. *A History of Protestant Missions in the Near East*, New York: AMS, 1970

Ridley, Jasper. *Lord Palmerston*, London: Panther, 1972.

Roberts, David. *The Holy Land, Egypt, Arabia, and Syria*, London: F. G. Moon, 1840.

——*The Holy Land, Syria, Idumea, Arabia, Egypt and Nubia*, London: Day & Son, 1855–6, 2 vols.

Rodinson, Maxime. *Islam and Capitalism*, New York: Pantheon Books, 1973.

Rosenthal, Steven. *The Politics of Dependency*, Westport, Conn., and London: Greenwood Press, 1980.

——'Minorities and Municipal Reform', in B. Braude and B. Lewis (eds), *Christians and Jews in the Ottoman Empire*, New York and London: Holmes & Meier, 1982.

Ruskin, John. *The Works of John Ruskin*, ed. E. T. Cook and A. Wedderburn, London: George Allen, 1903–12.

Said, Edward. *Orientalism* (1978), New York: Vintage Books, 1979.

——'Orientalism Reconsidered', *Race and Class*, 27, Autumn 1985, pp. 1–15.

——*Culture and Imperialism*, London: Vintage Books, 1994.

——'East Isn't East – The Impending End of the Age of Orientalism', *Times Literary Supplement*, 3 February 1995.

St. John, Bayle. *Two Years' Residence with a Levantine Family*, London: Chapman & Hall, 1850.

St. Laurent, B. and Riedlmayer, A. 'Restorations of Jerusalem and the Dome of the Rock and Their Political Significance, 1537–1928', *Muqarnas*, 10, 1993, pp. 76–84.

Salzenberg, W. *Alt-christliche Baudenkmale von Constantinopel*, Berlin: Ernst & Korn, 1854.

Sandes, E. W. C. *The Military Engineer in India*, Chatham: Institution of Royal Engineers, 1933–5.

——*The Royal Engineers in Egypt and the Sudan*, Chatham: Institution of Royal Engineers, 1937.

Saulcy, Félicien de. *Histoire de l'art judaïque*, Paris: Didier, 1858.

Scharabi, Mohamed. *Kairo: Stadt und Architektur im Zeitalter des europäischen Kolonialismus*. Tübingen: Wasmuth, 1989.

Schick, Conrad. 'Die Baugeschichte der Stadt Jerusalem ...', *Zeitschrift des deutschen Palästina-Vereins*, 17, 1894, pp. 266–8.

Schwab, Raymond. *The Oriental Renaissance: Europe's Rediscovery of India and the East, 1680–1880*, trans. G. Patterson-Black and V. Reinking, New York: Columbia University Press, 1984.

Scott, George Gilbert. 'The Study of Medieval Architecture', *Building News*, 3, 1857, pp. 279–80.

——*Personal and Professional Recollections*, London: Sampson Low, Marston, Searle & Rivington, 1879.

Searight, Sarah. *The British in the Middle East*, London: Weidenfeld & Nicolson, 1979.

Sekula, Alan. 'The Body and the Archive', *October*, 39, Winter 1986, pp. 3–64.

Semmel, Bernard. *The Governor Eyre Controversy*, London: MacGibbon & Kee, 1962.

Senior, Nassau W. *Conversations and Journals in Egypt and Malta*, London: Sampson Low, Marston, Searle & Rivington, 1882.

——*A Journal Kept in Turkey and Greece in the Autumn of 1857 and the Beginning of 1858*, New York: Arno Press, 1977.

Sepp, J. N. *Jerusalem und das heilige Land*, Schaffhausen: Hurter, 1863.

Serageldin, Mona A. 'Urbanization and Social Change in a Foreign Dominated Economy: Cairo, 1805–1930', unpublished Ph.D. thesis, Harvard University, 1972.

Shaw, Stanford. 'The Population of Istanbul in the Nineteenth Century', *International Journal of Middle East Studies*, 10, 1979, pp. 265–77.

Shaw, Thomas. *Travels or Observations Relating to Several Parts of Barbary and the Levant* (1757), Edinburgh: J. Ritchie, 1808.

Silberman, N. A. *Digging for God and Country: Exploration, Archeology, and the Secret Struggle for the Holy Land, 1799–1917*, New York: Alfred A. Knopf, 1982.

Silverman, Deborah. 'The 1889 Exposition: The Crisis of Bourgeois Individualism', *Oppositions*, 8, Spring 1977, pp. 70–91.

Smith, Tony. *The Pattern of Imperialism*, Cambridge: Cambridge University Press, 1981.

Solomon-Godeau, A. *Photography at the Dock*, Minneapolis: University of Minnesota, 1991.

Spivak, Gayatri C. 'The Rani of Sirmur: An Essay in Reading in the Archives', *History and Theory*, 14, 1985, pp. 247–72.

Steegman, J. 'Lord Lindsay's *History of Christian Art*', *Journal of the Warburg and Courtauld Institutes*, 10, 1947, pp. 123–31.

Stephens, W. R. W. *The Life and Letters of Edward Freeman*, London: Macmillan, 1895.

Stevens, MaryAnne (ed.). *The Orientalists: Delacroix to Matisse*, London: Thames & Hudson, 1984.

Stocking, G. W. 'What's in a Name? The Origins of the Royal Anthropological Institute (1837–71)', *Man*, September 1971, pp. 369–90.

——*Race, Culture, and Evolution*, Chicago: University of Chicago Press, 1982.

Stokes, Eric. *The English Utilitarians and India*, Oxford: Clarendon Press, 1959.

Street, Arthur E. *Memoir of George Edmund Street RA 1824–81*, London: John Murray, 1888.

Street, George E. 'On Colour as Applied to Architecture', in Associated Architectural Societies, *Reports and Papers*, London: J. Masters & J. H. Parker, 1854, vol. 3, pp. 348–66.

——*Brick and Marble in the Middle Ages*, London: John Murray, 1855.

———*Unpublished Notes and Reprinted Papers*, New York: Hispanic Society of America, 1916.

Summerson, John. 'An Early Modernist: James Wild and His Work', *Architects' Journal*, 69, 1929, pp. 57–62.

Sumner-Boyd, H. and Freely, J. *Strolling through Istanbul*, Istanbul: Redhouse, 1973.

Sweetman, John. *The Oriental Obsession*, Cambridge: Cambridge University Press, 1988.

Temperley, Harold. 'The Last Phase of Stratford de Redcliffe', *English Historical Review*, 47, 1932, pp. 226–31.

Texier, Charles. *Description de l'Asie Mineure*, Paris: Ministère de l'instruction publique, 1839–49.

———*Description de l'Arménie, la Perse, et la Mésopotamie*, Paris: Institut de France, 1842–52.

Texier, Charles and Pullan, R. P. *Byzantine Architecture*, London: Day & Son, 1864.

Thackeray, William. *Notes of a Journey from Cornhill to Grand Cairo*, London: Smith, Elder & Co., 1869.

Thomas, Nicholas. *Colonialism's Culture: Anthropology, Travel and Government*, Cambridge: Polity Press, 1994.

Thompson, J. P. *Into All Lands: The History of the Society for the Propagation of the Gospel in Foreign Parts, 1701–1900*, London: SPCK, 1951.

Thornbury, Walter. *Turkish Life and Character*, London: Smith, Elder & Son, 1860.

Thornton, Thomas. *The Present State of Turkey*, London: J. Masoman, 1809.

Tibawi, A. L. *British Interests in Palestine, 1800–1901*, London: Oxford University Press, 1961.

———*A Modern History of Syria*, London: Macmillan, 1969.

Tillett, Selwyn. *Egypt Itself: The Career of Robert Hay*, London: SD Books, 1984.

Toon, Peter. *Evangelical Theology 1833–56*, London: Marshall, Morgan & Scott, 1979.

Tregaskis, Hugh. *Beyond the Grand Tour, the Levant Lunatics*, London: Ascent, 1979.

Tsigakou, Fani-Maria. *The Rediscovery of Greece*, London: Thames & Hudson, 1981.

Turner, Bryan S. *Marx and the End of Orientalism*, London: George Allen & Unwin, 1978.

Tylor, E. B. *Anthropology: An Introduction to the Study of Man and Civilisation*, London: Macmillan, 1881.

Unrau, John. *Ruskin and St. Mark's*, London: Thames & Hudson, 1984.

Van Zanten, David. *The Architectural Polychromy of the 1830s*, New York and London: Garland, 1977.

Vatikiotis, P. J. *The Modern History of Egypt*, London: Weidenfeld & Nicolson, 1969.

Vaughan, W. 'The Englishness of English Art', *Oxford Art Journal*, 13, 1990, pp. 11–23.

Vereté, M. 'Why Was a British Consulate Established in Jerusalem?', *English Historical Review*, 85, 1970, pp. 316–45.

Viollet-le-Duc, E. *Entretiens sur l'architecture*, Paris: Morel, 1863–72.

Vogüé, Le Comte de. *Le Temple de Jérusalem*, Paris: Noblet & Baudry, 1864.

———*Syrie centrale*, Paris: Baudry, 1865–77.

Volait, Mercedes. 'La Communauté italienne et ses édiles', *Revue de l'Occident Musulman et de la Méditerranée*, 46, 1987, pp. 137–55.

Von Hagen, Victor. *Frederick Catherwood Archt*, Oxford and New York: Oxford University Press, 1950.

———*Frederick Catherwood: Architect-Explorer of Two Worlds*, Barre, Mass.: Barre, 1968.

Warren, Charles. *The Temple or the Tomb, Giving Further Evidence in Favour of the Authenticity of the Present Site of the Holy Sepulchre*, London: R. Bentley, 1880.

Waterfield, Gordon. *Layard of Nineveh*, London: John Murray, 1963.

Watkin, David. *Thomas Hope (1769–1831) and the Neo-Classical Idea*, London: John Murray, 1968.

Webb, Benjamin. 'On the Adaptation of Pointed Architecture to Tropical Climates', *Transactions of the Cambridge Camden Society*, 1845, pp. 199–208.

———*Sketches of Continental Ecclesiology*, London: J. Masters, 1848.

Wells, Thomas. 'On the Influence of Eastern on Western Art', *CEAJ*, 30, 1867, pp. 77–83.

Welsh, P. J. 'Anglican Churchmen and the Establishment of the Jerusalem Bishopric', *Journal of Ecclesiastical History*, 8, 1957, pp. 193–204.

Whewell, W. *Lectures on the Results of the Great Exhibition of 1851*, London: G. Barclay, 1852.

Wightwick, George. *The Palace of Architecture*, London: James Fraser, 1840.

Wilkinson, J. G. *On Colour and on the Necessity for a General Diffusion of Taste among all Classes*, London: John Murray, 1858.

———'The Saracenic Style Distinct from the Byzantine', *Builder*, 19, 1861, pp. 193–5, 205–7.

Williams, George. *The Holy City*, London: J. W. Parker, 1849.

———*Dr. Pierotti and His Assailants*, Cambridge: Deighton, Bell & Co., 1864.

Williams, Robert. *Architecture and Alexandria. How to Beautify the City*, Alexandria: n.p., 1905.

Willis, Robert. *Remarks on the Architecture of the Middle Ages. Especially of Italy*, Cambridge: Deighton, 1835.

Wilson, Captain Charles, *et al. The Recovery of Jerusalem*, London: R. Bentley, 1871.

Wright, Arnold (ed.). *Twentieth Century Impressions of Egypt*, London: Lloyd's, 1909.

Wright, Gwendolyn. *The Politics of Design in French Colonial Urbanism*, Chicago and London: University of Chicago Press, 1991.

Wyatt, Matthew D. *The Industrial Arts of the Nineteenth Century*, London: Day & Son, 1851.

———'Orientalism in European Industry', *Macmillan's Magazine*, 21, 1870, pp. 551–6.

Young, Robert J. C. *Colonial Desire: Hybridity in Theory, Culture and Race*, London: Routledge, 1995.

INDEX

•

Page numbers in *italic* refer to plates.